Best Friends

PROMISES
A ROMANCE

Best Friends

DEBRA WHITE SMITH

Chariot Victor Publishing
A Division of Cook Communications

Chariot Victor Publishing,
Cook Communications, Colorado Springs, Colorado 80918
Cook Communications, Paris, Ontario
Kingsway Communications, Eastbourne, England

BEST FRIENDS
© 1999 by Debra White Smith.
All rights reserved.
Printed in the United States of America.

Editor: L.B. Norton
Design: Bill Gray
Cover Illustration: Matthew Archambault

1 2 3 4 5 6 7 8 9 10 Printing/Year 03 02 01 00 99

Library of Congress Cataloging-in-Publication Data
Smith, Debra White.
     Best friends / Debra White Smith.
          p. cm. -- (Promises, a romance)
     ISBN 1-56476-721-3
     1. Romantic suspense novels. gsafd. I. Title. II. Series.
PS3569.M5178B47   1999   98-36831
813'.54--DC21   CIP

*Dedicated
to my wonderful friends at
Christian Blind Mission,
International,
Greenville, South Carolina*

Author's note

I enjoy weaving the classics into my novels and hope that will be one of the hallmarks of my works of fiction. The classic I have drawn upon for *Best Friends* is Henry James' *The Aspern Papers* (1888). I am deeply indebted to James for the role Michael Alexander plays as "scoundrel on the search."

One

*T*his was going to be much easier than Michael had anticipated. He could pose as a tourist, and Beth McAllister would never suspect his motive. As he waited to pay his lunch bill in the small-town restaurant, Michael Alexander examined the brochure he picked up from the counter.

McAllister's Bed and Breakfast, it read, *A Taste of Home Away from Home.* Both the antique interior and pillared exterior of a turn-of-the-century mansion were depicted against the Arkansas Ozarks. On the last page Beth McAllister, a welcoming smile dimpling her cheeks, stood near the mansion's massive white doorway. Michael hoped she was as naive as she appeared.

When he arrived in Eureka Springs only an hour ago, Michael knew he must get his hands on what he was after and get out before Beth suspected. How to do it was another matter. Now the plan had been miraculously laid before him, almost as if by fate.

Smiling in satisfaction, he glanced around the lunch crowd of tourists and town regulars eating their gourmet hamburgers and steaks and cheesecake. As a new pot-pourri of food smells wafted from the kitchen, he wondered if Beth McAllister would be as easy to get along with as the drop-dead gorgeous brunette cashier who had doubled as his waitress.

"That will be seven ninety-five," she said in her deep Southern drawl, smiling in what he interpreted as feminine appreciation for his blond, movie-star looks.

He produced his most charming, most manipulative smile and held up the brochure. "Lauren . . ." he said, reading the name on her badge as he handed her his credit card, "would you happen to know how to get to this bed and breakfast?" Michael caressed each word. "I think it's exactly the kind of place I'm looking for. I plan to be in town a while and want a place where I can have some privacy."

The cashier's smile broadened, her blue eyes twinkling with pleasure. "Sure. That's my sister's place, and there's a map on the back. Just go about a mile south. Then you'll be turning west here." She pointed to the map. "This road winds up the side of the hill. There's a three-story pink house right next door to McAllister's. If you come to Crescent Drive, you'll know you've gone too far. It's pretty simple, though. You won't miss it."

Her arms full of groceries, Beth McAllister entered her spacious, old-fashioned kitchen and came knee-to-face with a pig. Tiffany, a forty-pound, coffee-colored, pot-bellied porker, had just one goal in life—to escape into the great outdoors. Every time Beth moved right, Tiffany trotted left. Beth felt as if she were square dancing with the creature rather than trying to outmaneuver her. Just then, the phone's shrill ring bounced off the kitchen walls.

"You know the rules, Tiffany," Beth scolded as she finally closed the door without catching the pig's flat snout. "You can't go back outside until I shut the gate."

Her round black eyes full of accusation, the pudgy animal sat on her haunches and glared at Beth.

With a chuckle, Beth deposited the two bags of groceries on the end of the polished cabinet and rushed for the persistent phone.

"McAllister's Bed and—"

"Cut the introduction. This is hot news!" Lauren's breathless words crackled with excitement. "There is a total hunk coming to check in at the inn. His name's Michael Alexander, and he looks like a blond Tom Cruise."

"So the brochures worked! Great!" Beth flipped her waist-length mahogany hair over her right shoulder. "I just had two guests check out this morning. I can—"

"Would you listen to me?" Lauren scolded. "Forget the brochures. I'm telling you this is your chance."

"My chance?"

"Yes. Not only is he good lookin', honey, but he's wearing a diamond ring that would choke Tiffany—and he drives a Mercedes! You need to fix your hair, put on some perfume, and—and nab him!"

"Nab him?" Beth rolled her eyes. Apparently Lauren had decided that her single sister, who had reached the advanced age of twenty-eight, needed a man in her life—whether she knew a thing about him or not. "Only two more months, and I'm counting the days."

Lauren's silence stretched several seconds, and Beth could imagine her brow wrinkled in confusion. "Till what?" she finally asked.

"Till you go back to college. You're driving me nuts!"

"Okay, fine! But don't say I didn't warn you." With a condescending huff, Lauren hung up.

"New guests?" Scott Caldwell asked as he descended the back stairway.

"Yeah." Beth glanced up to return Scott's dimpled smile. "Somebody who saw my brochure at Mom and Dad's restaurant."

"Great. I guess I fixed the faucet in the nick of time."

"Right, and thanks a bunch, too." She reached for her burgundy leather purse. "How much do I owe you?"

Scott held up a muscular arm. "No, no. You know the set-up—"

"Set-up? What set-up?" she asked.

"The 'this is summer and I'm here to help' set-up." His emerald eyes held the determined glint that Beth had first encountered the day they entered kindergarten.

She placed her hands on rounded hips. "Look, I

didn't ask you to help out this summer for free—"

"I'm not working for free. I greatly anticipate my payment. The doctor says I need to gain a few pounds." He rubbed his flat stomach, the product of his rigorous exercise regimen. Scott never asked his students to perform a workout he wasn't willing to do himself. "I plan to join you for supper every evening till school starts again."

"Oh." Beth blinked at this news. As usual, Scott had made plans for her only to reveal them at his leisure.

"I figure the best place to gain weight is at your table. I still say you make the best apple pie in the South."

"The Lord knows I hate to admit it," Beth said as she removed sugar and flour from her grocery bag. "But you're right, and my weight shows it. The doctor says I need to lose ten pounds."

Shame and inferiority marched into the pit of Beth's stomach and dug their claws into her very soul. Overweight. She had always been just a bit too plump, and others perceived that as a bit less attractive, a bit less worthy of friendship . . . of courtship. She swallowed against the lump in her throat and tried to force the lump from her heart. Did God also see her as less worthy? A nagging voice said He did.

"Ah, come on, Bet," Scott said, leaning against the counter as he nabbed a sugar cookie from her always-full cookie jar. "You can't weigh more than a hundred and twenty."

She turned to place the flour in a cabinet. "Try one-thirty," she mumbled in defeat. "And that doesn't sit too well on a five-foot-one frame. I'm built just like Aunt—Aunt Naomi." Beth stumbled over the name. Her eyes misted, and she was glad her back was turned. Was it really six long months ago that her favorite aunt had died? It felt like six days.

"And we all know what she looked like before she died," Beth continued. "Bless her heart, she was pushing one-eighty. I got my apple pie recipe from her. That stuff's lethal!" She pointed to the freshly baked pie sitting on the counter.

"Well, you look just fine to me," Scott said in brotherly approval.

Beth turned to face him. Tanned, dark-haired, handsome. She returned his warm smile. "You're a pal, Scott. You'll make somebody a good husband one day."

"I know," he said mischievously, then popped the last of the cookie in his mouth.

Tiffany's low grunt reminded Beth that she had promised the pig a romp outside. But just as she reached for the back door, the front desk bell rang. "Be right with you," she called over her shoulder. "Would you please shut the back gate and let Tiffany out to play, Scott? I think my new guest is here."

He rolled his eyes with disgust as Tiffany stared at him in blatant hostility. "Okay, but this is going to cost you an extra piece of pie. I still say you oughta make bacon out of this—"

"Shhh," Beth said, her eyes rounded in mock horror. "She'll hear you."

"Yeah, right," Scott growled.

Giggling, Beth hurried toward the antique front desk only to swallow a faint gasp. Lauren was right. The man did look like a blond Tom Cruise. Handsome, aristocratic. Her pulse skipped a beat as she quickly swished her hair into place. Maybe she should have listened to her sister.

After releasing his worst enemy into the backyard, Scott walked toward the inn's reception area. He had noticed a light bulb out in one of the crystal lamps and planned to change it.

"I want a room for the summer, actually," the man was saying as Scott approached.

"I can accommodate that," Beth returned with a lilt in her voice.

Scott stopped in his tracks just outside the room. If he didn't know better, he would say Beth was flirting with the guy. His stomach tensed. Unseen, Scott examined the guest and Beth. They made a striking couple, the newcomer's fair good looks contrasting with Beth's mane of dark hair and startling blue eyes.

Scott's stomach knotted anew. His summer goal, to somehow get Beth to fall in love with him, could be completely demolished by one blond, debonair guest.

He pursed his lips and breathed a prayer. *No, Lord, no. You promised.*

When had it happened? When had he fallen in love with his lifetime friend, his buddy, his pal? Beth McAllister, the girl with whom he had shared his childhood. The girl who encouraged him, an underprivileged, scrawny kid, to pursue his coaching dream. The girl whom he had never seen as a woman until he moved back to Eureka Springs last fall. Somehow, that girl had snared his heart. With this realization came a peaceful certainty, a promise from the Lord, that Beth was the answer to his year-long prayer for a godly wife.

Scott knew breaking through their "friendship barrier" was going to be a challenge, even with God's promise. But now . . . now . . .

Like a great oak rooted in unyielding clay, Scott stood and watched his worst nightmare come to life. Beth, beaming at the intruder. Beth, her eyes twinkling as if she wished to share some secret but didn't dare. Beth, fussing with her incredible mahogany hair as if she wished it were combed. And the guest taking in each feminine cue as if she were already his.

"Might I say, Ms. McAllister," the blond stranger continued in his smooth voice, "you have the most remarkable eyes. Please forgive me if I'm too forward, but I just can't help noticing."

A blush. Beth was actually blushing like a teenager!

Nausea crept up Scott's throat, and he swallowed like a man drowning in terror.

"Thank you," Beth returned in a tone that said, *You ain't so bad yourself, honey.*

And Scott, his fists curling into tight wads, suppressed the age-old male possessiveness that nearly raged out of control.

He had carefully planned the whole summer. He was going to spend all his spare time at the inn, going to spoil Beth with his handyman skills, going to slowly woo her until she awakened to his love and hopefully hers. Now, those plans were mere air castles crumbling at his feet.

Lord? Where are You? You promised!

"If you'll just follow me up these stairs," Beth continued as she rounded the desk, "I'll show you to your room." She bent to pick up his one piece of designer luggage.

"I can get my bag." The intruder's hand reached the suitcase handle immediately after Beth's, only to linger against her fingers in something resembling a caress.

Scott couldn't stand any more.

"I can get your bags," he said as he rushed into the room. A stiff smile in place, he laid a possessive hand on Beth's shoulder. "I worry about Beth hurting her back."

Beth's questioning glance barely preceded her words. "Since when—"

"Oh . . ." the stranger said in a crestfallen voice. "I—I didn't realize you were married."

"We're not—I mean I'm not—I mean he's just a friend, a family friend," Beth rushed as if trying to disqualify any claim Scott might seem to have on her.

"I'll take your bag," Scott said again, forcing the anger and jealousy from his voice. "What room, Bet?"

"The blue room."

He picked up the leather bag and deftly removed the key from her grasp. "I'll see to him." Another stiff grin. "That way, you can get back to your work in the kitchen. I don't want anything to spoil my chances of a high calorie dinner."

"Oh, well, okay," she said, disappointment in her voice and eyes.

"Nice to have met you." The blond stranger took her hand in his, bent, and touched his lips to her fingers as if she were the Queen of England and he were her devoted subject.

"The feeling's mutual."

Scott wanted to groan. "The blue room is this way." He started toward the winding staircase with "Blondie" on his heels.

"Oh! Dinner's at six if you care to join us!" Beth called after him.

"I'll be there."

Not wishing to witness any more of Beth's admiring gaze, Scott kept his eyes riveted to the stairway.

Wrong, wrong. You were wrong, a scornful voice mocked. *God never promised that you would marry Beth.* If that voice were right, then Scott knew he didn't have a clue about perceiving God's will.

Two

*B*eth stared into the full-length cherry antique mirror. In the last fifteen minutes, she had French braided her hair, then twisted it into a chignon, then pulled it into a golden clip, and finally let it fall down her back in a rose-scented, mahogany cloud. With a resigned huff, she hurriedly ran the brush through her layered bangs and decided to leave well enough alone.

The dress. Was it too much? Pivoting, she peered into the mirror at her not-so-thin figure in the blue, polished cotton print, trimmed in lace. A definite summer masterpiece. And it did hide her extra pounds. Sighing, she wondered if she would ever be thin.

Would Michael Alexander suspect she had dressed just for him?

"Who cares if he does?" she mumbled.

Maybe Lauren was right. Maybe she did need a man in her life. And Michael made no attempt to hide his interest. He acted as if he didn't notice those extra pounds.

Could he be the one for her? No sense in playing hard-to-get with Mr. Right. She bit her lip. It was definitely too soon to start thinking in those terms. She had only just met the man and didn't even know if he were a Christian.

Obviously, his good looks had thrown her common sense into a tailspin. The same common sense that had stopped her from marrying her college sweetheart. The same common sense that assured her the Lord would provide the man to whom she could give her whole heart. The same common sense that had been wrong.

Here I am. Pushing thirty. Still unmarried, with absolutely no prospects.

With a furtive glance at her silver wristwatch, Beth rushed to the cherry highboy, grabbed Aunt Naomi's diamond pendant from the crystal jewelry box, and fastened it around her neck.

"Forget common sense," she muttered. "Common sense left Aunt Naomi an old maid." *And don't worry about his being a Christian. You can win him to the Lord later.* The words seemed to settle around her neck like an albatross, and Beth didn't dare pray for God's will in this. Praying for God's will had left her single. And whether she admitted it to Lauren or not, she was tired of being single.

Trying to run from the uneasiness her heart, Beth rushed out of her room, down the stairs, and into the kitchen.

"Oops, caught in the act," Scott said, a huge bite of apple pie halfway to his mouth.

"Scott! You turkey! You've ruined the pie."

"Hey, don't I deserve it?" he asked, then crammed the bite into his mouth. "After all, I did mow the yard and take your sorry excuse for a dog on a walk."

She raised her chin in feigned indignation. "Tiffany is not a dog substitute."

"Yeah, right, tell her that."

Beth laughed and grabbed a green-checked apron to tie around her waist. "She does act rather, um, canine-ish, doesn't she?"

"Yeah—here, let me help with that apron. You're all thumbs."

"Thanks. I guess I'm just a little nervous. I always get that way when a new guest arrives." *But not this much.* She turned her back to Scott.

His close, exaggerated sniff tickled her ear. "Wow, ma'am, you smell like a rose garden," he said as he pulled the apron strings into a snug bow.

Beth whirled around. "Is it too much?" she whispered, not even trying to hide her expectancy. It was no use, anyway. Scott could read her like yesterday's news. "This was Aunt Naomi's perfume, and I didn't realize it was so stout."

His full lips tilted into a smile, half in brotherly indulgence and half in something Beth couldn't define. "It's just right. Who's the lucky guy?"

Snorting, she rummaged through a drawer for some pot holders. "Need you ask?"

"Oh, Mr. Blondie." Scott rolled his eyes. "Can't you do better than that?"

"Better than that?" She playfully slapped his tummy with a floral pot holder. "You've been away from home too long. Guys like him don't come through Eureka Springs every day. Now, grab the salad on the top shelf in the refrigerator." Beth started to pick up the tray of appetizers sitting on the counter, then paused. "Oh, and Scott?"

"Yes?" He turned from the refrigerator, and something in his emerald-colored eyes made Beth slightly uncomfortable.

She took a breath, determined voice her thoughts. "Please don't tell that corny joke about the cat running out of gas."

Those words, spoken like a sister to a brother, filled the air like stifling, acrid smoke. Then that certain, latent something in Scott's eyes sparked into blatant recognition. Anger, hurt, resentment.

She recoiled from her own insensitivity. For the first time in five years, Beth saw lurking in Scott's eyes a shadow of the poor, soiled little boy he had once been.

"Oh, I'm sorry, I didn't mean to—"

"Do I embarrass you, Bet?" He gripped the crystal salad bowl until his fingers grew white, contrasting with his tanned skin and the dark hair on his arms.

Beth swallowed. She hadn't noticed until now that Scott had gone home to shower and change from his grubbies into stylish jeans and a crisp white oxford shirt. His near-ebony hair was still damp at the neck.

"No, of course you don't embarrass me," she said hurriedly. "It's just—I—I so want to make a good impression—"

"Take my word for it, you already have," he clipped.

"What's that supposed to mean?"

"Knock, knock, anybody home?"

It was Lauren, pushing open the kitchen door.

Floundering in confusion, Beth glanced toward her younger sister. Even in such an awkward moment, Beth noticed Lauren's brunette beauty and felt inferiority grip her own stomach.

"Never mind," Scott mumbled and rushed past the two sisters toward the dining room.

"What got into him?" Lauren whispered as she watched Scott's retreat.

"I have no idea," Beth whispered back. "He's been a little weird ever since he moved back from New York. Haven't you noticed?"

"No. Probably because I haven't been in town." She turned to face Beth. "Forget him. Tell me about Mr. Wonderful." Her almond-shaped, light-blue eyes sparkled with excitement. "Did he check in?"

"You mean Michael?" Beth, rearranging celery sticks on the crystal appetizer tray, tried unsuccessfully to hide her own excitement.

"You know who I mean. Didn't I tell you he was gorgeous?" Lauren grabbed a carrot stick from the tray, and Beth slapped her hand.

"Stop it. You and Scott are going to eat up the whole

dinner before it gets served."

Lauren sniffed the air delicately. "Do I smell pot roast?"

"Yes. Care to join us?"

"Didn't think you'd ever ask. Mom and Dad are still at the restaurant, and I'm ready to eat. I'm just in jeans, though. Does it matter?"

"No, Scott's in his jeans too."

"Well, you certainly aren't. Is that dress new?"

"Uh, yeah. I sorta ran out and bought it this after-noon."

"Oh. I see. I guess that means *Michael* will be joining us."

"Don't say it like that." Beth hid a smile.

As Lauren grinned, she focused on the two-carat dia-mond pendant around Beth's neck.

"It was Aunt Naomi's," Beth explained to Lauren's unasked question. "I found it in the back of her jewelry box." She swallowed against the lump in her throat. Along with buying her new dress that afternoon, Beth had also visited her aunt's grave with a bouquet of yellow roses. Tomorrow was her birthday.

"Oh," Lauren said. The hurt, so evident at Aunt Naomi's death, still haunted her eyes.

"Lauren, I don't think she loved me more than you, I really don't."

Aunt Naomi's decision to leave the prosperous bed and breakfast to Beth had created a chasm between the sisters. With eight years between them, sibling rivalry had never been a big issue . . . in spite of Beth's awareness of her sister's head-to-toe beauty. Now, the whole complexion of their relationship was changing.

"I'll take this to the table," Lauren said quickly. She grabbed the appetizers. "And hurry with that roast. I'm starved!"

Lauren walk toward the dining room, her slender hips swaying in jeans that always fit perfectly. Everything Beth had missed in life, Lauren had been blessed with. The perfect figure. The perfect teeth. An all-expenses-paid trip to college.

Beth, on the other hand, always struggled with her weight, wore braces through adolescence, worked her way through her cum laude business degree and graduate school. When Beth left for college, her parents hadn't made the success of the restaurant they now enjoyed. She knew all this was the reason Aunt Naomi had favored her in the will. She just wished Lauren understood.

Lord, please heal Lauren. Help her see, Beth prayed as she removed the fragrant pot roast from the oven.

But when are you going to see?

She blinked, wondering where that disturbing thought had come from. What was she supposed to see? Lauren was the one with the problem.

Sighing, Beth decided to do what Lauren had done—shove the issue of Aunt Naomi's will from her mind and concentrate on something else.

Like dinner with Michael Alexander.

Three

ould you care for dessert, Michael?" Beth asked in her most dignified Midwest accent. From the meal's beginning Scott cringed every time Beth spoke. Gone was Beth's natural, "sweet southern girl" drawl. She replaced it with her sanitized Midwest accent, the one which accompanied her from Oklahoma State University. This was obviously part of her plan to make a good impression.

"Oh yes, you've got to have a piece of Beth's apple pie," Lauren chimed in. "It's the best in the South."

"I wouldn't miss it, then," Michael said, an apprecia-tive twinkle in his eyes.

A twinkle Scott wanted to snuff out. In all the years he had known Beth, he had never seen her so animated. Not even when she thought she was in love with that guy from college, Darren Chandler. And certainly not for Scott.

It's hopeless, man. You might as well give up. How can you, plain, everyday Scott, compete with the likes of Mr. Blondie?

"What exactly do you do for a living, Michael?" Scott asked with slight distrust. Beth might accept him at face value, but something about Michael Alexander made Scott suspicious. Why would a man of his obvious wealth want to spend the summer in a small Arkansas town? Sure, Eureka Springs was a tourist attraction, but so was France. And France seemed more in Michael's league.

Scott, fingering Beth's best crystal goblet, awaited Michael's reply.

"I'm a writer, actually." Michael, his lips twisted in a knowing smile, seemed to realize Scott's feelings for Beth. Or was it just Scott's imagination?

"Oooo . . . how exciting!" Lauren crooned.

"What do you write?" Beth asked as she placed a piece of pie before him with a clink of silverware against china.

"Oh, this and that. Mainly mystery novels." He seemed to be groping for details. "It's really more of a hobby and has gradually become my main interest."

The flash of his diamond ring underscored his emphasis on the word "interest." Apparently Michael Alexander didn't need an income.

And I'm a mere high school coach who tells embarrassing jokes, Scott thought as his dreams for the summer, and his trust in God's promises, shriveled like wilting roses.

Beth's expressive, shocking-blue eyes didn't hide her instant fascination. His revelation had produced the exact effect Michael probably hoped for.

"What have you had published?" she asked as she finished serving the pie.

Michael turned his complete attention to her, where it had remained most of the meal. "Well . . ." he hesitated, as if debating exactly how to reply. "I have yet to see anything in print, actually."

Scott wanted to groan. He didn't believe for half a second that this guy had written so much as a grocery list. *I don't know who you really are, or what you're here for, buddy, but you're going to get a fight from me before you make an idiot of Beth McAllister.*

"So you're a writer, are you?" Scott drawled, crossing his arms.

Beth blankly stared at Scott as if she didn't understand his point. Lauren, more attuned to Scott's words, widened her eyes. And Mr. Blondie observed Scott in condescending reproof.

Scott scowled for emphasis. "I know a line when I hear one, and you are feeding these ladies a line. We aren't quite the local yokels you seem to think we are," he said. "Beth holds a master's in business administration. She quit her job teaching junior college to run this bed and breakfast. Lauren, here, is working on a pre-law degree. I hold a B. S. in education. And guess what, mister," he continued in his best hillbilly accent, "we even have telephones, electricity, and runnin' water." Stopping for added emphasis, he scowled. "And none of us enjoys being lied to."

A slow, dawning light surfaced in Michael's eyes, and Scott knew the visitor realized he had misjudged them.

"Scott," Beth gasped. "Mr. Alexander is my guest."

"I don't care who he is. He's stringing you a line."

"So you caught me in the act." A twisted, defeated smile. "But then, what man hasn't lied to try and impress a beautiful woman?" His ardent gaze turned to Beth. "Your friend is right. I'm not a writer. I'm a mere investment manager on the east coast." Michael, pushing out his full lower lip, produced a penitent pout that made Scott want to groan anew. "Forgive me?"

With a quick flip of her hair over her shoulder, Beth chuckled as if she were glad he had lied to her. "Don't worry about it," she said, her tone implying that he had already greatly impressed her, book or no book.

Lauren, obviously enjoying the fix Michael had gotten himself into, chuckled in support of Beth's attitude.

"Since when do you care so little about honesty, Beth?" Scott snorted, unable to contain his disdain.

Beth's eyes had never been colder, her lips never so firm, her peachy cheeks never more flushed. "Scott, I need to speak with you in the kitchen," she said through gritted teeth. "Now."

He grabbed the red napkin from his lap, wadded it, and tossed it onto his plate.

"Fine. I'll be glad to join you," he growled.

Beth turned on him as soon as the kitchen door closed behind them. "How could you!"

He thought her cheeks couldn't get any redder than they were at the table. He was wrong.

"How could I what?" Scott hissed back. "The man was

lying to you, and I called him on it. Since when do you—Miss Honest America—cater to lying?"

"And since when do you—Mr. Congeniality—act so rude to anyone, let alone my customers?"

Since your customer started playing up to the woman I love. "Since you started making an idiot of yourself over—"

"An idiot of myself? Listen, you . . . you . . ."

A sealed volcano, prohibited from erupting, that's what Beth resembled. Scott blinked at her fury. He had never seen her so angry.

"You . . . turkey! I'm not anybody's idiot!"

Scott wanted to shake her shoulders until she reconnected with her usually present, but recently defunct common sense. "You were practically swooning over the—"

"And I guess you've never swooned before?" she challenged. "And while we're on the subject, I suppose you're also going to tell me you've never lied to a woman to impress her?"

He opened his mouth to deny the accusation, only to snap it shut again. Six summers ago, on a visit home, Scott had done just that, letting an attractive tourist think that he came from a wealthy Boston family. Beth had promptly, although inadvertently, refuted his claim.

"That was before I was a Christian, and you know it," he whispered, his chest tightening. "And the only reason I lied then was because of my past. You know how I feel about my past."

Poor white trash. That was the image he lived with all

his childhood. Until Beth had requested he not tell his cat joke, Scott thought God had healed his childhood wounds. Now, he wasn't so sure. For as those words of only an hour ago left Beth's mouth, he once again felt like the filthy little boy with whom people were ashamed to be seen.

Maybe that was part of the reason he had grown to love Beth so. She never refused her friendship just because of his father's inclination for alcohol and loose women and a dirty house. Some days, Scott felt as if he had always loved Beth.

"And you know how I feel about my reputation as a businesswoman." She stabbed the center of his chest with her index finger.

"It's not that reputation I'm worried about right now! What about your reputation as a Christian? And what about your influence on Lauren? The man is obviously not a Christian, and you obviously have decided you don't care!"

As Beth averted her eyes, something urged Scott to grab her and kiss some sense into her. He suddenly needed the assurance that one day she might be his, that perhaps she could grow to love him, that maybe even now she was attracted to him. His frustration rising, mingling with his need to feel her close, he reached for her shoulders only to stop as the kitchen door opened.

"Er, excuse me, Beth," Michael Alexander mumbled, a mischievous gleam in his eyes. "Lauren asked me to come tell you that your pet pig is digging up the neighbor's geraniums, and the neighbor doesn't seem very happy. Lauren is chasing the pig now."

Scott dropped his hands. *Well, great. Tiffany strikes again.*

Four

*B*eth rushed from the house, down the massive porch stairs and onto her lawn. She stared across the street at the turbulent trio: Tiffany, trotting recklessly through Mr. Juarez's flower bed; Lauren, trying to tackle the pig, her designer jeans splattered with soil; and the elderly Mr. Juarez in his red Bermuda shorts, railing in Spanish and waving a dilapidated broom over the pig's head.

The anger Beth had only moments ago directed toward Scott found a new target. This was the third time Tiffany had escaped to wreak havoc in a neighbor's yard. Beth's patience snapped.

"Tiffany, get yourself out of that flower bed and over here this minute!"

At the sound of Beth's firm voice, the guilty pig jumped, then slowly turned to face her mistress. One red geranium hung from her snout while another graced her right ear. Lowering her eyes, Tiffany trotted toward her yard, intent on trying to bypass Beth at the greatest distance possible.

"Oh, no you don't," Beth said, rushing toward her.

"Ah Bet," Scott said, stepping between Beth and the pig. "Leave her be. She's just doing what comes naturally." He chuckled. "You'd dig around in Mr. Juarez's flowers too, if you were a pig." His eyes sparkled with mirth as he glanced toward the furious neighbor.

"Since when do you take up for Tiffany?" Beth asked, enraged anew. "The last I heard, you were ready to take her to the butcher!"

Tiffany scooted behind Scott and ran for the backyard.

Beth's hands curled into involuntary fists. First, Scott was rude to her customer. Then he questioned her Christianity. Now he had the audacity to defend the rebellious Tiffany. What was the matter with the man?

"Uh, excuse me, but I think this is the problem," Michael said from nearby.

Suppressing a groan, Beth turned to her guest. What must he think of her? In a matter of moments, her carefully planned dinner had turned into bedlam.

Michael held up what appeared to be part of a rusty gate latch. "When I tried to lock the gate, this fell off."

"So the latch is broken," Scott said. "That's the reason Tiffany got out, Bet." He reached for the rusting piece of metal. "Why didn't you tell me your gate needed to be repaired?"

"I kept forgetting." She rubbed her temples, wondering why Aunt Naomi had ever adopted a sow. Why not a cat or a dog or a python? Even a rhinoceros would be less trouble. "I bought a new latch last week. It's in the storage shed on the worktable."

"Beth, I think you'd better go over and calm Mr. Juarez," Lauren said as she entered the yard. Another swift brush of her dusty jeans. "My Spanish isn't what it should be, but I think he's muttering something about the police and the animal shelter."

"Oh no, not the police again."

"Again?" Michael asked.

"Oh yes," Scott supplied with a satisfied smirk. "Last month Tiffany trotted three doors down to a neighboring inn and helped herself to the outdoor dining area. By the time the fiasco was over, there was a continental breakfast for twelve on the ground along with Mrs. Scully and—"

"Scott, would you please repair my gate now?" With a pointed smile through gritted teeth, Beth suppressed the urge to tell him he could shut up while he was at it. He seemed intent on leaving the worst impression possible with Michael.

If Beth didn't know better, she would think he had reverted back to adolescence. Where was her Christlike, cheerful, dependable Scott? He seemed to have vanished before her eyes, replaced by a difficult, unpredictable, haunted-eyed stranger.

"Sure, I'll fix your gate." A jaunty, triumphant grin. "But I'll need your help."

"Fine." Beth's nostrils flared as she gritted her teeth again. He was acting as if their heated conversation of only moments before had never occurred.

"I could help," Michael offered.

"Oh, that's okay," Scott said rudely. "I don't need your help."

Until that second, Beth had doubted the existence of temporary insanity. But with her stomach churning in rage, hot blood rushing to her face, her legs trembling like overcooked pasta, she briefly thought about chasing Scott down and strangling him.

"Oh, Beth," Lauren said in a sing-song voice. "I really do think you should go calm Mr. Juarez now. He's heading inside."

"Okay," she said, turning to cross the street. Michael kept pace with her, and she spoke to him, quietly but intensely. "I'm sorry Scott's acting so . . . being so rude. He's never—"

"Don't worry about it." Michael's lips tilted in a half-grin. "By the end of the summer, I may be a little crazy too. Please forgive me if I'm too forward, but I imagine that living so close to such beauty as yours would be enough to drive any man out of his mind."

Beth, her face reheating, scrambled for an appropriate reply while her stomach fluttered like a sixteen-year-old's on a first date.

"Now, if you'll excuse me," Michael continued nonchalantly. "I think I'll go have a nice chat with Mr. Juarez." And before Beth knew what was happening, he was across the street standing on the white porch, soothing the irate neighbor.

"Wow," Lauren whispered.

"Ditto," Beth muttered, but a doubt plagued her. Had Scott been right? Was associating with Michael sending a negative message to Lauren? Or risking her Christian reputation? Or even worse, affecting her relationship with the Lord?

Of course not! You've only shared one meal! It's not like you're marrying the man, a pragmatic voice argued. But another voice softly muttered, *Don't be unequally yoked.* It was a voice Beth desperately tried to ignore as she returned Michael's smile from across the road.

Please Lord, don't ruin this for me.

Clamping his jaw, Scott stared at the remnants of the rusty lock swinging from one last bolt. If only Beth knew he was ready to clobber that Michael Alexander. After their argument, Scott resorted to the only defense available. Pretend as if all were well. And he had done a good job of it until that last remark. Every time Beth looked at that jerk, though, Scott's heart felt as if it were being ripped from his chest.

One afternoon. Only one afternoon with that blond interloper, and he and Beth were already at each other's throats.

Lord, where are You when I need You?

With great relish Scott thought of the fire and brimstone God had sent to destroy Sodom and Gomorrah, and fleetingly wondered what the chances were that He would do the same against Michael. A troubling conviction rumbled through Scott's heart and crushed his vindictive thoughts.

Un-Christlike . . . Un-Christlike . . . Un-Christlike . . . The word echoed through the corridors of his soul and summed up his actions of the last hour. How could he condemn Beth when he wasn't acting like a Christian?

"Forgive me, Lord," he muttered, not wanting to think of the restitution that must follow.

"I'll get the gate latch," Beth called, her voice tight.

With a feigned innocent smile and a casual whistle, Scott studied the gate to determine his options for repair, hoping Beth didn't sense his internal turbulence.

Tiffany, poking her flat nose out the gate, stared up at him as if to say thanks. For the first time, the small pig seemed glad to see Scott. She even rewarded him with a slight twitch of her curly tail.

Great, just great, he thought sarcastically. *I'm winning the pig's friendship while making an enemy of her owner.* Scott had no idea why he had defended the sow. Perhaps some perverse desire to needle Beth for the betrayal he felt every time she smiled at Michael. Why couldn't Beth see through that man's slick lines?

Tiffany's tail twitched again.

"Oh, go get in your doghouse, Tiffany," he muttered.

"I didn't really mean that I wanted to be friends." He scratched her soft ear. "But then, maybe I could use a friend right now."

"Here's the latch," Beth bit out from behind Scott.

Smile, just smile. Don't let her know her voice makes your heart melt. "That was quick." Taking in the fresh scent of her rose perfume, he turned to face her, grin intact.

"And you can wipe that fake smile off your face, Scott Caldwell," she hissed, her cheeks flushing with the fury churning in her eyes. "I have never in my whole life been so humiliated!"

"I'm sor—"

"Don't you 'I'm sorry' me, buster, because you aren't sorry, and we both know it!" She flicked her hair over her shoulder. "And if you ever resort to such rudeness again, I'll—I'll . . ."

"You'll what?" Scott asked like a bothersome brother. "Beth, can't you see what that fake Bozo is up to?"

"Listen you . . . you . . . I'm telling you for the last time. You stay out of my business. Just because we're friends doesn't give you the right to start running my love life. Now stop it!" She stomped her foot for emphasis.

"What about God? Does He have any say in your love life?"

Silence, the kind that yells "touché," filled the space between them. Beth stared at him, her eyes rounded in blank surprise. But her stunned expression was rivaled by the halo-like effect the setting sun created around her hair.

Breathless.

Her beauty left him breathless, and Scott struggled to concentrate on the words reverberating between them.

What about God? What about God? What about God?

"Here's the latch," Beth finally said as if he had never asked her God's opinion. "You know where the tools are."

"Thanks," he said, biting his tongue to keep from saying more.

"Excuse me, Beth?" Michael's smooth tone brought their conversation to a close.

With a last, warning glance for her best friend, Beth walked toward "Mr. Blondie."

Scott, staring at the aged gate, strained to hear the retreating conversation.

"Yes?" Beth asked, anticipation in her voice . . . anticipation that made Scott feel sick.

"It's such a lovely evening. I was wondering if you wanted to go for a walk," Michael continued. "Lauren said there's a historic hotel and quaint church not far from here?"

A delighted laugh. "Yes, it's about a mile away. But it's such a steep walk up the hill, it would be better to drive. . . ."

Their voices blended with the cooing of the doves resting in the eaves of the neighbor's garage.

That's when Scott knew what he had to do. Rushing for the ancient storage shed, Scott deposited the latch and tools and grabbed a piece of rusty wire he'd seen lying on the workbench. *Perfect. This will do the trick for now. It will keep Tiffany in, and I can fix the latch tomorrow.*

One twist, two twists, three twists of the wire, and the dilapidated gate was temporarily fixed. He would come back tomorrow and build a whole new gate. That would give him a good excuse to be nearby. Right now, though, Scott wasn't about to let Beth out of his sight.

Five

Michael smiled into Beth's unsuspecting eyes while his spirits soared. She believed everything he told her. If she only knew the truth, she would probably shove him off the terrace.

"Isn't this beautiful? You can see for miles," she said, gazing across the wooded hills of the Ozarks.

"Beautiful," Michael said, his gaze never leaving her flushing cheeks.

She had given him a brief tour of the quaint Catholic church across the street. Now they sat on the terrace of the historic, mountaintop Crescent Hotel overlooking the tree-lined valley where Eureka Springs was nestled. A cool mountain breeze, scented with pine and cedar and earth, danced between the tables and whispered for Michael to make his move.

With growing confidence he reached across the white metal table to wrap his fingers around Beth's, and her chilled hand actually trembled. He suppressed a chuckle.

Michael never imagined his "mission" would find such a willing participant.

"I noticed a horse-drawn carriage when we entered the hotel. Would you like to take a ride?"

"I'd love to," she said almost reverently.

"Let's go." Standing, Michael graced her with a charming smile. The smile that never failed. Women were so dense, so naive.

And Beth McAllister seemed the epitome of naiveté. Michael had to admit she was attractive, in a simple fashion. Not nearly as gorgeous as her sister. If the situation were different, Michael would have made a play for Lauren and never glanced twice at Beth. But it was Beth, not Lauren, who possessed what Michael was searching for . . . or so he hoped.

In the lobby of the Crescent Hotel, Scott sat on the red velvet Victorian sofa, holding an outdated newspaper in front of him. Oblivious to the rich decor of antiques and white pillars, he glanced around the paper toward the elevator. Still no Beth and Blondie. Would they ever come back down? They had been upstairs thirty minutes! Thirty minutes of pure agony.

Another furtive glance toward the elevators, and his heart thudded in fury as Beth and the jerk exited. Beth, her dimpled smile turned toward the jerk. The jerk, softly chuckling at something she had said, holding her hand as if he owned her.

Scott clamped his teeth and gripped the paper in his damp palms. He suppressed the urge to race over and yank their hands apart.

Dear Lord, You're going to have to give me strength.

Then they were walking right past him, within touching distance, close enough for Beth's heavenly rose perfume to tickle Scott's senses. *Oh Bet, if only you'd worn it for me.*

"Are you sure you don't want to go back home and grab a sweater?" Michael said, his smooth voice grating along Scott's spine. "The carriage might be cool once night falls."

"No. I'm used to it."

A cautious glance toward the stately door, and Scott folded the paper. They were heading for the horse-drawn carriage, the *romantic* horse-drawn carriage.

Beth settled onto the worn leather seat next to Michael. Casually, he placed an arm around her shoulders as if they had always known each other.

"I am so glad I decided to come to Eureka Springs," he breathed. "It looks as if this is going to be an exciting summer."

Demurely smiling, Beth couldn't concentrate on

Michael's words. She couldn't concentrate because her mind raced with what she had seen in the hotel lobby. Either Beth was hallucinating, or Scott was following her.

She would recognize his worn-out penny loafers anywhere. After Tiffany chewed the toe of the right shoe last week, Beth volunteered to buy him a new pair, but he refused. "These are just getting broken in good, and I like 'em," he had said. "Besides, I barely notice the teeth marks."

Well, Beth noticed the teeth marks. She had seen them as she neared that person hiding behind a crumpled newspaper in the hotel lobby, a person she would have never noticed if not for the shoes.

Another moment, and her suspicions were confirmed. Scott, worn-out loafers, dark sunglasses and all, slipped from the hotel entrance as if he were a spy. *Scott Caldwell, you would go broke as a PI,* Beth thought, trying to force the anger from tilting her emotions.

As the carriage began to roll toward the tunnel of trees and Michael muttered something low, Beth had a new, disturbing thought. She stared vacantly toward the clop-clopping gray mare. What if Scott were having some kind of emotional problems or a nervous breakdown? That would explain his strange behavior. Her heart, once beating with anger, now beat with sympathy.

Scott's father had died last year, leaving Scott without a family. Could all the stress from his childhood, all the grief from losing a father he never really knew, be finally culminating to cause some kind of crisis? If that were the case, he probably needed Beth. Needed her to hold his hand through his pain. Needed her to pray and cry with him. Isn't that what friends were for?

While Michael continued speaking, Beth gripped the cool leather seat and started to order the hooded carriage's halt. She must go to Scott, go to him now.

A glance into Michael's fathomless gray eyes, and she couldn't speak. Those were the kind of eyes a woman felt as if she were falling into. When Michael's words became clear, her worries about Scott blurred.

"What would you say if I said I wanted to kiss you?"

A hard swallow against a throat suddenly dry, and Scott's accusation swarmed through her mind. *The man is obviously not a Christian, and you have obviously decided you don't care.*

Slowly, deliberately, Michael leaned toward her.

"Uh . . ." Beth placed a restraining hand against his chest. Another compulsive swallow. "Uh . . . We—we only just met," she said, her voice a mere, hoarse whisper. "I—"

His eyes clouded with apology. "Please forgive me," he pleaded, his voice thick with propriety. "I think I must have lost my head. You're so beautiful, I just couldn't help—"

"It's okay," Beth said lamely, scooting an inch away, and feeling miles away from the Lord. *Dear Lord, don't abandon me!* But Beth couldn't help but wonder who was abandoning whom.

"Your cheeks," he said, his words as much a caress as his index finger stroking her face. "You're blushing."

Feeling like a Victorian prude, she blinked in chagrin and stared toward fragrant pines lining the road. Should she let him kiss her? True, they had only just met. True, she had always progressed slowly, cautiously, in her relationships. Yet she had already vowed to ignore common sense. But was it common sense she was ignoring or God's voice?

Not wanting to answer that question, she once again thought of Scott. Of his warning. His anger. His obvious need for her at this time.

A cautious glance toward Michael's limpid eyes, and she steeled herself against involuntarily leaning into his arms.

No.

She simply couldn't. What would Scott think of her if he knew she had let Michael kiss her? More importantly, what would God think?

Marilyn Douglas Thatcher, tears blurring her view, stared unseeing across the tree-lined valley. Five years ago that scenic valley had served as the backdrop for her wedding on this very terrace.

As if she had been a spectator, her mind replayed the scene. The petite blonde bride, almost ethereal in the morning light. The tall, adoring groom, his loving green eyes fixed on his new wife. The smiling minister, eyes alight with the joy of the moment. Her parents. His parents. And two dear friends.

A simple ceremony performed after sunrise.

Marilyn thought it was a scene she would cherish the rest of her life. But the memory that once brought joy now brought heartache.

Biting her bottom lip, she stared in disbelief at the untanned mark on her ring finger—just the size of her wedding band. A simple gold ring, that's all. But today was the first day she removed it. The pain was almost as poignant as the day she learned of Greg's desertion.

When he asked her to marry him, Greg tried to buy her a diamond, but Marilyn had insisted on simplicity. He had yet to complete graduate school. They were starting their ministry with a small congregation. Marilyn hadn't wanted to put them under any financial strain. The wide band had meant more to her than any diamond could ever mean.

If only it had meant as much to Greg.

Noiselessly she swallowed the last of her soda and steeled herself against any new onslaughts of agony.

The divorce was final. There was nothing she could do to reverse it. The Reverend Gregory Thatcher, Ph.D. had chosen his path.

Marilyn stood, paid for her Coke, and boarded the aging elevator. Her three-year-old daughter, Brooke, needed her affection, encouragement, and steadfastness. Marilyn must be strong for her.

Lovingly, Marilyn's parents welcomed their daughter

and granddaughter into their home. Her father declared he would fill the void in Brooke's life that Greg left. If not for their emotional support, Marilyn would have crumbled.

Denying the tears, she clamped her teeth, straightened her back, walked through the massive Victorian lobby, and climbed into her royal blue Toyota. She inhaled deeply of the new car smell, and her urge to cry abated.

One last glance around the parking lot, and a lone figure caught her attention. A brooding, dark-haired man about her age leaned against a forest green sports coupe. He stared into midair and absently tapped the face of his watch.

Marilyn was hit with a sudden memory of a gangly teenage boy with adoring green eyes, and she recalled Scott Caldwell. She hardly spoke to him in school, but she had known him. A lot of her classmates would have rather died than have their names linked with his. Marilyn, on the other hand, always felt sorry for him. Their senior year, he gave her a rose on Valentine's Day and asked her to the sweetheart banquet, but she already had a date.

He'd changed so much, Marilyn wouldn't have recognized him except for that thick mop of dark hair and the stubborn set of his square jaw. The longer she watched him, the longer she wanted to watch him. Marilyn soon found herself gaping at the transformation adulthood had rendered.

Then a twist of guilt. After all, she was married. Marilyn glanced at her ringless finger. Groaning, she gripped the steering wheel all the tighter.

When would she stop feeling married? When would she stop expecting Greg home at four o'clock? When would her heart understand he no longer wanted her?

Perhaps when she started rebuilding her life.

With new determination Marilyn put her car into gear, backed out of her parking place, and steered toward the green sports coupe. Maybe Scott Caldwell would remember her.

Scott, exasperated with waiting for Beth's return, jerked open his car door, plopped into the driver's seat, and slammed the door behind him. How long had Beth and that jerk been gone? Impatiently, he checked his gold and silver Timex again. His eyes widened. How could it have been only fifteen minutes? Each minute felt like an hour.

Sighing, Scott knew he couldn't continue this vigil. He was going to drive himself insane with worry if he didn't just go home and try to get his mind off Beth. She was grown now, and hopefully had the firmness she need-ed to deter men like Michael Alexander.

But did she want to deter him?

I refuse to answer that question. I refuse to think about this anymore. I refuse to allow Beth McAllister to consume my every thought.

"Women," he muttered under his breath. "Lord, why couldn't You have made them more like men?"

He was acting like a man obsessed. A week ago he would never have dreamed of spying on Beth. Scowling, Scott cranked his car, put it in reverse, and began backing out.

A horn honked from behind. He slammed on his brakes and guiltily glanced in his rearview mirror. A blue Toyota with an attractive blonde at the wheel sat directly behind him.

"Sorry," he mumbled.

With a carefree smile and a friendly wave, the blonde drove on.

Was that Marilyn Douglas? Scott thought he was seeing things. She had been his idol in high school.

Marilyn Douglas. Head cheerleader. Long blonde hair. Perfect figure. Great smile. Had his mind, in his frustration over Beth, conjured her up?

Like a man seeing a mirage, he shook his head to clear it. What he needed was a bucket of popcorn and a fast basketball game on television. Then maybe he would feel like his old self again.

Six

O ne hour later, Beth stood at the base of the inn's staircase and smiled up at Michael. "Thanks for the carriage ride. I hope you enjoy your stay here." Unintentionally, she had slipped into her professional voice. But her thoughts were so consumed with Scott and his odd behavior that she paid little attention to the present. She could only think of going to see Scott immediately.

"You didn't enjoy yourself." Disappointment dripped from Michael's voice.

"Oh no. I did enjoy myself. I had a lovely time. I'm sorry. If I sound a bit distracted it's because—well, because I am. I have a friend who's not doing too well right now, and—"

"I didn't know." Michael nodded as if that answered all his questions.

"Well, I don't feel that I can share any of the details, but my distraction has nothing to do with you. As I've already said, I had a lovely time."

"As did I." Michael lifted her fingers to his lips.

The light kiss flustered Beth.

"Thanks for the pleasure of your company. I hope you'll be planning to repeat our time together."

"Of course." Beth swallowed against her heart's flutter. At least Tiffany's escapade and Scott's ill humor hadn't discouraged Michael's interest in her.

Despite the excitement of such a debonair guest, as soon as he turned to ascend the stairs, Beth dismissed him from her thoughts. With purpose, she rushed past the clean dining room and kitchen and into the den where Lauren sat reading. "Did you do the dishes?"

"Yeah." She closed her Jane Austen novel. "As a matter of fact, I just sat down."

"Thanks a bunch."

"So how did it go?" Lauren asked with anticipation.

"Fine. But I've got to go to Scott's for a minute. Would you be able to watch the inn a wee bit more?"

"Sure." Lauren, exposing Beth to a questioning frown, relaxed against the burgundy sofa.

"He followed me to the hotel, Lauren." Beth reached for her shoulder bag sitting in the wicker chair.

"Scott?"

"Yes."

"Strange."

"Very strange."

"Did he sit with you and Michael, or—"

"No. He waited for us in the lobby, then spied on us

as we rode away in the carriage."

"Do you think he's losing it?"

"I don't know what to think. But I'm going over to talk with him right now."

"Call if you need me to bring a strait jacket." Lauren giggled.

"Very funny."

The drive to Scott's took about three minutes. For an additional five minutes, Beth sat in her worn-out yellow Camaro and debated whether to approach Scott or go back home. Finally, she decided she hadn't driven three streets over for nothing.

He answered the door immediately.

"Hello," Beth said awkwardly.

"Hi." Scott stared down at her, an unspoken question in his eyes. "I was wondering if you were going to sit out there all night."

"You saw me drive up?"

"Yeah."

Now what? Beth asked herself as a tense silence stretched between them, broken only by the whippoor-wills. The smell of the petunias lining Scott's flower beds filled the air with sweet poignance.

Should she tell him she saw him at the hotel? Why had she even come? Something had urged her to drive to his home the moment she and Michael returned to the inn. That urgency said Scott needed her.

She glanced toward the porch swing. "Care to join me?" she asked.

"Uh, sure. Nice night, isn't it?" he said as if they were two polite strangers.

"Yes. The moon's full. Did you notice?" She sat on the swing's cool boards, and it creaked with Scott's added weight.

As she pushed with her feet, Beth remembered the many times during adolescence she awaited Scott on this very swing. Back then, the house hadn't been in top repair as Scott had recently rendered it. The paint had been chipping. The flower beds were choked by weeds, the floors layered in grime. It had once been a neat house, when Scott's mother was alive. The deterioration followed her untimely death twenty years ago. Beth was glad to see the house at its full potential.

Savoring the evening's cool air, she decided to plunge into the reason she had come. She and Scott had always operated that way. No secrets. No hidden motives.

"I saw you at the hotel," she said to a potted fern hovering near the eaves.

Silence. Tense, loaded, cold silence.

Beth chanced a glance out of the corner of her eye.

Scott, his face an impassive mask, stared straight ahead.

"It was your shoes. I'd recognize Tiffany's teeth marks anywhere."

A laugh, low and rumbling, extinguished the silence. "And you're not irate?"

"I was at first." She glanced at the swirling floral print of her new dress and pinched the stiff cotton. "I mean, after all, I'm all grown up now. I don't need a chaperone. Then I started thinking. . . ."

"And?"

The words spilled from her of their own volition. "Scott, you aren't acting like yourself. At first, I was furious, but now—now—" Turning, she grasped his forearm. His muscles tightened beneath her grasp. "I'm so worried. Is there something wrong? Are you—are you having—a nervous breakdown, or—or—is it because of your childhood, because of your father's death—I—"

"It's not," he snapped, turning an iron gaze to her and deliberately removing her hand from his arm.

Beth felt as if he had slapped her. "I was just going to offer my support," she whispered weakly. "We've always been there for each other. If you need Christian counseling, I wanted you to know I'd be glad to go with you. Oh, Scott, the Holy Spirit can heal so much if you'll only let Him."

Then why don't you let Him?

The alien thought stopped Beth's words. Where had that come from? She didn't need healing. Scott . . . Lauren . . . They needed to be healed.

"I don't need healing. I need—" He stopped, his eyes the shadowed orbs of an eagle mesmerizing his prey. "Never mind."

Beth pushed herself to the swaying swing's corner. She'd never seen Scott like this.

"Have you said all you came to say?" he demanded, his voice never rising.

"Yes," she squeaked.

"Then I need to go to bed. It's getting late."

"Okay." And with that, she stood on trembling legs to race toward her car.

Turn the ignition. Blink against the stinging tears. Don't let your heart know how badly this hurts. One last glance toward the house, a last glance that showed Scott standing on the porch's bottom step as if he had thought of pursuing her.

His form, nothing but a silhouette under the star-studded night, spoke to Beth on a level she could not comprehend. Despite his rude treatment, Beth's heart moved for the little boy who had survived his father's alcoholism, for the teenager who had been her sturdy ally, for the man whose eyes now stirred with something she couldn't identify.

Scott, grinding his teeth, watched Beth's car lights fade from view. He felt as if those lights were his heart, speeding away. For Beth and only Beth held his heart.

Oh Lord, what do I do? I thought I had Your promise. Now . . . now I don't even know if I'm able to comprehend Your voice.

Six years ago Scott accepted Christ. He had been home from college for summer break, and Beth badgered him into attending a revival service. Scott never regretted going. Once he surrendered to Christ, the Christ Beth had shown him through the years, he experienced a new joy, a new love that flooded his heart.

Free.

He was free for the first time in his life. Free to laugh. Free to hurt over his father's abuse. Free to accept the healing only the Holy Spirit could render.

And nothing, nothing had disturbed his peace since that day. He had mourned his father's loss, as any human being would, but the peace . . . the peace was still there. Tonight, however, as he stared at the empty street where Beth's car had been minutes before, Scott's soul churned in distress.

Wrong, wrong, he had been wrong. God hadn't promised Scott he would marry Beth. And if Scott had been wrong about that, could he have been wrong in feeling God's unconditional love? Could the whole thing have been a hoax?

No.

The word, accompanied by chills up his spine, refuted any doubts. Scott sighed. No, God did love him—loved him unconditionally.

If only Beth would.

Scott strained to hear the last purr of her car and wondered at his own abrupt behavior. He had been fine until she mentioned the counseling. That's when frustration overpowered him, and he had growled at her. Now he wondered if he should have obeyed his instincts, chased after her, told her he loved her.

But that would have meant another emotional reaction. Something within whispered that he must take control of his behavior. Since he first saw Michael, Scott had been pushed to the brink of human feelings. First disillusionment, when Beth responded to Michael's flirting. Then fury, when she ignored the jerk's lying. Next the irrational, when Scott followed Beth to the hotel. Now frustration, and he had taken it out on Beth.

Chasing after her, proclaiming his love, would only add to his growing list of rash reactions. Furthermore, her knowledge of his love would cramp their relationship at the very best. At the worst, it would drive her away. He had to be sure that she loved him, or at least was attracted to him, before he let her see his love. As long as she didn't suspect, he could at least feed on the crumbs of her presence. But if she knew, he might risk losing her forever.

O Lord, don't let me lose her.

Seven

*M*ichael Alexander closed the door behind him as he hungrily examined his room. This was the perfect opportunity to begin his quest. From the top of the stairway, he had listened to the rise and fall of Beth and Lauren's voices. Then Beth drove away, leaving Lauren in the back den.

His room, positioned at the front of the house, left Lauren well out of hearing distance. He could press and tap on the walls to check for any hidden doors or sliding panels. The two rooms next to his were empty. Only the guests across the hall could possibly hear him. And if they reported the tapping, so would he. He might even suggest a squirrel or rat as the source. Beth would never suspect Michael. Carefully he lowered the blinds, then closed the navy blue curtains.

After checking into the inn, Michael had superficially searched his closet, looked under his bed, and even examined the room's antique wardrobe. That search rewarded him with a lone pair of worn-out house slippers abandoned by a previous guest. Michael suspected that each room of the old mansion would have to be methodically examined before he found his treasure.

He stared at the ornate antique dresser beside the matching bed. Including the mirror, it stood taller than he. The monstrous thing looked as if it dated from the eighteenth-century French aristocracy. *Too bad,* he thought, crawling onto it. After standing, he had an unusual attack of guilt and kicked off his alligator loafers onto the bed's navy blue quilt comforter. Michael began examining the wall. As he alternately pressed and tapped against the textured blue and burgundy wallpaper, his mind wandered to the carriage ride he had shared with Beth.

He had been truly disappointed when she deflected his kiss. Like magic, the evening twilight had transformed her blue eyes into an infinite sea, her flushing cheeks into velvet, her dark waist-length hair into shimmering satin.

For an amazing second, Michael seemed to be able to see her thoughts. The dear girl had no concept of the power of her simple beauty. And that within itself increased the power. Michael had entertained gorgeous women, too many gorgeous women, who used their looks as manipulative tools. Compared to them, Beth McAllister seemed a rare rose among a field of thorns.

He blinked in confusion. His lips turned upward.

Michael D. Alexander, for the first time in his life,

found himself critical of the very manipulative skills on which he had relied since late adolescence. How many times had he used his looks to his advantage? A smile, a wink, a flirting quirk of the brow. Those and much more had worked "miraculously" to serve him opportunity after opportunity.

Until tonight. Tonight, for the first time in his adult life, Michael had been refused.

Beth McAllister. Had the aunt been anything like the niece? If so, no wonder his father had fallen.

Michael steeled his mind against any more straying thoughts. He had come to McAllister's Bed and Breakfast Inn for one thing, and nothing would stand in his way. With renewed determination, he lowered himself from the dresser to the floor.

Beth might have kept him at arm's length, but she was not unaffected by his charm. Smugly, Michael assured himself that she would capitulate sooner or later. While he faced the challenge of searching her home, he would rise to the personal challenge of Beth herself. By the time Michael discovered the object of his pursuit, Beth would be clay in his hands.

Having examined the wall above the dresser, Michael turned his attention to the wall behind the dresser. Carefully, he strained to lift a corner of the ancient piece of furniture and slid it toward the matching bed.

Patiently, he tapped. This time, the tapping sounded a bit more hollow than it had before. His heart thudded in anticipation. With a new surge of bravado, he knocked against the wall in front of him, then reached to knock against the portion of wall he had previously examined. The area behind the dresser definitely sounded more hollow.

A triumphant thrill zipped through his gut. Tentatively, Michael peeled away a strip of the blue and burgundy floral wallpaper, knowing the ornate dresser would hide any mar he created. Just as he had suspected. Drywall.

He needed something to cut it. Licking his lips, Michael let his gaze move around the room. Nothing. He thought of the storage shed he noticed outside when that blasted pig escaped. Perhaps Beth owned a small handsaw.

First, a quick peek out the window. Beth's old Camaro was still gone. Without another thought, Michael silently moved from his room, down the stairway, and out the front door. No sense in alerting Lauren.

He slipped through the storage shed's rickety door. The smells of motor oil and gas greeted him as he let his eyes adjust from the moonlit night to the darkness of the shed. A moonbeam pierced the lone, dusty window to reveal a bare light bulb attached to a white socket in the wall. Michael pulled the short, rusty chain hanging from it.

Wasting no time, he scanned the piles of clutter lining the shelves and floor. Expended gas cans. A lawn mower. An edger. Rakes. Water hoses. A large tool chest.

Deftly, Michael stepped over the water hose to open

the top drawer of the tool chest, decorated in smudges of grease and rust. Nothing but the typical scattering of screwdrivers, wrenches, and even a dilapidated butcher knife. The next drawer held even fewer tools. The remaining drawers were empty.

Would the butcher knife work? He had never cut through drywall before, but he knew from his teenage escapades that a doubled fist would penetrate it.

He grabbed the butcher knife, a screwdriver, and a hammer. Perhaps he could use the hammer to tap the screwdriver or butcher knife through the drywall and get a start on a hole. If there were a doorway under the drywall, he needed a space only the size of a small window to crawl through.

Hands loaded with tools, Michael reached to pull the light chain. Simultaneously, a pair of headlights pierced the enveloping darkness. He chanced a glimpse out the dirty window. Beth parked her yellow Camaro and got out. Breathless, Michael waited as she ascended the porch steps and entered the mansion.

Now what? Should he try sneaking to his room? As if he were watching a movie, Michael's mind played a hypothetical scene of his creeping up the stairway, laden with tools. How would he explain if Beth caught him?

Then he remembered the garment bag he had left in his car. The perfect means for smuggling the tools upstairs. He needed to get it anyway. Fate must be smiling on him.

Beth, her mind numb with Scott's rejection, dashed away the last traces of tears before entering the den where Tiffany dozed at Lauren's feet. Engrossed in *Sense and Sensibility*, Lauren never stirred from the corner of the overstuffed sofa.

For a moment Beth contemplated telling Lauren of her odd conversation with Scott. Immediately she canceled the thought. Even though Lauren was keeping up appearances, she seemed more distant with Beth every day. Beth no longer felt the depth of comradeship they had shared before Aunt Naomi's death.

Discreetly, she cleared her throat.

Lauren jumped, dropped the book, and let out a puppy-like yelp. Covering her heart, she looked up. "You scared me to death."

Tiffany, shifting her position on the thick Oriental rug, responded with a grunt.

"Sorry." A chuckle. "That's what I was trying not to do. Did I get any calls?"

"No." Lauren, narrowing her eyes, peered at Beth. "Have you been crying?"

"Not much." She ignored Lauren's prying gaze and whistled for Tiffany. "It's time for you to go outside."

The sow, intent on staying in, scurried toward the hallway.

"No go, Tiffany," Beth said, cutting her off. "You know

the rules." Purposefully she prodded the pig out the back door.

With a discontented grunt and a scornful glance over her shoulder, Tiffany trotted toward her outdoor abode.

Hoping Lauren would drop her previous question, Beth nonchalantly plopped into a wicker chair and grabbed the remote control. Not that she particularly felt like watching television, but anything was better than having to dissect her feelings at the moment.

"Are you going to explain?"

Beth heaved a tired sigh. Looked as if Lauren wasn't going to take the hint.

"Did Scott make you cry?" The protective edge in Lauren's voice surprised Beth. The rift between them had obviously not lessened Lauren's loyalty to her big sister.

Still, Beth chose not to answer. Even with Lauren's genuine concern, she knew examining her feelings would only increase her pain and cause more tears. Scott had never mistreated her before. Why had he started now?

"You don't want to talk about it?"

Beth's eyes watered. Her lips trembled. Her throat tightened. "I can't." She turned on the television and began clicking the channels to find the classic movie station—the only station she ever cared to watch.

"Okay." Standing, Lauren tucked her novel under her arm, curiosity churning in her eyes. "I'm heading home then."

"Thanks for watching the inn for me."

"Anytime." She turned for the door, only to do an abrupt about-face. "Okay," she said again, her voice several notes lower. "You're not going to get away with this." She deposited herself in the opposite wicker chair, leaned forward, and pointed her slender finger at Beth's nose. "I want details!"

"Lauren," Beth began in an exasperated tone, "I already told you I cannot talk about Scott right now."

"I don't want to hear about Scott! What happened with you and Michael? When you came back, all you said was that Scott followed you. I want to know how your date went. Here I've been for the last two hours, reading a romance novel that's almost two centuries old"—she held up her book—"while you're out living a romance. I'm the one who sent Michael here, then covered for you while you went out with him. Don't you think I deserve a rundown?" Her blue eyes wide, Lauren dared Beth to refute her.

A spontaneous gurgle of laughter chased away the melancholy Scott had poured into her soul. "You're going to make a great lawyer one day."

Beth briefed her sister, but the details of her date with Michael blurred in comparison to her concern for Scott. He must have developed a terrible emotional problem. She wouldn't take his rejection personally. Instead, she would concentrate on being a pillar of support during his time of need.

Michael bent over the opened trunk of his rented Mercedes, stashed the tools in the bottom of the garment bag, and zipped it. Nonchalantly he walked toward the inn, up the steps, and into the mansion.

Beth and Lauren approached from the dining room, smiling congenially.

He schooled his features into a bland mask. "Just retrieving the rest of my luggage."

"Okay." Beth's faraway expression barely acknowledged him.

She had mentioned a friend she was concerned about. Perhaps that friend would be Michael's salvation, something to keep her focus off of him. For the moment, anyway.

"I'm going to try to catch an old movie in the den." Beth turned from opening the door for Lauren. "So if you need anything, you can find me there." Her voice, although warm, held that professional politeness from earlier.

"Thanks." He headed up the stairs, barely able to suppress a triumphant smile. He had just smuggled in a collection of tools right underneath the woman's nose. On top of that, she had innocently told him she would be in the back of the house for at least a couple of hours. This task might be easier than he had imagined.

Within minutes, Michael locked his door, collected the tools, and positioned himself behind the dresser.

Quietly he pressed the butcher knife's point against the wall and used the hammer to deliver an experimental tap against the handle.

A pause. He listened for any movement in the hallway. No one stirred.

Then another idea occurred to him. He rushed to the bathroom and returned with a folded washcloth. He held it against the knife handle and delivered a harder blow, using the washcloth to muffle the noise. This time, the blade sliced through the drywall. Impatiently, he cut and tore at the wall until he had carved out a jagged square about the size of a hubcap.

He retrieved his penlight, clicked it on, and aimed the beam into the hole. "Bingo."

As he had suspected. A doorway. But where it led, Michael couldn't tell. The wide door frame appeared to have been a doorless walkway.

A new plan crossed his mind. This door might lead to a secret storage room Beth didn't know of. If the treasure were hidden there, she was probably ignorant of its existence. Tonight he could secretly leave, taking his find with him. Beth would never know where he had gone, never suspect what he had taken.

His father would have called it embracing opportunity. But his mother called it stealing. A flame of guilt flickered in his soul. Michael snuffed it out. His plan had progressed too far for that nonsense. The piece rightfully belonged to him, not Beth McAllister. If she knew of its existence, he would purchase it as his father had instructed. But if by some chance Michael could remove it without Beth's knowledge, he would.

He checked his Rolex. Thirty minutes had elapsed since he found the tools in the shed. Should he postpone further searching until Beth was gone? But this was a huge house. The exploration could take six months if he didn't use time wisely. Michael decided to move ahead quietly, swiftly.

Within forty-five minutes, he had cut and torn away a waist-high hole the size of his room's window. But with its jagged edges and uneven circumference, the hole more resembled the gaping mouth of a jack-o'-lantern.

Brushing the beads of sweat off his forehead, Michael pulled a penlight from his shorts pocket. He swept aside a veil of spider webs and dipped through the hole. As he pulled his left leg into the darkness, his thigh scraped against a protruding point of drywall, leaving a stinging reminder of his venture. He straightened and curiously peered into the web-lined corridor.

What he had expected to be a hidden storage closet was actually an unused hallway. The musty smells of mothballs and dust permeated his nostrils. He felt as if he had stepped onto the movie set of a haunted house. The dark walls seemed to constrict him like a shrunken glove on a swollen hand. The consummate claustrophobic, Michael wanted to rush back to his room.

Then common sense urged him forward. If he were going to find the object of his pursuit, he must overcome his fears. That included spiders. Twisting his mouth in distaste, Michael took several steps, tore at a nose-high, gauzy web, and hoped the retreating furry spider wasn't poisonous.

Not twenty feet away, an arched walkway identical to the one he stepped through claimed a spot at the end of the hallway. As in his own room, a sheet of drywall blocked entry. Must be the guest room next to his. Earlier, he had noted that the room was empty.

Why would these two rooms be connected by a private hallway when they shared the main hall? Michael, trailing the penlight's beam along the walls, found the answer to his question. A narrow flight of stairs. His mouth watering in anticipation, he rushed for the steps.

Then he made the mistake of glancing over his shoulder. The light from his room seemed the faint gleam of a star from another solar system. He fought an impulse to run, to claw his way back to his spacious room and clean air.

Leaning against the wall's cool planks, Michael forced himself to take a deep breath; forced his will to control his fears. Slowly he brushed the penlight's beam against the wooden stairwell, searching for any signs of decay. At last his light revealed a doorway at the top of the stairs. Perhaps that doorway would lead to the treasure.

Greed bubbled within, leaving no room for fear. With renewed bravado, Michael began his gradual ascent of the stairs. The impulse that had bade him flee only minutes before now bade him hasten for the doorway above. But Michael once again obeyed his common sense and progressed cautiously. Crashing through a rotting board wouldn't be the most convenient thing to do.

Finally he stood in front of the door. Turning for a last glance behind, he shined the penlight over the stairs to see another dark spider dropping from the ceiling, mere inches from his face. With a stifled grunt he swatted at the creature, only to have it land on his bare forearm. Eight tiny legs seemed to sink into his very bone as Michael wrestled to remove it from his arm.

As a five-year-old, he had endured an older cousin's tormenting him with a pet tarantula. After that summer, Michael's attitude toward spiders had never been healthy. A shiver accosting his spine, he ground at the spider with the heel of his loafer, not satisfied until the creature was nothing more than a dark streak.

At last he gripped the rusty metal knob, twisted it, and pushed against the resisting door. Carefully he squeezed through the narrow opening, slowly pushing against a tall stack of boxes blocking the door. Now he stood between the wall and a double row of aging clothing. The smell of mothballs, stronger than on the stairway, seemed to beckon him farther.

Michael shoved aside the clothing. A quick flick of his penlight. The hidden hallway accessed a cluttered, walk-in closet; a closet with another door that he figured opened onto the third-floor hallway.

Could his treasure be hidden here?

Eagerly he crawled under the bottom clothes rack. He stood erect in the middle of a narrow room and trailed the penlight's beam across rows of hat boxes stashed above an out-of-date wardrobe. The clothing must have belonged to Beth's deceased aunt.

When Michael discovered the hallway behind his dresser, he hoped Beth knew nothing of it. But because the stairway door wasn't visible in the closet, he was almost certain she didn't know about it. The hallway would give him the perfect escape should Beth approach while he searched the closet . . . a closet that held a wealth of possibilities.

But before his search began, Michael needed to learn exactly where this closet was located within the house. He clicked off the penlight and allowed his eyes to adjust to the velvet darkness. Then he grasped the cold metal door knob, turned it, and prepared to ease the door open.

He heard the faint tap of approaching footsteps. Breathlessly he waited as the footsteps neared, then stopped. Fearfully, he counted each thud of his heart. Compulsively, he gripped the knob all the tighter, afraid it would expose him with a click were he to release it.

Yet Michael's curiosity demanded some answers. He inched open the door the width of a grass blade and observed Beth McAllister unlocking her bedroom door and closing it behind her. Then the faint noise of the lock being re-engaged.

With caution, Michael opened the door several inches and examined the area before him. As he suspected, the third floor hallway. When he had checked in, Michael noticed an open stairway leading up here. Now he had his own secret access.

A smirk crawling onto his lips, he opened the door wider to see another stairway in front of him. This one led to yet another door. Consisting of no more than ten steps, this second stairway seemed to lead to an attic or storage room.

Old attics usually held old treasures.

Fresh triumph invaded his soul like a victorious army claiming new territory. Even though he hadn't found his prized piece tonight, Michael had discovered a passageway that led to the attic and a closet that deserved as thorough an exploration as the attic.

Enough exploring for one day. Even though Michael's impatience tempted him to search the closet tonight, he couldn't risk Beth's hearing him.

Furthermore, the time to take his sleeping pill was approaching. Though Michael could survive a few hours without his habitual dosage, the thought of putting himself through the consequent anxiety, headache, and sweating held no appeal.

The closet would be there all summer. The attic would be there all summer. As soon as the opportunity presented itself, he would be back.

Eight

*B*eth watched from her kitchen window as Scott, whistling cheerfully, unloaded a stack of yellow timber from the bed of his father's dilapidated truck.

What was he up to?

Earlier, when she took Tiffany for her usual walk, Beth wrestled with the wire Scott used as a latch substitute. Then she vowed to call a repairman to fix the gate. After last night, she assumed Scott wouldn't be available to help her. He had been so angry. Now, his face was rested, relaxed. All vestiges of anger had vanished.

Wrinkling her brow in confusion, Beth turned toward the stack of cookies she had just finished baking for her guests—one of Aunt Naomi's traditions. With a flick of her wrist, she tore a paper towel, folded it, and placed four of the cookies in the center. Then she poured a mug of the French vanilla coffee she and Scott favored. Perhaps cookies and coffee would work as a peace offering and smooth the problem between them.

Unseen, she approached him, contemplating exactly what the problem was. Scott denied being troubled about his childhood or his father's death, but Beth had almost convinced herself that was the issue. He had snapped at the very mention of his father's death, as if she touched a raw nerve.

From a few feet away, she watched while he unloaded the last piece of lumber. His muscles rippled beneath his blue shirt. He wore his usual chore attire, T-shirt, faded denim cutoffs, and Nikes. They fit Scott as if they were a part of him. She blinked with the new feeling stirring in the pit of her stomach. Had he always been this attractive, or was the morning sun playing tricks on her?

Dismissing the foreign thought, Beth cleared her throat. "Mornin'," she said tentatively.

"Oh, hi!" Turning to face her, Scott smiled.

"Thought you might like a coffee break." Beth extended the peace offering, and he took it.

"I'm always game for your chocolate chip cookies. Didn't you bring some for yourself?" He gingerly set the cookie-laden napkin on the hood of his rusty truck.

"No, I'm trying to lose a few pounds. And I've already had three cups of coffee this morning."

"Too many." He shook his head in brotherly disapproval.

"You know me and French vanilla. We go way back." The tense knot inside her was slowly uncoiling. Could this be the same man who had practically pushed her off his porch the night before?

As their meaningless chat continued, Beth peered into his eyes, hoping to find the answer to her mounting questions. But Scott wouldn't make eye contact for more than seconds at a time. How strange that he should act as if nothing ever happened. Beth's knot of tension began to recoil.

Something was wrong.

Scott, the strong, the dependable, never acted angry only to pretend everything was well.

"What's the lumber for?" she asked, hoping her voice didn't reflect her now churning emotions.

"Oh, I forgot to tell you." A dimpled smile—the smile that had brightened Beth's life for as long as she could remember.

Had Scott's smile always been so endearing? His dimples so deep?

"I decided to rebuild your gate."

"But—"

"No buts, lady. The thing is about ready to fall apart. Even if I put a new latch on, I doubt this gate would last another six months."

Biting her bottom lip, Beth stared at a clump of wood fern growing under her kitchen window. Should she accept his help? The question, so new to her, defied answering. She had never hesitated to call Scott for help before. And the gate did need to be replaced.

"Okay, but I'm paying you. It's not fair for you to spend your summer—"

"Nope," he clipped and drained the last of his coffee. "No deal." With that, he resumed his whistling and turned toward his task as if to dismiss her and her protests.

Searching for words, any words, Beth continued to stare at his lean form. If he hadn't been so . . . so . . . however he was last night, Beth would push the issue of her paying. But a new wave of uncertainty swept over her. Uncertainty about his reactions, his motives, him. Immediately, Beth knew the Lord couldn't use her to help him heal if Scott kept pushing her away. Better to hold her tongue and comply with his wishes.

Deep in thought, she walked toward her front porch to find a smiling Michael Alexander sitting in one of the wing-backed wicker chairs.

Scott stopped whistling. Beth thought he was nuts. He could see it in her expressive eyes. They seemed to scream, *What is the matter with you?*

He gazed at Michael's expensive vehicle sitting in the driveway. Until that moment, Scott had been so proud of his new, forest green sports coupe—a mere Chevrolet. It now paled in comparison. With sinking clarity, Scott realized he would never be able to offer Beth what Michael could.

At least he could be comforted in knowing she was

still speaking to him. After last night, he'd wondered. Scott decided to play like nothing happened and hope she would play along. She had. Just like a pro. Why did he ever doubt his Bet?

A soft voice, deep in his soul, suggested that he owed her and Michael an apology. That quick, repentant prayer yesterday had cleared him with the Lord, but he knew God expected restitution. He had acted anything but Christlike with Michael and Beth.

As something akin to cold rocks settled in his stomach, Scott propped his hammer against the decaying gate and walked toward the front porch.

Lord, I'd rather be buried in ants than apologize to that—that— Okay, okay, I'll apologize. But not to Beth, Lord, not right now. Please, please understand. I'm afraid if I start an apology I might tell her everything.

Scott knew telling her everything, of his love, of his hopes for their future, could lead to her rejection. And he was not ready to encounter that rejection.

When Scott saw Michael smiling at Beth as she approached the front porch, his resolve to apologize nearly dissolved.

"Hello, Beth," Michael said, standing.

"Good morning," Beth said, surprised at his presence. She had been so engrossed with Scott's problems she hadn't given Michael one thought.

"What are your plans for the morning?"

"Hmmm, excuse me." Scott's voice floated across the spacious porch, and Beth's heart lurched with its mellifluous tone.

Michael's brows rose in sarcastic query, and Scott looked as if he were having to eat escargot with whipped cream.

"Uhh, I—I just wanted to apologize for yesterday, Michael, for being so rude, and, um, obnoxious." A new determination stirred Scott's eyes. "I'm a Christian, and I know there are a lot of people who say that and don't live like it. I'm one of the ones who says it and means it. So's Beth," he added.

His pointed glance splattered guilt across Beth's very soul.

"I acted anything but Christlike yesterday, and I'm sorry."

Michael's smirk turned to surprise. "I won't give it another thought."

"Good," Scott said. "Sorry for interrupting, Beth. I'll get back to my work now."

Breathless, Beth rushed forward. "Scott?"

His troubled glance, a glance that recalled the sobbing boy who had lost his mother to cancer, stirred Beth's emotions to a level she had never felt for her friend. Suddenly, she wanted to hug him. Following that prompting, she took three quick steps.

Then stopped.

"Uhh, uhh . . ." Clearing her throat, she tried to

steady her trembling voice. "Thanks," she finally croaked. "Not many men would have apologized. You don't know what it means to me."

"Yeah." And he was gone.

"I was just going downtown," Michael said as if nothing had happened. "From what I understand, it's like taking a trip back in time. Want to go with me?" He twirled a pair of flashy sunglasses by the earpiece.

Beth forced her mind to focus on Michael. In his white cotton shorts and designer turquoise shirt, he looked as if he had stepped from the pages of *Gentleman's Quarterly*. But for some reason Beth couldn't appreciate the effect.

"What did you say?" she asked, forgetting what her mind had registered only seconds before.

"I said, would you like to show me around historic Eureka Springs?"

Wake up! a pragmatic voice demanded. *The most handsome man you've ever met is asking you for a date! This is not the time to be worried about Scott!*

"I'd love to," she blurted, hoping he didn't sense her earlier distraction. "But I've got a ton of work to do around here. Plus, I have to stay close to the front desk in case new guests arrive." The disappointment cloaking her mind virtually dripped from her voice.

"Oh, hang your chores." His eyes crinkled with his coaxing words. "When was the last time you took a day off?"

Beth, walking toward the door, tried to remember.

Even on Sundays, after attending church, she listened for the front desk's electric bell. In essence, her time was not her own, including the three days a week the maid, Mrs. Spencer, came. Last night, Lauren had stayed by the desk. Lauren wasn't here today.

"I really can't," she said, hoping upon hope that he believed her. She didn't for one second want him to think she didn't want to go. Why discourage opportunity? "I have a business to—"

The merry toot of Lauren's Volkswagen horn stopped Beth's words. "Hello," Lauren called in her cheery voice as she climbed from the car.

"Hello yourself," Beth called back, a twinkle of hope igniting. Maybe, just maybe Lauren wouldn't mind watching the desk once more.

"Let's see if we can get her to help you out again," Michael said under his breath, then squeezed her hand as if they were two conspirators.

Beth, reveling in the feel of Michael's fingers against hers, watched as Lauren bounced up the sidewalk in her jeans and red T-shirt.

"Mom and Dad don't need me today because Sherry's finally back from maternity leave," Lauren announced. "So I thought I'd drop by and see if I could help you out." As she passed Beth, Lauren produced an exaggerated, although secret, wink.

"Well, I could use you. Michael and I were thinking of going downtown. Would you mind—"

"Not in the least. You two go on." She waved her hand

toward Michael's car. "I can answer the phone." Lauren beamed like a satisfied lion who had just outwitted a sheep.

Beth thought of Lauren's summer project to see her older sister happily married, and she had the uncomfortable feeling she was being manipulated. With a cautious glance toward Michael's charming smile, she wondered if Lauren had somehow arranged for him to appear this summer. No. Lauren might have a manipulative streak, but she wouldn't go that far.

Besides, didn't Lauren realize that Michael wasn't a Christian?

Well, what about you? an insistent voice asked; the same voice that had prohibited her from finishing her devotions that very morning. As she had done then, Beth tried to smother the voice.

A moment later, she climbed into Michael's Mercedes and fastened her seat belt. Scott was busy at the gate. His lips puckered in a whistle, he turned from his task to walk toward the storage shed. That's when their gazes locked. As if by some supernatural force, he focused on Beth, sitting in the luxury car's plush leather seat. Her hands stilled as guilt, cold, constricting, gripped her heart. The look in Scott's eyes, even at this distance, seemed the gaze of one betrayed.

But why betrayal? Since when did Scott care whom she dated?

"I can't tell you how much I'm looking forward to the day," Michael said, reaching to lace his fingers with hers.

She tore her attention from Scott and looked at Michael, searching for confirmation for her friend's warnings. But all she saw were Michael's adoring gray eyes, wispy blond hair, and full-lipped smile.

No.

Scott was wrong.

There was nothing to be afraid of.

A cautious glance back at Scott. He remained unmoved, still staring as if to somehow will her from the car.

Purposefully Beth glanced at the hand enveloping hers, to Michael's diamond ring, winking at her as if to say, "Don't worry about Scott. Just enjoy yourself. This might be your chance at happiness. No need to let Scott's petty problems ruin your future."

Please, Lord, understand, Beth pleaded as an icy hand sunk its talons into her chest. *I know he's not a Christian, but guys like this don't come along everyday, especially not for girls like me.*

She thought of her lonely teen years, of being dubbed "fatty," of braces, of acne, of never being part of the "in" crowd. She thought of the romantic relationships that dotted the years that followed. Then she thought of the one person who had been like a rock through it all. Scott. Scott Caldwell had been her friend, even during the most humiliating experience of her life . . . but she wasn't going to think about that now.

As Michael backed out of the driveway, Beth wanted to lunge from the car and run for Scott who turned, defeated, toward the gate. A crazy impulse. A senseless impulse. An impulse that would surely push Michael from her for good.

Taking a slow, deliberate breath of the leather-scented air, Beth turned a flirtatious smile to Michael.

"Scott seems a nice guy after all," Michael said, eyeing her curiously.

"Yes."

"Good of him to apologize." A derisive snort. "I certainly wouldn't have."

"Well, that's just Scott." Beth took a deep breath as a thought struck her. Maybe she could use this as an opportunity to witness for Christ.

"Like he said, he takes being a Christian seriously. So do I, actually. I—"

"That's nice." He raised her hand to gently kiss her knuckles. "But I'm more interested in taking you seriously."

Beth swallowed against her quickened pulse as her desire to witness faded in the face of his ardent words.

Scott, deliberately turning his back on Beth, repressed the urge to jump into the dilapidated work truck and follow her. He couldn't continue spying on her, he knew that. And seeing the two of them flirting made him crazy enough without adding to the torture by watching them on a date. Beth would simply have to take care of herself.

Lord, please protect her. . . . and re-engage her common sense!

Grabbing a hammer, he pounded a plank for no reason.

"What's got you in an uproar?" Lauren's teasing voice floated from the kitchen window.

Scott scowled in her direction. "Who says I'm in an uproar?" he demanded.

"Uh—sorry I asked." Her smile faded.

Sighing, he gripped the top of the truck's bed, hung his head, and took a deep breath. "Sorry I snapped at you. I plead temporary insanity." But another quick glance told him Lauren was gone.

His gut churning, Scott tackled the gate and vowed he would avoid Beth the rest of the summer. Too many more days like today, and his insanity would be permanent.

So much for God's promise that I'll marry her.

Nine

*M*arilyn Thatcher ruffled her daughter's blonde curls and plopped behind her on the giant spiral slide. They had been playing in the park almost an hour, and both were dusty, tired, and anticipating a trip to McDonald's.

"Okay, this is the last time down," Marilyn said. "Are you ready?"

"Ready!" the three-year-old cheered.

Down they zoomed to an abrupt stop amid giggles and girlish screams.

"Let's do it again, Mom!" Brooke urged, her pleading brown eyes so like her mother's.

"No, that was the last time. Mom's tired. Aren't you ready for your Coke?"

"Can I have a hamburger and Fench fies, too?"

"You bet!"

"YIPPEE!" Brooke exclaimed, racing for their car.

Marilyn, usually full of energy, trudged behind. Her

mother seemed to think her listlessness resulted from the stress of the divorce. Marilyn knew her mother was right.

After seeing Scott Caldwell yesterday, she suspected another cause for her lingering depression and listlessness. She desperately needed to begin rebuilding her life. That would start with her application for a part-time job at the local veterinary clinic. But she also needed new friendships.

The image of Scott Caldwell leaning against his green sports coupe floated back into her mind. Last night, Marilyn had discreetly asked her mother about him. With a few vague questions, she learned that Scott never married, recently returned from New York, and was the high school basketball coach. Did he have room in his life for a friend? A friendship with Scott would take Marilyn back to a time in her life before she had ever met Greg Thatcher. Those days had been carefree, delightful, joyous.

The days before heartache.

Michael Alexander steered the Mercedes into the inn's driveway. Beth had shown him the highlights of downtown Eureka Springs and, much to his astonishment, he had enjoyed it. In the gourmet candy shop, he held her hand. And by the time they got to the quilt shop, he had taken the liberty of slipping his arm around her waist a few times. For a brief hour, he had even lost focus of the reason he was playing up to Beth.

Even now, with a dot of chocolate on her nose, she was by far more interesting than most of the women he had encountered. Character, his mother would call it. Somehow Michael knew his mother would approve of Beth McAllister.

A tendril of uneasiness twined through his soul as he thought of the wrongs his trusting mother had endured at the hand of her wealthy husband. For years Michael adopted his father's scornful attitude about the gullibility of women in general, his mother in particular. Now, at the age of thirty, he doubted that his mother was the one who deserved his scorn.

As he stopped the car, Beth glanced his way and caught him watching her.

Michael smiled indulgently. "You've got chocolate on your nose."

"Oh, no! I ate that chocolate-covered apple an hour ago! Why didn't you tell me before?"

"I just now noticed. It's not that much."

Beth reached for the vanity mirror, but Michael stopped her. "Let me get it off."

He slowly extended his index finger to blot the tiny smudge. Then taking advantage of the spark of reaction in her eyes, he brushed his thumb across her cheekbone, stroked her neck, and inched toward her. A fire ignited in him as she hesitantly tilted her chin upward.

Then something changed in her eyes. The spark was

replaced with a shadow—perhaps a memory. Michael couldn't define the emotion, but he felt as if an intruder had wedged his way between them. Just as Michael's lips were about to caress hers, she turned from him.

Disappointment settled in his chest. Whether he wanted to admit it or not, Beth McAllister, the woman he had come to dupe, was affecting him. Affecting him deeply.

None of this romancing is for your pleasure, Michael reminded himself. *Beth is merely an expendable stepping-stone. Nothing else. You must keep your head.*

With his focus reestablished, Michael smiled in self-mockery, cleared his throat, and moved away from her. "I guess I'm to be content with a handshake," he teased.

"Sorry," she squeaked. "I usually take my relationships slowly." The plea in her eyes was exactly what Michael had hoped for.

He knew her capitulation was only a matter of time. He wouldn't push. Whatever happened, Michael wouldn't anger her. He must not, for she owned a treasured possession he desperately desired.

Beth, staring at the geraniums encircling her massive white porch, didn't dare look at Michael again. Her stomach flip-flopped, and she willed herself to open the car door. She could feel him watching, waiting, as if he still hoped for a kiss. But something within her couldn't allow him any closer. As desperately as she wanted him to take her in his arms, there was a granite-like wall inside her that repelled his presence.

Was the wall because of Scott? As much as she tried to lock him out of her mind, she felt his look of betrayal boring into her back the whole afternoon. Twice she glanced over her shoulder, expecting to meet him. Instead she encountered the curious expression of a stranger.

Was the wall because of the Lord? Her chest felt as if it were in a giant's iron grip. No. She wouldn't feel this way. She wouldn't allow her religious beliefs to snatch away her chances with Michael.

Look at Aunt Naomi, she firmly reminded herself. Aunt Naomi wound up living her whole life unmarried.

Beth so desperately desired a husband, desired children. The thought of letting Michael slip away because of her faith—or because of Scott—seemed ridiculous. Suddenly, she wanted to throw herself into Michael's arms. Her heart pounding, she turned back to him, ready to speak, ready to tell him whatever he wanted to hear.

His smile, jaunty and assured, stopped her. It was the smile of a ravenous wolf. An overwhelming urge to run replaced Beth's thoughts of surrender.

As if he had read her initial intentions, Michael once again leaned toward her.

"I—I—just—just remembered I hadn't thanked you for the delightful trip," she stammered, placing one foot outside the Mercedes. The feel of the paved driveway beneath her sandal seemed to connect her with reality. Cautiously, she chanced another glance toward him to see the disappointment of a twelve-year-old draped across his features. Her imagination was working overtime. Surely, he hadn't really looked like a wolf only seconds before.

"I enjoyed it too," he whispered, stealing a last caress of her cheek.

A caress that sent a weakening, frightening chain of fire to the pit of Beth's stomach.

Just as strongly as she had wanted to embrace Michael, she now wanted to escape him. Wasting no more time, Beth stepped from the car. Instinctively, she glanced toward her backyard gate.

Was Scott still working? No.

Disappointment stabbed her soul; a disappointment more poignant than any fire Michael had produced.

At 11:30 P.M. Michael cautiously eased open the door of his room and glanced up the wide hallway. The other guest rooms seemed locked securely for the night.

After the date with Beth that afternoon, Michael rested in his room, ate dinner at a local restaurant, went to a movie, and returned late. Then he waited in his room until he heard Beth ascend the steps to the third floor. That had been an hour ago.

By midnight, he would be forced to take his sleeping pill. He had taken the small green gel caps for about seven years. If he missed his twelve o'clock dosage, he grew sweaty, shaky, nervous. In thirty minutes, the pill would beckon, but thirty minutes was long enough for a quick search of the downstairs closet he noticed at breakfast.

Belting his monogrammed, designer bathrobe, he tiptoed down the stairway that led to the inn's entry room. That morning, when no one was looking, he tried the handle of the closet off the kitchen to see if it were locked. A quick peek inside revealed a narrow room lined with shelves stacked with who knew what. Now, Michael planned a thorough investigation of that room.

The closet upstairs and the attic still beckoned, but Michael planned to save that search until Beth was not at home. Meanwhile, this downstairs storage closet called for exploration.

He silently turned the aged metal knob, pulled the string that hung from a bare light bulb, stepped into the closet, and noiselessly closed the door behind him. The smells of rust, stale paint, and machine oil greeted him. Like a lion hungrily scouting a tribe of gazelles, Michael inspected the room's six crowded shelves.

Buckets of paint, streaked in green and yellow and white. Household tools—a hammer, pliers, electric drill. A wooden box, overflowing with nails of various sizes. A mixed assortment of liquid cleaners. Two old shingles. A bag of wild birdseed. An ancient sewing machine.

Eagerly he began his methodical search. Careful not to rearrange the contents, he gradually inched each item from its spot and firmly pressed the wall behind it. If a secret stairway led from his room, he might discover a secret storage space in this closet. Obviously, the object of his desire did not openly reside on one of the stained, wooden shelves. However, it could easily have landed behind the shelves. Old treasures had a way of arriving in the least suspected places.

His father gave the priceless piece to Beth's aunt when Michael was a toddler. Three months ago, Edgar Alexander had lain in a hospital bed, ashen with the pain of cancer, and recounted the story to his only son. He had stayed at Naomi McAllister's quaint bed and breakfast inn merely by accident. Traveling to Eureka Springs to soak up nature's beauty and solitude, he also stumbled upon a beautiful woman. Not giving a thought to his wife or small son, he spent the summer with Naomi. When Edgar exited, he left behind a brokenhearted, disillusioned woman and, in her possession, an item now worth a great deal of money.

Edgar Alexander, having never been a good husband or father, had recounted the story to Michael in an attempt to ease the tormenting guilt of the dying.

"I want somehow to make it up to you, Michael," he rasped.

Michael's hands stilled against a streaked paint bucket as he recalled his father's fading eyes, white hair, and angular face.

"It's worth a fortune by now. Except for your trust fund, everything I own is going to your mother. But this—this— If you can get Naomi to sell it to you, it's yours. You deserve it. I should have been with you and your mother when I gave it to her. Please—I—I—" Tears had pooled in his eyes; tears of regret.

And Michael, for the first time, had felt a true bond with his father. Swallowing against a tightening throat, he had floundered in confusion, wondering how to respond. Throughout Michael's whole life, his father had provided materially for him. So bent was he on pursuing his career and his mistresses, he had taken precious little time to build a relationship with his son.

Still, everyone said Michael was the exact image of his father, in looks, in disposition, in attitude. Until the last few days, Michael had been proud of his successful womanizing and luxurious lifestyle. But for some reason, perhaps because of his father's deathbed regrets or his mother's steadfast loyalty, Michael was suddenly questioning his life.

Once more he focused on the streaked bucket of paint and remembered his quest. He also remembered his dwindling trust fund. If he were going to continue living on the same level of luxury that had characterized him thus far, he must find his prize. His mother, so dedicated to her church work, had already given heavily to missions. Michael knew without asking she wouldn't support his luxurious lifestyle. She would support him, he had no doubt of that. But her support would likely include his moving into her mansion, listening to her incessant sermons, and having his every move known.

Or he could work. If he wanted to continue in independent, unbridled pleasure, Michael would be forced to work. No doubt family friend Gaylon Sadler would give him a well-paid position that included international travel. But the thought of being tied down to any position, no matter how prestigious, left Michael feeling sick.

With renewed determination, he began quietly removing the paint from the shelves and carefully placing it near his feet. Along with the cleaning supplies and other items, the cumbersome buckets must be removed to thoroughly check the wall behind them.

Beth couldn't sleep. Her eyes ached. Her forehead pounded. And her mind raced with thoughts of Michael and Scott and Scott and Scott. Scott's defeated stance when she drove away with Michael. Scott's following her and Michael to the Crescent Hotel. Scott's unpredictable behavior.

She had expected him for dinner, but he hadn't called all evening. Three times she picked up the phone to call him, and each time changed her mind.

She also thought about her conflict with Lauren. Lauren had been so sweet to watch the inn today while Beth and Michael went into town, but Beth still sensed a tremendous amount of tension from her. Would Lauren be happy if Beth sold McAllister's Inn and split the profit with her? Somehow, Beth didn't think that would solve a thing.

Sleep wasn't going to come. Beth decided to go downstairs and make a cup of tea. Wishing she could erase the speeding thoughts from her mind, she opened the china hutch in the dining room to remove her favorite tea cup, white with an elaborate pattern of cranberries. A soothing cup of cinnamon herbal tea would still her thoughts.

As she turned from the hutch, she noticed the door of the storage closet ajar, allowing a shaft of light to escape the narrow room. Squinting, Beth tried to remember the last time she opened the closet that day. After retrieving some dust cloths, she was almost certain she had turned out the light and closed the door.

But that had been the moment before she made her final decision to call Scott, and then not to call Scott. Sighing, she plodded toward the closet.

By midnight, a sea of disappointment drowned Michael's anticipation. Nothing. He had discovered nothing. No hidden closets. No treasure behind the cluttered shelves. No hint of where it might be.

Fingers trembling, he rubbed his gritty eyes and decided to go on to bed. The time had come for his pill. Tomorrow would bring new challenges; new potentials for his search.

The caution that had accompanied him to the closet now deserted him, driven by a hasty need to swallow the green gel cap. Without thinking, Michael opened the door, only to see Beth walking from the kitchen into the dining room, mere feet from the closet.

His heart thudded in a panicked tattoo.

Afraid of any noise he might make, he didn't dare risk closing the door or pulling the string to click off the light. Instead, he held his breath, flattened himself against the shelves, and desperately searched for a plausible excuse for being there.

He felt a gauzy tickling on his right ear. Slowly he turned to see a furry, gray spider scurrying toward the center of her web, a web his ear had invaded. Michael swallowed. He felt as if he were a stallion caught between a panther and a jagged cavern. If he moved to kill the spider, Beth might see the movement. If he didn't kill the spider, it might bite him. The terrified child within urged him to knock the spider to the floor and smash it with his heel. But the man he had grown into insisted he remain still. To add to his anxiety, he recognized too well the evil cobra uncoiling in his gut. His body was beginning the demand for its little green pill.

With each of Beth's nearing footsteps, a new film of sweat oozed from Michael's body. First his upper lip, then his forehead, next his spine. Desperately he tried to keep his breathing even. If Beth discovered him now, her suspicions would be roused. His chances of finding the treasure would be demolished.

She will see you.
She will grow suspicious.
She will ask you to leave.
You will never achieve your goal.
Work, work, work. You will be forced to get a job.

Beth inched open the door. With her back to Michael, she bent to replace some fallen dust cloths. So close was she, a sigh could have rustled her hair. Michael swallowed, licked his lips, and tried to look casual. But how did you look casual in your bathrobe in the middle of the night in a storage closet with a spider inches from your ear?

Then, without turning to face him, she pulled on the light string, exited, and clicked the door shut behind her.

His icy fingers tingled. His heart thudded. Every ounce of his blood felt as if it drained to his feet. Quickly, silently he jerked away from the web and reveled in the quiver of relief dancing down his spine.

Michael had learned his lesson.

Caution.

If he were going to proceed with his search, he couldn't use enough caution. This enormous house could take months to search. The summer stretched before him. He would not allow his greed or exhaustion or thoughtlessness to overrule his caution again.

Ten

Scott entered Beth's spacious kitchen. "Wow, something smells scrumptious."

Sniffling, she turned from the cutting board where she was chopping a large onion.

"It's the brisket," she said through a torrent of tears.

"Hey, what's the matter?" Scott steeled himself against rushing to her side.

"Nothing." Another sniffle. "The onion gets me every time."

A soft chuckle. They hadn't spoken since his apology the week before. After rebuilding her gate, Scott had kept to his decision to avoid her. He hadn't wanted to see her with "Blondie," and hoped to avoid the sight by staying away. But it seemed everywhere he went, he saw them anyway. Just yesterday he had been jogging and spotted them out for a stroll, Beth laughing at some witty thing Blondie had said. If only she were laughing for him.

She called him an hour ago to ask a favor. "Could you

please come and see if you can get the air conditioner in the pink room to work? I turn it on, and nothing happens."

Even though Scott planned to avoid her the rest of the summer, her sweet southern girl drawl had dissolved that resolution. Like a loyal coonhound, Scott arrived as if he had been awaiting her summons. He was simultaneously disgusted with himself and elated at her needing him. Having made short work of the task, he came downstairs to find Beth in her kitchen.

"Your air conditioner wasn't plugged in," he said indulgently.

"Oh." She stared at him in round-eyed chagrin. "Thanks. I've got a new guest arriving and everything needs to be working." A vague smile.

"Does that mean you'll have three rooms occupied now?"

"No, six. Three more couples have signed in since I last saw you."

"You're full, then. Great. Looks like it's going to be a profitable summer."

"Yeah. I've invited Mom and Dad over for supper to celebrate. Care to join us?"

Eager acceptance poised itself on Scott's tongue. Then he checked himself. He had no desire to eat dinner with Michael Alexander. Seeing his Bet ride away with that jerk last week made him feel as if she were never coming back. Indeed, he felt as if he had already lost her; lost her, before he ever held her.

"No, I've already got supper planned," he said, thinking of the stale TV dinner he intended to eat.

"What had you planned?" Beth demanded, turning and placing her fists on her jeans-clad hips.

"I . . . um . . ."

"Oh," she said with a tinge of disappointment.

Like a man drowning in despair, Scott grabbed at the hope that maybe she missed him; maybe her invitation was more than just propriety; maybe she really wanted him at dinner.

"Is Michael going to be here?" he asked, his voice blunt even to his own ears.

"No," she said, turning back to her onion. "He's gone to Branson for a couple of days to see the music shows."

"And you didn't go with him?" he asked, a sarcastic twist to his words.

"He asked me to." Her back stiffened.

And Scott remembered her stomping her foot and demanding that he stay out of her love life. If only she knew he wanted to *be* her love life.

"But I couldn't leave the business." She turned to wash her hands, and an expectant silence settled between them. Finally she spoke again. "So, will you stay for dinner?"

"Sure." The word popped out before Scott realized he had spoken. He was annoyed by his own weakness and delighted with her relieved smile.

"Hello, Michael here."

"Michael, my man," a familiar New Jersey voice said over the phone. "How are you progressing?"

"Not nearly as fast as I thought, Gaylon." He glanced around the glass-and-brass first-class hotel suite only miles from Beth's inn. "I've searched my room, a closet, one other guest room. I discovered a hidden staircase leading from my room to the third floor, near the attic. But I still haven't found it."

"Have you searched the attic?"

"Not yet. Last week, she almost caught me in the closet. That slowed me down a bit. If she suspects anything, that ends the whole operation."

"Are you sure it even exists?" Gaylon asked.

"Dead sure. You know he told me about it just before he died. People on their deathbeds don't usually lie."

"Then it's got to be there."

"I hope I find it soon. There's a guy here who doesn't trust me." Michael reflected over Scott Caldwell's amazingly correct intuition. Regardless of the apology, Michael knew Scott still didn't appreciate his presence.

"Well, it's up to you whether you want to keep looking. You're the one who'll get most of the money, but I could sure use the sales commission."

"Just how badly do you need it?"

Silence.

"What are you implying?" Gaylon asked, a hint of conspiracy permeating his tone.

"I went into this planning to buy the piece and resell it." Michael hesitated.

"Yes?"

"What if I find it tucked away somewhere, and Beth doesn't even know it exists?"

"I assumed you would somehow manipulate the situation to make her aware of its existence, then make an offer."

More silence. Gaylon was adept in maneuvering the law to his benefit. What Michael was about to suggest wouldn't be Gaylon's first effort to assist a friend in a tight spot.

"But why lay out the cash if you could slip out without her ever missing it?" Gaylon murmured.

"Could you arrange a false passport and driver's license?"

"I'll see what I can do."

"Good. I'll have some passport photos made and overnight them to you."

"Okay. And I'll use them for your driver's license as well."

A stretch of silence. Michael waited while Gaylon's sharp mind sorted this turn of events. "Perhaps I'll get an express package from you in the next week?" Michael asked.

"You can count on it."

"And do you happen to have a customer who would

make the purchase and keep it quiet?"

"Of course. I know just the client. There's no sense in putting this one on the international market for bids. That would only alert the authorities if—"

"I won't get caught," Michael insisted. "Especially not if I can make a quick exit from the country under an assumed name."

"Right. But the best thing to do is stick to your first plan," Gaylon said in a fatherly tone. "It will be less risky."

"I will. I will. If Beth knows about the piece, I have no choice. I can't waltz out of the house with it and not expect her to miss it. But if I do find it hidden somewhere . . ."

"Just be careful. The last thing you need is an all-expenses-paid trip to prison."

"Right." That would be worse than working. "Well, I guess I need to go. I'm heading back to the B & B. I told Beth I wouldn't be back till tomorrow morning, but I'm starting to get bored."

"Good luck. And don't give up."

"Oh, I won't." As he hung up the receiver, Michael set his jaw in new determination. The last week he treaded lightly for fear of arousing Beth's curiosity. Even though the third-floor closet and attic tantalized his curiosity, the downstairs closet episode shook his bravado.

But he had spent the time wooing Beth, an important part of the grand scheme. Every time she had a free minute, he placed himself in her path. Regardless of her holding him at a distance, Michael sensed her growing pleasure in his company. And despite himself, he found that he looked forward to the pleasurable gleam in her eyes.

That was part of the reason he faked a trip to Branson. He came to Eureka Springs for one reason. He would leave when he gained his goal, whether honestly or dishonestly. He couldn't afford to let this woman's simple charm get to him.

These two days away from Beth had refurbished his purpose, reinstated his courage, and left him hungry for more exploration.

Marilyn Thatcher, chewing her fingernail, stared at the traditional black telephone gracing her mother's oak end table. Should she call Scott? She had never called a man in her life.

All week she hoped she would run into him by chance, but to no avail. She was even tempted to attend his church. But that would have meant breaking the vow she made when Gregory left her: no more church. Her life as a pastor's wife revolved around church. Now she could barely stomach the thought of entering a sanctuary.

Sighing, Marilyn paced the homey room, feeling like a lost little girl in a tangled, mocking forest. Yesterday her parents had taken Brooke on a trip to visit Marilyn's older brother, Drew, in Little Rock. Marilyn couldn't go because she had started her new job at the veterinary clinic.

Marilyn assumed some time alone would do her good. Now she questioned that assumption. All this free time only intensified the loneliness that constantly lurked outside her heart's door, awaiting the first opportunity to slip through the keyhole.

Well, Mr. Loneliness had slipped through tonight and planted himself firmly in the center of her soul. Staring at the fuchsia-and-black Oriental rug, Marilyn made her decision. She would call Scott.

Beth, smiling in anticipation, placed a German chocolate cake on the table. The delighted groans from her family and Scott increased her smile.

"You've outdone yourself, Beth," her father said.

"Yes," Frances McAllister echoed, her blue eyes alight with pride. "We weren't expecting you to do so much."

"Oh, well." A nonchalant shrug. She sliced the coconut-laden cake. "I enjoyed it."

"Bet's the best cook in Eureka Springs," Scott said, his eyes strangely disturbed.

"Second only to her mother," Don McAllister qualified, patting his wife's plump hand.

"Well, what about me?" Lauren feigned a pout.

"I think you'd better concentrate on a career, dear." Frances's eyes lighted with mirth.

"Yeah, and marry a chef," Scott added, then filled his mouth with the fragrant cake.

"Ah, Scott, I'd counted on marrying you," Lauren teased.

"No, you can't have Scott." Beth jumped into the ongoing joke between Scott, Lauren, and herself. "We're set to get married in our old age."

Scott sputtered, wheezed, then coughed compulsively.

"Are you okay, son?" Don asked, his eyes full of concern.

"Fine . . ." A dry hack. "Fine . . . I—I just choked on a piece of cake."

"Here, let me get you a glass of milk to wash it down," Beth said. "You always liked milk with your cake, anyway."

Rushing into the kitchen to get the milk, Beth thought of how empty her house had been last week without Scott. Even when he lived in New York, she hadn't missed him this much. Of course, she hadn't lived in a sprawling mansion then, either. Perhaps the big house was the problem. Even with guests here, Beth felt alone.

Alone physically and spiritually.

At the age of fifteen, Beth asked Christ to forgive her sins and come into her heart. From then on, no matter how alone she was, no matter how others treated her, she felt that constant sweet presence that initially filled her being. A few years later, Beth humbled herself at an altar to surrender her everything to the Lord, in essence, to make Him Lord of her life. And a steady, inner peace descended upon her, a peace that remained, regardless of life's storms. Now, that peace, that sweet presence seemed miles from her. And Beth, for the first time in thirteen years, felt lonely spiritually.

Nervously, she grabbed one of the crystal milk mugs from the glass-front cupboard and forced herself to think of the physical. Thoughts of the spiritual led to thoughts against dating Michael, something she enjoyed this last week, something that made her feel of true worth for the first time in years.

Early in the week, Beth hired Mrs. Spencer's college-age daughter, Sheila, as a part-time receptionist and clerk, freeing Beth to spend evenings with Michael. They had sat and talked for hours. They had strolled at dusk. They had shared several old movies. He had even taken Tiffany for her walks and won the pig's lifetime loyalty.

But despite Michael's steady companionship, Beth still thought of Scott. When she invited him to dinner only hours ago, she held her breath. He had obviously distanced himself from her after last week's episode, and she didn't want anything to taint their lifelong friendship.

Maybe he was like the trusty house slippers she had worn for years and years. They fit. They were comfortable. Two years ago, she left them at a hotel while vacationing in Florida. She resorted to drastic measures to get them back.

And Beth had done the same with Scott. With a calculating smirk, she poured the milk. What would Scott think if he knew she had unplugged that air conditioner herself? "Lauren McAllister, you aren't the only one with a manipulative streak," Beth muttered.

***

"Mom, did you notice the couch by the door when you came in?" Lauren asked. "Beth had it recovered last week."

Lauren, seeming more tense than Scott ever recalled, laid down her fork. "Come on, and I'll show you."

Still recuperating from choking, Scott discreetly hacked at the last piece of coconut lodged in his windpipe. When Beth mentioned their getting married, he compulsively swallowed.

That had been his mistake.

He eyed his china coffee cup. The old marriage joke he and Beth started in high school had turned into a cruel twist of irony, ready to choke the life out of him physically and emotionally. The very woman he had joked about marrying for years was now the one he desperately desired.

Oh Lord, am I forever destined to dull bachelorhood? I want to wake up to Beth every morning. I want a house full of children. And I really thought You promised!

As his coffee cup blurred, anger, like a white-hot knife, sliced his thoughts. What if God really had promised? What if the peace Scott felt was indeed God's confirmation of answered prayer?

New anger.

Anger with God for allowing him to feel such infinite peace, only to have it shattered by Beth's continual indifference. *Why did You promise if You weren't going to follow through?* Scott pleaded inwardly, his frustration exploding to new levels.

"How long have you been in love with her?" Don McAllister mumbled after the women left the room.

A quick glance into Don's keen brown eyes told Scott that denying it would be useless. "Is it that obvious?" he whispered as cold desperation pierced his heart.

"Only to me, I think."

"I hope."

"If it's any consolation, I think it's high time Beth married, and I don't think she could find a better man."

"But . . ." Scott shook his head, a pall of defeat snuffing out his momentary joy over Don McAllister's approval.

"Just give her time." A fatherly smile.

"It seems she would rather spend her time with somebody else."

"Ah yes. The famous guest," Don said with feigned reverence.

"You've met him?"

"No, but Lauren has told us all about him."

"I'm really worried. The guy's obviously not a Christian, and—"

"Just leave it in the Lord's hands, son. Beth is a strong Christian. She'll come around."

"That's what I initially thought. Now I don't know." Scott toyed with his napkin.

"Well, I have a firm conviction that she will, and when she does, I believe she'll turn to you. Frankly, I think the two of you would have an excellent marriage. Friends make the best spouses. I ought to know."

"Were you and Mrs. McAllister friends first?"

"Yeah. And she almost had to beat me over the head before I woke up to the fact that she was the most intriguing woman I had ever met."

"How exactly did she wake you up?" Scott asked, eager for advice.

"Well, we were at a Fourth of July church picnic." Don squinted as he recalled the event. "And the pastor had sent us to his truck to retrieve the watermelons. It was high noon and about a hundred degrees. And, well, I turned around from the truck and there she was, looking up into my eyes with those big baby blues. And do you know what she did?" A reminiscent laugh. "She just grabbed me, kissed me, and then said, 'There's more where that came from if you're interested,' and walked back to the picnic."

Scott laughed, the kind of laughter that rolls the stomach and cleanses the soul. "Mrs. McAllister? I can't believe—"

"Well, you better believe, son, because that's exactly what happened."

"And what did you do?"

"I stood there gaping like a zombie for about five minutes. Then I decided that was the best kiss I'd ever had and I wanted more. I showed up on her doorstep that night with a bouquet of roses, and the rest is history."

"What stories are you telling about me?" Frances McAllister asked from the dining room doorway, hands on hips in typical McAllister fashion.

"Oh, just chatting with Scott." Don's expression was the epitome of innocence.

"Okay, here's the milk." Beth entered from the kitchen. "Sorry it took so long, but somebody called to make reservations for next month."

"Great." Lauren's eyes clouded. "Looks like you've got it made in the shade."

"No, I don't." Beth shook her head. "You know Aunt Naomi didn't leave me a lot of cash, and this place needs a roof. Besides, I just hired another part-timer and have that salary to worry about now." She set the pitcher on the table.

"Some of these people have been coming to Eureka Springs every summer for years and years, and they always expected Aunt Naomi. I was worried that business would slack off when they didn't find her here."

She sat next to Scott, her soft rose perfume tantalizing his senses. What would it be like to wake up to that smell every morning?

"Well, I wish she were still alive," Lauren rushed, her cheeks flushing. "I'd like to ask her why—" And she stopped, guiltily glanced toward Beth, then dropped her eyes to her empty dessert plate. "I'll start clearing the table," she said instead.

Eleven

*A*re you okay, Lauren?" Frances McAllister's voice
floated over the clinking of dinner dishes in the
sink.

Coffee urn in hand, Beth entered the kitchen.

"I'm going to be fine," Lauren whispered, her back to
Beth as she filled the porcelain sink with water.

Beth frantically searched for the right words. Why did
they always come to her hours or even days after she
needed them?

Lauren and she were closer than most sisters growing
up, probably because Beth had been more like an adoring aunt than an elder sister. Beth still remembered the
day her mother brought the tiny infant home from the
hospital, and everyone said that Beth, at eight years old,
was a "little mother."

Now, she could hardly bear the tearing in their relationship. And all because a doting aunt had left more of
an inheritance to Beth. The matter seemed so trivial to

erode a relationship, but apparently not to Lauren.

But was that the only reason their relationship seemed strained? Biting her lip, Beth looked with envy at Lauren's slender hips in her crisp denim skirt.

Why was she suddenly so obsessed with her appearance? Beth thought she had accepted long ago that she wasn't attractive. Now old scars were erupting into new wounds and filling her heart with a raw pain she thought was long gone. As the haunting laughs of high school classmates echoed through her mind, Beth wondered if the pain had ever died. Perhaps it had only lain dormant for a time.

Only days before she thought Lauren was in need of the Lord's healing. Now, she wondered if perhaps Lauren wasn't the only one. Beth told Scott that the Holy Spirit could work miracles, but right now she felt as if He were miles from her.

Shoving aside her musings, Beth busied herself with the leftovers.

Suddenly Lauren screamed.

Jumping, Beth fought to balance the bowl of potatoes teetering against her palms.

"What's the matter? What is it?" Frances rushed to Lauren's side.

"It's only me," a muffled voice called from outside the window.

"Oh." Lauren placed a flattened hand over her heart. "You scared me to death."

Michael. Michael was back. Beth's pulse, which had

raced in fear, now raced with excitement. She couldn't exactly say she had missed him, but his distinguished voice had a way of affecting her.

"What is it? What's the matter?" Scott rushed from the dining room with Don close behind.

A faint knock preceded the back door's opening and answered Scott's question.

"I am so sorry," Michael said, entering with a bouquet of roses. "When I saw you at the window, I thought you were Beth and just wanted to surprise her."

"When Lauren saw you, she thought you were a peeping Tom," Frances said, eyeing Michael suspiciously.

"Mom, Dad, I want you to meet Michael Alexander. He's a guest—and a friend of mine."

"Michael, I believe Lauren mentioned you last week." Don extended his hand, and Michael exchanged pleasantries with Beth's parents.

"I brought these for you." Michael, an admiring twinkle in his eyes, handed Beth the roses.

"For me?" A rush of pleasure. "Thanks. I've got the perfect vase for them. It matches Aunt Naomi's crystal. Scott, would you—" She turned to ask Scott to fetch the vase from the china hutch, but she was talking to air. The sound of a cranking car in the driveway punctuated his disappearance.

Lauren, casting a nervous glance to Beth, cleared her throat. "I guess he had to leave."

"Must have." Beth wanted to run after him. Even though her house was full of company, it felt strangely empty once more. "Well . . ." She feigned a bright smile. "I'll get the vase then, and as soon as we clear the table, I'll put the roses in the center."

❧❧

By 11:00 P.M. Michael was pacing his room like a prisoner sentenced to life. The attic. Tonight he would search the attic. He would climb the stairs from his bedroom, sneak up the attic stairs beside Beth's room, and begin the hunting, just as soon as Beth was asleep.

She went upstairs thirty minutes ago, and he lay on his bed, light off. Now adrenaline flowed through his veins as if he were struck by the lightning flickering on the horizon. He had a full hour before he needed to take his sleeping pill. But one hour in the attic would be a good start.

Remember caution, he admonished himself. *Caution.*

If his treasure weren't in the attic, Michael would have to continue his search, prolong his stay. No sense in getting caught. Suddenly, he wished with his innermost being that he would find the treasure tonight. He had to get away from Beth McAllister.

Keeping company with her was getting risky.

He hated to admit it, but he missed her these last two days. Something about her smile touched him as he had never been touched—perhaps because it wasn't tainted by greed. Other women had been more interested in his pocketbook than they were in him. Their motives hadn't bothered Michael much, because he was preoccupied with his own equally ulterior motives. Now, next to Beth's genuine interest, the thought of their greed disgusted him.

Michael couldn't lose sight of his reason for being here. Beth McAllister was not it. Financial independence was.

You have got to get away from her.

✦

After a relaxing bubble bath, Beth collapsed into her antique poster bed and, for the first time in a week, reached for her Bible. Between her duties with the inn and Michael's constant companionship, she had barely found time for the Lord. After that first failed attempt at witnessing, Beth hadn't mentioned God to Michael again. And if she were honest, she would admit she hadn't purposed to. Not that she was ashamed, but she sensed that Michael wasn't interested.

So why are you developing this relationship with him?

Beth bit her lip and thought of all the fun they shared. The boat ride. The music shows. The glass chapel. All the usual tourist attractions that were old news for Beth came alive when she was with Michael.

Why was she dating him?

Because for the first time since she remembered,

Beth felt as if she were worth something. When she gazed at his near-perfect face, she wanted to pinch herself. To think that a man of his appearance and wealth could be falling in love with her. . . .

Please God, Beth pleaded while staring at her unopened Bible. *Please understand. This might be my one shot at happiness. I don't want to be single my whole life. I want a husband and children and grandchildren. Please God, please.* . . . The warmth seemed to slowly recede from her heart, replaced by a chilly foreboding and Scott's haunting question.

What about your reputation as a Christian?

Thoughts of Scott turned her attention to the cordless phone sitting on her cherry night stand. Should she call him? What would she say? Since he left so abruptly, Beth felt as if she should apologize for something.

"Nuts," she muttered in consternation, wondering exactly what that "something" was.

She knew why Scott left. He made no attempt to hide his dislike of Michael. Well, Beth couldn't help that, because she did like Michael.

Pulling the cool, fresh-smelling sheet over her legs, she placed her unopened Bible on the night stand and clicked out the light. For thirty minutes, Beth debated with herself.

It's too late to call him.

Then she remembered the little boy from grade school, the disenchanted teenager, and her heart whispered, *You know he's a night owl. He won't be asleep. Call.*

Her hand, of its own volition, reached for the phone.

That's when she heard the creaking. Creaking. As if someone were walking up the nearby attic stairs. Beth's pulse leapt.

The third floor consisted of Beth's spacious bedroom, a bathroom, and Aunt Naomi's private library. All six guest rooms were on the second floor. That meant nobody—*nobody*—should be on the third floor with Beth.

A faint rumble of thunder was followed by a gust of wind, sending an oak's branch squeaking against her window. Beth exhaled. The wind. Maybe that was what she heard.

But the creaking persisted, despite the wind's lull. Beth's stomach knotted, and she swallowed against a painfully tight throat.

Without thinking, without a prayer, she lunged from her bed, reached for her satin robe, and grabbed the flashlight from the drawer of her night stand. Perhaps the noise was only the house settling. Or mice. Or . . . or Tiffany.

Silently she tiptoed from her bedroom. The hinges on the attic door squeaked. And she knew she would not find mice or Tiffany.

The thunder's mumbling filled the musty-smelling hallway and penetrated the halls of Beth's mind in ominous warning. Whom would she find? Was he or she dangerous? Should she call the police?

Or Scott?

Scott hammered the basketball against his new back-yard court. He executed a perfect lay-up and dribbled back to half court. But with every bounce, with every echo against the fragrant night, the sound of leather against cement seemed to mock his aching heart.

Hopeless. Hopeless. Hopeless. Your love is hopeless.

He had been so sure of God's promise when he set out to woo Beth that he had plunked down several thousand for a one-carat diamond engagement ring. The futility of that purchase seemed to fill the night with scornful laughter . . . a laugh much like Michael Alexander's.

Earlier, when Michael waltzed through Beth's back door as if he owned the house—and Beth—Scott had been forced to run. Run, or face the consequences of his masculine instinct, which told him to punch "Blondie" right in the nose and tell him to keep his hands off Beth. Then once again Scott would have been apologizing to that jerk for acting un-Christlike.

Maybe I should move back to New York, he mused.

Scott took a leave of absence from his teaching position in New York and came back to Eureka Springs because his dad was dying with emphysema. As the dreaded illness progressed, and Scott's visit stretched longer and longer, he realized just how much he had missed his hometown; how much he had missed Beth. So when the Eureka Springs school board offered him a coaching position, Scott accepted.

That acceptance opened several opportunities for him to contribute to the welfare of the town. Currently he was planning a charity basketball game to raise funds for the refurbishing of several abandoned historical churches. The game would pit local clergy against the high school staff and was the third such game Scott had planned. Proceeds from the other two games benefited the humane society and a home for battered women.

All these events enhanced Scott's fulfillment as a teacher, and he hadn't doubted that coaching in Eureka Springs was the right choice. Now he wasn't so sure. For somewhere between Beth's endless supply of potluck and smiles and her holding his hand through the funeral, Scott had fallen. Fallen hard. Fallen hopelessly.

At dinner tonight he stopped doubting that God promised to fulfill his love. He couldn't deny the peace that swept over him during his initial prayers for a godly wife, the peace that ushered in thoughts of Beth and an awakening of the love turned tormentor.

Once again, anger washed over Scott as he weighed the situation. Why wasn't God following through? Why would He so freely promise, then allow such turmoil?

Gritting his teeth, Scott glided through another lay-up, wiped sweat from his brow, and headed for the door. But something within him shriveled at the prospect of going in. He had thought that a complete facelift on the house would wipe away the bad memories collected in the corners, in the attic, on the porch.

He had been wrong.

Even this morning, he remembered the forgotten months that followed his mother's death, the weeks when his father, in an alcoholic stupor, blamed Scott for his wife's cancer. Those weeks started the pattern of verbal abuse that depicted the rest of Scott's childhood.

Scott held no animosity toward his father, only pity for a miserable soul. He thought the Lord had healed him from his past.

Then this morning he poured a bowl of cereal and remembered the countless times his father had let Scott's cereal sit until it was soggy as "punishment." Not punishment for anything specific, just punishment. How many mornings had Scott eaten soggy cereal before going to school? He couldn't remember. He hadn't remembered.

Until this morning.

Forgetting his anger with the Lord, Scott began to pray. *Oh Father, You'll have to heal this memory too. I'd forgotten. Please, please, Lord, release the pain and make me whole.*

One last shot at the basket. He missed and chased the stray ball toward his driveway. Once he caught it, he aimlessly dribbled the ball, forcing himself to trudge toward his house.

His empty house.

No wife.
No children.
No laughter.

Twelve

Marilyn, her forehead perspiring under her helmet, pedaled her ten-speed through the quiet neighborhood. The hills and valleys of this Arkansas town were just as steep as she remembered, the fresh smell of a country night still as poignant. After trying to call Scott three times and getting only his answering machine, she decided to chase away her blues with exercise.

Eleven thirty P.M. wasn't the usual hour she biked, but nothing in her life the last few months had been usual. So why not? With Brooke gone, Marilyn was free until morning to do what she wanted when she wanted.

Her aimless riding took her through street after street of shadowed frame houses occasionally caressed by the flickering of lightning on the horizon. Neighborhoods full of laughter, joy, families. Thoughts of families sent an ache through her heart, and she recognized "Mr. Loneliness" sitting on her handlebars. Sighing, Marilyn wondered if she would ever shake him.

Eventually her pedaling led her to Scott's neighborhood. Marilyn didn't try to analyze her motive. She simply wanted to cruise past his home. For some reason, she felt unusually drawn to him, to his potential friendship.

As she neared his house, she slowed to hear the pounding of a ball against pavement. Then she glimpsed an angular, shadowed figure walking up the driveway. And Marilyn Douglas, who had never called a man in her life, did something else she had never done in her life. She decided to surprise Scott Caldwell with a spontaneous visit.

One of Greg's comments before he filed for divorce had been that Marilyn lacked spontaneity. *Well, this one's for you, Reverend Greg Thatcher,* she thought sarcastically.

❦

Fingers trembling, Beth clicked on her flashlight, then immediately turned it off. No sense in alerting the person prowling in her attic. Holding her breath, she leaned against the wall as a jagged bolt of lightning bathed the hall in yellow light. A cautious peek around the corner, up the short flight of stairs, and her racing pulse stopped only to pound in hot horror.

Someone stood in the attic doorway, a ghostly silhouette against a new streak of lightning.

Run . . . Run . . . RUN! a voice urged. *Call the police!*

Would Aunt Naomi have run? a stronger voice queried. *No!*

"Excuse me," she said impulsively, amazed at how her firm tone contradicted her trembling knees. "But this floor is off limits."

The figure pivoted to face her, and a new blink of lightning only heightened his blackness. The walls vibrated with the nearing thunder as if the house itself were warning her.

One silent second. Beth poised to race for her room, to do what she should have done in the first place. Alert the police.

"Beth?" a bewildered voice called.

"Michael?" She exhaled in relief as hot blood rushed to her cold face. New caution quickly followed. What was he doing up here?

"I seem to be lost," he said, closing the attic door and descending the steps.

Beth flipped on the nearby hall light to encounter Michael in a black bathrobe, his eyes those of a pleading boy, and her suspicions melted.

"I'm so glad you found me. I—I—" He shuddered. "I hate to admit it, but I'm a chronic sleepwalker. I woke up at the base of those stairs. I thought I was on the first floor. Then when I got to the top . . ." Like a gallant knight, he bent, drew her hand to his lips, and kissed her fingers. "Thank you. I think you just saved my life."

With a nervous giggle, Beth pulled her hand from his warm mouth. For some reason, there were no tingles.

Perhaps because she had been so scared. "Well, I wouldn't say that I saved your life."

"Ah, but the lady is modest."

Another crash of thunder, closer, louder, resounded through the hallway, and Beth jumped as if she had been struck. "Sorry," she breathed. "Storms always give me the jitters."

"Hey," he soothed, reaching to pull her into his arms. "It's okay."

Stiffly, she leaned against him, his expensive after-shave filling her senses. She didn't relish being alone on the third floor with Michael. Scott's warning echoed through her mind.

I'm worried about your reputation as a Christian.

"Want some tea?" Michael asked, pulling away, his eyes the epitome of innocence. "I always like tea on a stormy night. I'm sure it would calm your nerves too. Would it be too much to ask?"

Her momentary doubt vanished, and her knotted stomach relaxed. "I'd love to make some tea."

"Hmmm, excuse me?" a feminine voice called.

Scott turned to face a vaguely familiar figure. Dressed in biker's shorts and a helmet, a woman pushed her bike around the freshly trimmed shrubs and to the edge of his lighted court.

"I was out for a late ride and heard you playing. I just thought I'd stop. I can tell you don't remember me."

As she removed the helmet, the years peeled away, and Scott recalled a bright-eyed cheerleader, all lanky legs and braces and dimpled smiles.

"Marilyn. Marilyn Douglas."

"Right!"

"Did I see you the other day at the Crescent Hotel?"

"You sure did. I was just going to stop and say hi when you got into your car."

"I thought I was seeing things." A smile. "You haven't changed a bit."

"I can't say the same for you," she said, the shadows hiding her eyes but not the appreciation in her voice.

Scott wasn't sure if the rush of pleasure was from the seventeen-year-old within or from the man he had grown to be. "What brings you to Eureka Springs? I thought you moved away."

"I did, but well, divorce happens, you know."

"Divorce?" he said, trying to hide the astonishment. "I thought you married a minister!"

"I did." A nonplussed shrug. "But he decided he liked his secretary better than me."

"Oh," Scott said, hearing the pain in her voice and not knowing what else to say.

"It shattered the church, my parents, his parents, me."

"I'm so sorry." *Now that was a brilliant cliché,* he thought sarcastically.

"Anyway, my little girl and I are staying with Mom and Dad a while until I get back on my feet." Another shrug. "After I saw you the other day, Mom mentioned that you were back in town, and I just thought—"

She glanced toward the house as if to incite an invitation, and the nearing lightning on the western horizon seemed to urge Scott to speak.

"Would you like to come in for a soda?"

"Sure."

With an encouraging smile, Scott reached for her bike. "Need any help?"

"Sure." She chuckled. " 'Sure' is the word of the hour. Did you know?"

"Sure, I did." He parked her bike beside the deck and ushered her inside his neat home. The way she surrendered the bike to him, the way she allowed him to open the door for her made Scott feel of use in a way Beth had never made him feel.

Beth seemed to view him as just plain ol' Scott. Always there. Always the same. Taken for granted.

Having a blonde-haired beauty smiling up at him left Scott wondering why he had been pining after a woman who never looked at him in appreciation.

"So what brings you back to Eureka Springs?" she asked as he settled her at the breakfast bar of his austere, black-and-white kitchen. "Mom mentioned that you had been teaching in New York."

Scott warmed with the knowledge that Marilyn Douglas actually knew something about him. "Well, my father was ill. Emphysema. He passed away not long ago."

"I'm so sorry." Her doe-brown eyes, filled with concern, reminded Scott of smoky topaz. "I forgot. Mom told me about that too. I know losing your father must have been heartbreaking."

"It was." Scott smiled sadly. He didn't feel like talking about his father, not with that cereal memory draped over his thoughts like a lifeless corpse. He didn't trust himself not to shed a few tears over his father's abuse, and tears were not the way to begin a new friendship.

"Do you like root beer?" he asked.

"Sure."

"And popcorn?"

"Sure."

"Microwave okay?"

"Sure," they answered together.

"Okay, I promise not to say it again, if you won't," she said over a girlish giggle.

"Scout's honor."

As the evening continued, Scott couldn't remember the last time he felt so elated. All the worry before his father's death, all the worry with Beth, all the worry with Michael Alexander had so robbed him of joy he had almost forgotten how good laughter felt.

Marilyn Douglas once snared his heart with her upturned nose, hair of honey, and a smile that could dazzle the sun itself. How easily she could snare his heart again.

By midnight, Scott discovered an old comedy on his

big screen television. They plopped themselves on his southwestern rug, munched their fragrant popcorn, and reveled in newfound friendship.

At two A.M. Marilyn finally insisted she leave, but Scott, hating to see her go, offered to drive her home. "The streets are so wet from the storm, I'd feel better if you'd let me drive you."

"What about my bicycle?"

"I'll drop it off tomorrow." *That will give me another excuse for seeing you,* he thought, images of Beth McAllister fading quickly.

"Works for me," she quipped, and he was almost sure she had read his mind.

Scott opened the front closet, grabbed a sweater, and deposited it around her arms. "I think that rain blew in a summer cool front. You might be glad to have this."

"Thanks."

He opened the front door, and they stepped onto the spacious porch. The smell of midnight rain coupled with the crisp morning air greeted them.

Soon Scott's Chevrolet rolled to a stop outside Marilyn's parents' home. "I'm really glad you stopped by," he said.

"Me too," she said warmly. "I don't make a habit of, um, dropping in on men, but—"

Sensing Marilyn's uncertainty, Scott reached to squeeze her fingers, which nervously picked at the hem of her biker's shorts. "As I said, I'm glad you did."

Marilyn's smile, sincere and relieved, seemed to

ignite a thousand candles in Scott's midsection. "You know," he rasped, stroking her cheek, "your ex-husband must have been crazy."

With a swallow, she closed her eyes. "Thanks. I needed to hear that."

Scott hadn't kissed a woman in a while. And he would be lying to himself if he pretended he hadn't missed affection from the opposite sex.

Scott knew for certain if he attempted to take Marilyn in his arms, she wouldn't protest. The feeling left him heady with anticipation. At the same time, he wondered if her sudden interest was in him or if she were simply on the rebound from her husband, a man she obviously once adored.

Several silent seconds elapsed.

Her hesitant glance instigated him to action. Slowly he leaned toward her. Suddenly Beth's fresh smile and candid eyes appeared between them.

Would kissing Marilyn be fair to Beth?

Would it be fair to Marilyn?

Wouldn't he be just as guilty of using Marilyn as that jerk was of using Beth? And what about God's promise to him?

Like a whirlpool, wild and raging, confusion swirled through Scott's soul. He reversed his impulsive decision.

No. Scott couldn't kiss Marilyn, not until he was more sure of his own feelings.

"Good night," he muttered, pulling away, her floral

perfume teasing his senses. "I'll bring your bike to you tomorrow."

"Sure," she said with a dry chuckle.

"Sure." Gently, Scott touched her hand.

Thirteen

ichael paced his room, debating whether to sneak up the hidden stairway into the third-floor closet. For a week that third-floor closet and attic had enticed him. Then, when tonight came, and he finally thought he could slip into the attic, Beth caught him.

The sleepwalking story was a stroke of genius. Beth's believing it had been a miracle.

But how had she caught him? He experienced the oddest paranoia that Beth possessed some supernatural power that allowed her to sense when he was snooping. After all, she almost caught him in the storage closet under the stairs. Would she also catch him if he went upstairs now?

Michael chewed his thumbnail. His sleeping pill was long overdue. With a spin on his heel, he checked the digital clock on the marble-topped night stand. "2:00" glared at him in neon red. Could he wait much longer before consuming the gel cap? His hands shook. Sweat rolled down his neck.

Immediately, all his greed focused upon the closet at the top of the staircase. Apparently, it was not original to the house, but had been added once the staircase outlived its use. Also, the closet was across the hall from Beth's room, while the attic stairway was on the same side of the hall. So even if he dropped something, Beth probably wouldn't hear him. And if she did, he would hear her footfalls before she opened the door to explore the noise. He could slip back into the stairway and close the door before she ever got near. Nothing about this venture was half as risky as the attic expedition.

He would do it. And if he was forced to stop and take the pill, he would begin later where he left off. Michael had dallied enough. He desperately needed to find his treasure and leave this inn.

If he found the treasure without Beth knowing, he could stash it in his car and leave. She would never suspect he had taken it. But if, as his father suggested, Michael tried to buy the piece, Beth might guess its true worth and not sell it. At the present, stealing it seemed the logical plan. The false identification Gaylon was sending would be his safety net.

Like a shadow chasing a chance at life, Michael slid the dresser away from the wall, twisted the bottom of his penlight, stepped through the hole, and slipped up the stairs. Within seconds, he was wrapped in the closet's mothball smell.

Now, where to start?

Hands unsteady, he brushed the penlight's beam across the stacks of boxes and the hanging clothing. First he would check behind the clothing. Then he would search the shelves.

Thirty minutes later, he had examined the walls behind the clothing, tapping and pressing for any hidden storage area. Nothing. By now, the shaking tormented him. Soon he would be forced to swallow the pill and let sleep claim him. If the shelves didn't reveal his treasure, the attic still beckoned. Michael must remain steadfast. The summer was young.

He bent to grip a cardboard box full of books. After sliding the box from under the clothing, Michael stood on it. The added height gave his six-foot frame plenty of visual advantage over the shelves' contents. Silently he gripped the penlight between his teeth and began lifting every hatbox, scanning the shelf underneath and behind.

When he lifted the third box, a slip of yellowed paper, folded in half, flitted to the floor. At first, Michael ignored it. Then he remembered that nothing should be askew; he must leave no evidence of his presence. He bent to retrieve the paper, and let his gaze wander over the words written there.

> *Dear Naomi,*
>
> *I am gone. I know this will be a great disappoint-ment to you, but the time has come for me to be honest. I am not single as I first told you. I have a wife and*

*child living in New England. Even though you will
always hold a special place in my heart, I must maintain my allegiance to them.*

*Thanks for the great summer. Please keep all I
have given you. I hope you will remember me fondly as
I will you.*

Best regards,
Edgar Alexander

Michael stared blindly at the letter. Somehow, the letter made him feel closer to his father than he had ever
felt. Growing up, Michael assumed his often absentee
father gave little heed to his family. But this letter, so old,
so forgotten, touched Michael as his father never had. At
least Edgar Alexander had thought of his son, if only
once.

Then a new thought struck Michael. A twisted grin.
For the first time, he also felt that he was close to discov-
ering his prize. Knowing it was too large to fit in the hat
boxes, he hadn't wasted time opening them. But even if
the treasure he sought wasn't in a box, perhaps a clue to
its location was.

Knowing this was his last venture for the night,
Michael climbed back onto his makeshift stool and
eagerly examined the contents of the boxes. Hats. Hats.
Hats. Then, he opened the ripped box he had picked up
when the letter fell to the floor.

Another smile. His heart, like a schoolboy's in love,
palpitated with anticipation. For this box held old pho-

tos of his dad, notes, and, most importantly, jewelry boxes. His father's letter must have fallen from this collection.

Just in case there might be more hidden jewelry, Michael quickly checked the rest of the hat boxes. Nothing but hats. His head pounding for the pill, he momentarily considered tapping against the walls above the shelves. No. The walls would have to wait. The gel cap's call was too insistent.

Careful not to spill any more contents, he gingerly gripped the box's sides, then rearranged the remaining boxes to fill the space of the one removed. After replacing his footstool, Michael slipped from the closet and hurried down the stairs and into his room.

Heady with triumph, he clicked on his lamp, deposited the box in the middle of his bed, and replaced the dresser. A quick a check of his room's lock. Safe.

Compulsively he tossed clothing from his suitcase until he found the white bottle that would end the anxiety, sweating, shaking, and headache. Chloral hydrate. Long ago, his first cousin, an MD, had prescribed them. They had been Michael's regular companion ever since. Like an alcoholic desperate for a drink, Michael fumbled with the lid, finally unscrewing it. Then he swallowed one of the gel caps without water.

Fifteen minutes. The pill would take effect in fifteen minutes. Until then, he could peruse the box.

His mind racing with the possibilities of those jewelry boxes, Michael couldn't open them fast enough. At last, he stared hungrily at what he calculated to be approximately fifteen carats worth of antique diamond jewelry. A gold and diamond bracelet, shimmering like a thousand stars. A silver ring with solitaire diamond. A necklace and matching earrings, studded in emeralds and diamonds. Each piece contained a card with his father's signature.

The necklace and earrings resembled something Edgar Alexander had given to Michael's mom. An unusual attack of loyalty gripped his heart. Michael fleetingly wondered if his mother knew Edgar had bestowed such treasures on another woman. Whether she did or not, the jewelry rightfully belonged to Michael. Edgar should have been home with his wife and child instead of dallying with another woman. Perhaps fate was repaying Michael for a father who cared only for himself.

Not understanding the onslaught of bitterness, he picked up one of his father's black-and-white snapshots. With hands almost shaking out of control, he tore it in half, right along the cocky smile, so like his own.

That's when he noticed another photo. One of a young woman who bore a family resemblance to Beth. A young woman standing beside the item Michael so desperately desired. An inferno blazed through Michael as he speculated what the piece might bring.

Half a million? Three-quarters?

It was here. He knew it had to be. The jewelry would be an added bonus, but even the diamonds didn't near the value of his prize.

❦

The next morning Beth cleared away the things left from the herbal tea she and Michael had shared the night before. Neither she nor Michael had been exceptionally communicative. Politely sipping tea with him had seemed an obligatory deed. As it was this morning, her mind had been with Scott.

Now, after an almost sleepless night, Beth knew she must see her friend. His abrupt exit after dinner had disturbed her sleep. And her morning seemed to lag with the weight of her troubled night.

She cleared the clutter from the continental breakfast she always served her guests. Next, Beth left the reception desk and the inn's chores to the care of Mrs. Spencer and Sheila.

"We'll take care of everything, don't you worry. Enjoy your morning," Mrs. Spencer encouraged.

A dear lady from Canada, Mrs. Spencer and her college-age daughter had truly been a godsend to Beth. Both worked part-time, and they wouldn't be back for two days. So Beth decided to take advantage of their presence.

Clad in blue linen shorts and crisp white T-shirt, she arrived on Scott's front porch before giving herself time to back out. Hesitantly she tapped on the door, wondering what kind of reception to expect. That was a new feeling. A few weeks ago, Beth would have never anticipated anything but open friendship from Scott. Now she didn't know whether she would meet good ol' Scott or the moody stranger who often appeared in his place.

Another knock. Firmer. Still no answer.

Then Beth glimpsed movement from the corner of her eye. There was Scott, dressed in blue jean cut-offs and T-shirt, riding a maroon bicycle to the porch steps. "Hello," he teased. "I'm a local knight in shining armor out on my trusted steed. Would you happen to be a lady in distress? If so . . ." He dismounted to produce an exaggerated bow. ". . . I am your humble servant."

"Very funny." A relieved smile. Good. Apparently, the brooding stranger wasn't in today.

"You just caught me. I was about to leave." Still smiling, he propped the bike against the stair's handrail, then virtually bounded up the steps.

"What's got you in such a good mood?" Beth settled on the white porch swing, and he sat next to her.

"Oh, I don't know. It's just a beautiful day. I love to wake up to a morning after a storm. Everything always smells and looks so clean. Isn't God's creation great?"

Beth couldn't remember the last time Scott's eyes, the color of emeralds, had sparkled so. This morning, they reminded her of gems aglow. Taking advantage of his exultant mood, she compulsively mentioned the previous evening.

"I just dropped by to invite you over for dinner again tonight, if you'd like to come. I hated the way last night ended. I—I know you aren't—aren't really fond of—

of . . ." And Beth began the floundering of a woman whose mouth has outrun her brain. Why had she even mentioned last night?

Scott stilled.

Beth examined the potted ferns hanging from the porch's eaves. "Um—fond of him, and I really didn't think he'd be home—I mean back last night or—or—"

"Will he be there tonight?" Scott asked quietly.

Beth felt Scott watching her; she felt it despite her stubborn inspection of the ferns. "I . . ." A compulsive swallow. The tension sprouting between them like angry weeds seemed to choke off her every breath. "I haven't invited him and don't plan to, but I can't force him not to come."

"What if you ate dinner here?"

The suggestion, so unexpected, brought Beth's focusing on the ferns to an abrupt end. Her eyes widening, she looked at Scott in surprise. "But you can't cook."

"I know that. But my index finger isn't broken." He held it up. "And you know I have a knack for ordering delicious pizzas over the phone. If you'll bring a salad, I'll furnish the rest."

"What about the inn? I can't just leave it."

"You left it now," he said. "And you sure don't mind leaving it for—" He stopped himself.

Beth, not knowing what to say, remained silent. For the first time in their friendship, she was beginning to feel that she must walk on eggshells around Scott. Nothing she said seemed the right thing.

"You have your 'no vacancy' sign out, don't you?" he said, the teasing lilt back in his voice.

"Yes." Beth scrutinized him. Was he really in such a grand mood or was his joy a mere mask?

"Well, just get Lauren to sit by the phone for you. I'm sure she won't mind."

After Lauren's near explosion last night, Beth wasn't as sure of that as Scott was. She deliberated. Despite her fun times with Michael, Beth had missed Scott. Other than their initial conversation, they hadn't really had an opportunity to chat last night. She missed his voice, his refreshing common sense that somehow colored her life with a certain stability. The feeling, which Beth had never before realized, was hard to comprehend. But nonetheless, she acknowledged for the first time that since Scott returned from New York, their friendship had deepened. Beth depended on him more than ever.

"Okay," she finally said. "I'll call Lauren."

"Good. I need help with some final plans for the benefit basketball game next week. This will give me the perfect opportunity to exploit your organizational skills."

"I should have known the pizza wasn't going to come free." Beth playfully punched him in the arm.

As if her touch annoyed him, Scott abruptly stood. "Well, if you're coming over later, I guess I need to get on with my chores for the day. I volunteered to take care of Mrs. Lee's yard this summer. Today's my day to mow for her." He pointed across the street where an elderly lady sat in a worn wicker chair under a massive oak tree.

"That's so nice of you, Scott." Beth thought of Michael. Would he mow the yard for someone who could never repay him? Would he even mow his own yard? Beth didn't want the answer to those questions; didn't want to contemplate the implications.

"There's nothing in the least nice about it," Scott denied, walking toward the steps as if he couldn't get away from Beth fast enough. "Mrs. Lee bakes the best chicken and rice casserole in the South. Believe me, I don't see that yard when I mow, I see layers of rice and chicken and cheese."

"Yeah, right. Like you wouldn't do it if she didn't cook for you." Beth followed him down the steps and tossed her hair over her shoulder.

Chuckling, Scott remounted the bike.

"Since when did you take up biking? I thought you were a diehard jogger."

"It's not mine."

"Oh?" She leaned against the handrail.

Making a big job of placing his right foot on the pedal, Scott seemed to hesitate before answering her unasked question. "Do you remember Marilyn Douglas from high school?"

"Yeah." She recalled the blonde cheerleader who had been friendly to everyone, including Beth. Marilyn never attempted to hide her witness for Christ, and she was one of the few who lived up to her testimony.

"Well," Scott said, narrowing his eyes. "She's back in town. She stopped over late last night on her bike, and I drove her home because of the storm. I'm taking the bicycle back to her."

"Oh. I thought she was married to a pastor and living in Maine."

"She was. He divorced her."

As a distasteful emotion crept up Beth's spine, she felt as if Scott Caldwell was trying to weigh her reaction. But that was ridiculous. Why would Scott care if she cared if he struck up a friendship with Marilyn Douglas?

But did she care?

Then a new thought struck her, and Beth, not used to guarding her words with Scott, spoke before she could stop herself. "No wonder you're in such a good mood this morning."

"Maybe," he said, a defensive edge to his voice. "And maybe it's just—" Scott averted his attention to the bicycle and concentrated on brushing a streak of dust from the handlebars.

"Just what?" Beth asked, while that distasteful emotion scurried from her spine and into her heart.

"Nothing." A pause. "I'll see you tonight."

And he was riding away before Beth could reply.

❦

Maybe it was just seeing you standing on my front porch, looking like the impersonation of a summer day, Scott finished in his mind as he pedaled the bike from his driveway. Discreetly, he stole a glimpse of Beth getting into her car.

She was totally oblivious of his feelings. She had no idea that he wanted to take her in his arms when she playfully punched him. She saw him as nothing but a brother, a buddy, a chum.

Frustration assaulted Scott anew.

Perhaps the time had come for him to get a grip on reality. First, Scott was ready to settle down, get married, and have a family. Second, the woman who was his first choice would probably place Scott as her last choice. Third, he was about to see Marilyn Douglas, who obviously found him attractive.

What man in his right mind would keep pining after Beth McAllister?

A man who has received a promise from God, a haunting voice echoed.

Scott smothered that voice and turned down Marilyn's street.

Fourteen

For the first time in a week, Beth stepped into her parents' spacious restaurant. Before going back to the inn, she desperately needed to talk with her father about Scott. He always confided in Don McAllister; perhaps her dad could supply Beth with some answers to Scott's odd behavior.

Beth's timing was perfect. The breakfast crowd was gone; the lunch crowd had yet to arrive.

With a grin and a wiggle of her fingers, Beth passed Lauren tending the cash register. Lauren flashed her a big smile in return.

Passing through the kitchen, Beth exchanged pleasantries with Sherry, the cook, and the other staff members, then entered her father's cluttered office.

"Hi there!" Don McAllister looked over his reading glasses and bestowed a warm smile on his elder daughter. "How's my businesswoman?"

"Busy as usual." She deposited her oversized handbag

on the corner of his functional metal desk and deposited herself in a straight-backed chair. Nobody could accuse Don McAllister of wasting a penny on his office furniture.

Don laid an invoice aside, removed his narrow black glasses, and stared at Beth with an unasked question in his eyes.

Beth often dropped by the restaurant for a quick greeting, but she didn't usually come here for counsel. However, this was an emergency—she couldn't wait until after business hours.

"Dad," she said, not really knowing where to begin, "I'm worried about Scott. He's really been acting strange lately."

"Really?" Don said, a slight glimmer in his brown eyes.

"Yes. Some days I can hardly speak to him without his snapping at me. Then other times he seems perfectly normal. It's like I'm dealing with two people in one body. I'm worried that he may be suffering from depression or—or—I don't know—multiple personality disorder."

"Really?" Don said again, and Beth couldn't deny that there was humor spilling from his eyes, though his face was perfectly impassive.

Her father sometimes had an off-beat sense of humor, but this was inexcusable. "Dad, I'm telling you, I'm very concerned about him. This is not funny. Is there something he might have confided to you that I should know?"

"How do you—um— What is your opinion of Scott, Beth?"

"You know how I feel about Scott. He's like—like the brother I've never had. I care as much about him as I do Lauren."

Don's lips twitched.

"If I'm going to help him, I need to know what's bothering him. That is, if you know. Do you know?"

Don covered his mouth to suppress a chortle.

For the first time since adolescence, Beth felt as if she and her father were not communicating in the least. "This is not funny," she insisted once more, trying to control her irritation.

Had everyone in her life suddenly gone bonkers? Scott was acting stranger than strange. Lauren had been in the pits of jealousy. And now her father was laughing at her serious concerns.

"I'm really sorry," he replied, trying to sober. "But— I—I can't discuss this with you. It would mean breaking a confidence."

"Okay, fine." Her irritation swelled to anger. "I'm just going to—to—"she grabbed her purse and stood—"to quit worrying about him, then. All this is just about to drive me nuts, and then you—you—laugh at me!"

Seeing her true distress, her father stood and rounded the desk. "I'm really sorry, Beth." He placed a loving hand on her shoulder. "Please don't think I'm laughing at you. It's just—" He shrugged and smiled.

With a huff, Beth turned on her heel, leaving him to

his laughter. "I'll see you later," she muttered.

She opened the door to encounter her sister passing by.

"Oh, hi!" Lauren said. "I thought you were with Mom."

"No. Talking with Dad. Where is Mom, anyway?"

"Loading dishes into the washer." Lauren wrinkled her nose. "I guess I'll go help her. We're fresh out of customers for the time being."

"You know," Beth said, "our mother married a man who has an odd sense of humor."

"Tell me about it!" Lauren rolled her eyes. "Last week he put a rubber snake in the cash register drawer. I almost went through the ceiling. He hasn't stopped laughing since."

"Oh, the burdens we all must bear," Beth said with feigned sympathy and an assuring pat on the back.

"Thanks a lot."

The teasing sparkle lighting Lauren's clear blue eyes seemed to wash away the worry Beth had harbored about her sister's jealousy. Was it only last night at the dinner table that Lauren exposed her negative emotions over Aunt Naomi's will?

"I'm glad to see you're feeling better," Beth said in sisterly approval.

"Feeling better?" Lauren asked blankly.

"Yeah, after last night, I—" Beth felt as if she were with Scott again, floundering for the right words—any words.

Lauren's eyes churned with pain. Or was that humiliation? And last night's tension descended on them in twice the potency.

A sigh. Beth's sleepless night, her conversation with Scott, her father's offbeat laughter, and the tension with Lauren all suddenly left her exhausted. Exhausted, at only eleven A.M. What had promised to be a carefree summer was turning into a nightmare.

"I'm sorry about last night," Lauren squeaked out. "I'm just having trouble trying to understand—"

"I know, Lauren." Beth didn't sound consoling even to herself. "But I just wish you wouldn't blame me for Aunt Naomi's choices." As soon as the words were out of her mouth, Beth wanted to hastily pluck them from the air before they reached Lauren's ears.

"Who says I'm blaming you?"

"Well, nobody." A helpless shrug. "That's just the way I feel."

"Do you care about the way *I* feel?" Lauren asked, her mouth quivering.

Hesitating, Beth wondered how their sisterly banter had deteriorated in just a matter of seconds.

"Of course I care, Lauren."

"Hello, dear." Frances McAllister, towel in hand, placed an arm around Beth's shoulder for a brief sideways hug.

"Hi, Mom," Beth said, her voice flat.

"What's the matter?"

Lauren and Beth exchanged a glance. Then Lauren

rushed toward the dining room. "I need to go make sure everything's set for the lunch crowd."

Beth fought the urge to shake some maturity into her younger sister. How could she be so childish, so difficult?

"This thing with Naomi really upset her, honey." Frances, an older, plumper version of Beth, peered into her daughter's eyes as if she were trying to make Beth understand Lauren's view.

"Well . . ." For the first time that day, Beth decided not to say what came to her mind. *Why does she have to take it out on me?* Instead, she muttered something about how she was sure Aunt Naomi never intended for Lauren to feel as she did.

"But it's deeper than that, you know."

"Really?" Beth knitted her brows.

"Yes, but—I really can't say more. It would mean breaking Lauren's confidence."

Suddenly, Beth felt as if her whole family were harboring secrets from her. Weary to the bone, she wished to run away from her own life.

Then Beth thought of Michael. Running away would mean leaving him behind. But was that so bad? Today, he seemed like nothing but another complication.

Sighing, she bade farewell to her mother, walked through the cheery blue-and-white dining room, and called a pleasant good-bye to Lauren.

Her sister, intent on replacing empty salt shakers on the blue tables, merely waved.

So much for asking Lauren to watch the inn tonight.

More depressed and confused than ever, Beth wondered if Sheila would agree to come back that evening while Beth went to Scott's house. Whatever Scott's problems, Beth had pledged to be there for him.

Fifteen

*H*i." Marilyn, holding an adorable blonde toddler, smiled at Scott from the doorway of her parents' rambling rock home.

"I brought back your bicycle," he said, pointing to the bike parked near a rose bush. "Where would you like me to put it?"

"Just leave it there, thanks. I'll get it later."

Scott purposed to force the image of Beth from his mind and focus on Marilyn's beauty instead.

"This is Brooke," Marilyn said.

"Hi, Brooke. Nice to meet you."

Brooke shyly turned her face into her mother's neck.

"Come in and meet my folks. They just got back from Little Rock."

Awkwardly Scott entered the home and found a sixty-ish couple sharing an early lunch in a cozy breakfast nook. They greeted Scott, questions in their eyes.

Scott felt as if he should assure them his intentions

were nothing but honorable. Instead, he joined them at the glass and brass dining table and commented appreciatively on their multi-colored flower garden outside the bay window. After a round of small talk and a shared cup of coffee, Marilyn offered to give Scott a ride back home.

Brooke, silent to this point, suddenly overcame her shyness. "We went swimming in Little Rock," she said, her brown eyes wide.

"Mom and Dad just got back from visiting my brother for a couple of days," Marilyn supplied. "They took Brooke with them."

"I see," Scott said. "Do you like swimming, Brooke?"

"Yes. I *adore* it."

The adults laughed.

"That's something she's picked up from her older cousin," Marilyn said. "She *adores* everything now."

"Would you take my mommy and me swimming?"

Again the adults laughed, and Marilyn colored slightly. "I'm sure Scott has plenty planned to do today."

"Actually, I'd love to take you swimming," Scott blurted. Anything to get his mind off Beth. "The high school pool is open for the summer, and it's not terribly crowded. Since I'm on staff, I can take you for free."

"Yippee!" Brooke squealed.

Marilyn glanced from Scott to Brooke and back to Scott.

"It's okay. Really," Scott said.

"Well, okay then," she said, dimpling into a smile.

Within an hour, Scott was twirling Brooke around

in the almost vacant pool, inhaling the odors of chlorine and sunscreen.

"Mama, I'm an airplane!" Brooke exclaimed, spreading her arms as Scott lowered her onto the cool water's surface.

With a motherly smile, Marilyn rumpled her daughter's hair. "You're a *sweet* airplane."

Scott playfully tickled Brooke's tummy, then threw her into the air to catch her. Amongst shrill giggles, Brooke landed in his arms with a splash.

If Marilyn were ever to marry again, the man would be doubly blessed. A beautiful wife and a delightful child. Scott could live with that combination, live with it easily.

Then he thought of Beth. Of God's promise. Of his love for her. Purposefully, Scott pushed those thoughts from his mind. He would not let his turbulence with Beth spoil his friendship with Marilyn.

To punctuate that decision, Scott directed a warm smile her way. "Your daughter comes up with great ideas."

"I'm glad you think so. I was afraid—" She stopped in midsentence.

"You were afraid you were barging in?"

She nodded.

"Don't worry. I came by my own choice, and so far—" He threw a squealing Brooke into the air once more. "I'm thoroughly enjoying myself."

"I just hope we aren't keeping you from anything."

"No. I arranged to have much of this summer off. I've

been helping a friend some." Scott didn't feel he should discuss Beth with Marilyn. "I'm free until tonight."

A lady in her mid-fifties had been steadily swimming laps since their arrival. On her final lap, she stopped near them before heading for the steps. "What a lovely family," she said appreciatively. "How old is your little girl?"

"Three," Marilyn supplied, "but—"

"What's your name, darlin'?" the lady crooned in a deep southern drawl.

"Brooke."

"Well, Brooke, you sure are lucky to have a mommy and daddy to take you swimming on such a hot day."

"This isn't my daddy," Brooke said, her giggles gone.

Marilyn stared helplessly at Scott.

"My daddy doesn't live with us anymore."

"Oh," the lady said, her eyes pleading forgiveness from Marilyn.

Strained silence stretched into an ache. Scott spontaneously tickled Brooke to relieve the tense moment. The kind, yet embarrassed, lady gracefully took her leave.

Laughing and splashing, Brooke seemed to forget the conversation. Until they were ready to leave.

"I wish *you* were my daddy," she chirped as Scott tossed her into the air one last time.

Marilyn groaned, and Scott, focusing on the child, pretended he didn't hear it.

"No, don't wish that. I'm sure your daddy loves you bigger than the sky. He'd be sad that you wanted somebody else for a daddy."

"No, he wouldn't," Brooke said, her brown eyes rounded in certainty. "He doesn't want me anymore."

His heart twisting, Scott couldn't resist hugging the little girl as Marilyn brushed away a tear. Silently she stared at Scott, as if begging him to cast away Brooke's fears.

"Well, I happen to know that all daddies especially want their little girls," he assured her, wondering what he would say next. "It's a known fact that even if daddies leave, they still want their little girls, and especially little girls as wonderful as you." Scott touched the end of her nose with his index finger. "Now what do you say we go get an ice-cream cone?"

"Yeah!" she yelled, and a smile chased away her solemnity.

"Thanks," Marilyn said as they followed Brooke toward the dressing rooms.

"Sure." Scott squeezed her hand.

"I've told her over and over again that Gregory still loves her, and he *does* visit her. But I guess she still feels rejected, no matter what I say."

"I think that's natural." Scott thought of his own childhood, of the times his father lambasted him for no good reason. Yes, Scott understood Brooke's feelings of rejection.

"I guess. But it doesn't make it any easier to deal with. Why don't men think before they break up a family?" she blurted, venom dripping from her words. "I think I can deal with his deserting me. But his own child?"

Studying the wet walkway, Scott could arrive at no suitable answer.

"Sorry. I didn't mean to dump all that on you."

A reassuring grin. "It's okay. You need somebody to talk to. I just wish I had some answers."

"I don't think anybody has those, except maybe Gregory himself. And I can already tell you I don't like his answers."

"Mama, a frog!" Brooke pointed to a harmless gray toad hopping across the walkway toward the fence. She bent to catch it.

"I guess you didn't bargain for a marriage proposal when we invited ourselves to swim with you," Marilyn said, changing the subject.

"I was just thinking what a sly woman you are to put your own daughter up to suggesting matrimony," he teased. "What did you do, slip her a note on our way to the pool?"

"Yeah. And considering she can't read, it was a brilliant move."

"Don't worry about it," he said with a smile. "I dated a single mom a couple of years back. She had adopted a little girl from Korea. Kaela proposed to me a dozen or more times before Tamarah and I stopped seeing each other."

"Was that in New York?"

"Yeah."

"And you never took Kaela up on her offer?"

"Well, I thought about it." As Brooke pursued the

toad, they stopped in front of the dressing rooms. Scott draped the damp towel around his neck. "But even though Tamarah and I got along great, we realized we weren't meant for each other." He shrugged. "Something just didn't click. Do you know what I mean?"

"Yeah. I've had the click." Marilyn's faraway gaze drifted past his shoulders.

So have I, he thought as the image of Beth emerged from the recesses of his heart where he had tried to hide it. Even though Scott had spent the day in the company of two charming ladies, his mind still trailed to Beth. Beth, who knew him better than any woman ever had. Beth, who would be sharing dinner with him that very night. Perhaps he was a hopeless case.

Beth's knock caught Scott off guard. She was early, and he was late. Mowing Mrs. Lee's yard took longer than he anticipated. He had just barely stepped out of the shower. "Coming," he bellowed as he hastily grabbed a gray plaid shirt, buttoned it, and tucked it into his jeans. Not worrying with his damp, tousled hair, Scott whipped open the front door.

There she stood, just as she had always been. Fresh as springtime; her understated beauty as natural as daisies, wearing a copper-colored short set that brought out her peaches and cream complexion.

Scott's stomach twisted. He bowed deeply. "Welcome to my humble abode, Lady Beth."

"Maybe Lady *Mac*beth would be better," she quipped, handing him the salad.

"Planning to kill someone, are we? The last time I read *Macbeth*, Lady M.B. had murder on the brain."

Her quizzical expression caught him off guard. When had Beth ever been unsure of him? As he had that morning, Scott sensed hesitancy from her, as if she didn't know what to expect from him. With an internal chuckle, Scott couldn't say that he blamed her. After all, he was rather unpredictable lately. Perhaps tonight would re-establish the right tone to their relationship.

Walking past him, Beth dropped her purse on the edge of his deep blue sectional sofa. "I've had another conflict with Lauren," she muttered, her voice revealing her heavy heart. "I'm a bit put out with her right now."

"Oh?"

"Yes. Today's spat was even worse than last night's." She turned to face him, hands on hips. "I stopped by the restaurant today. To make a long story short, by the time I left, Lauren was in tears. All I said was 'I'm glad to see you're feeling better.'" Beth raised her hands in exasperation. "It went downhill from there."

Not knowing what to say, Scott looked at her in silence.

"Well?" she said.

"Well what?"

"Aren't you going to say something like, 'I'm so sorry.

I wish things were better between you two, I'll pray for the situation' or something?"

"Is that what I'm supposed to say?" Scott smiled indulgently.

"Yes." She rolled her eyes, and a smile dimpled her cheeks.

"Okay then. I'm so sorry. I wish things were better between you two. . . . And what was the other thing you said?"

"Ha, ha, ha. Have you ordered the pizza?"

"Not yet." Scott turned for the phone. "I'm glad that worried look is off your face. I'd hate to know I had to share my pizza with a brooding woman."

Scott, heady with the smell of Beth's rose perfume, deposited the salad on a nearby table and dialed the pizza parlor number he had long ago memorized. Did Beth even suspect his teasing was a cover for the electrical storm raging within? How long could one man stand such torment? Why had he even asked her over? If Scott was going to maintain his sanity, perhaps he should recommit himself to keeping his distance.

Confidently, he ordered their usual hamburger and mushroom pizza and hung up. Then he watched Beth toying with his stereo, searching for the classical station they both enjoyed.

He had spent most of the afternoon with Marilyn and Brooke. As in the pool, they'd had a blast, but all Scott could think of was his pending dinner engagement. Despite his earlier resolve to ignore God's promise and face reality, Scott found himself hoping all the more that perhaps Beth would awaken to his love. If she didn't, could he ever get over her? Did he even want to? Helplessly, he picked up the salad and turned for the kitchen.

Beth tapped him on the shoulder. "Hello in there! Anybody home?"

"What?" He spun to face her.

"I just asked you a question, but you must have been in never never land. All I got was a blank stare."

"Sorry." A sheepish grin. "You know how it is with us great thinkers. Always distracted."

"Yeah, right." Beth rolled her eyes again.

She seemed to be relaxing a little with him . . . something he hadn't experienced since Michael's arrival.

"So what did you ask?"

"Besides mowing your neighbor's yard, what did you do today?" Beth walked toward the kitchen.

He followed. "I—um—" He hesitated, wondering if she would even care that he had spent half the afternoon with Marilyn.

"Have you forgotten or something?" As he deliberated, she opened the ebony refrigerator.

"No, I haven't forgotten. I'm not *that* old." He laughed. "Actually, I was with Marilyn Douglas and her daughter, Brooke, most of the day."

"Oh."

The word hung between them like a ticking time bomb. Scott would have paid a cool million to see Beth's expression. Had her back tensed? Or was he infusing his own wishes into her reaction? Perhaps the simple "oh" meant she couldn't care less.

"I'm helping myself to a soda. Want one?" she asked.

Scott was reaching around her to grab a bottle of salad dressing when Beth turned, two sodas in hand. And she stood within kissing distance.

Michael could not believe his good fortune. Beth was gone, and he could freely explore the attic. Earlier, he asked her to share dinner with him, but she explained her previous engagement with Scott Caldwell.

"Three cheers for Scott Caldwell," Michael muttered as he moved the antique dresser away from the secret doorway.

Within seconds, he stood at the attic's door, practically salivating over the prospect of what he might find. Like an archaeologist opening an ancient tomb, Michael turned the doorknob, stepped over the threshold, and caressed the beam of his penlight across the dimly lighted, dust-laden clutter. This was more like a room than an attic. Nearly the size of his guest room, with about a fourteen-foot ceiling. Midway up the outside wall, a tiny, smudged window allowed minimal light across the sea of junk.

Boxes. Boxes. Boxes. An ancient set of encyclopedias.

A basketful of rag dolls. An antique bureau. A dilapidated artificial Christmas tree. A rickety ladder. And more.

Hungrily Michael peered onto every visible surface, but to no avail. With the smell of accumulated dust filling his senses, he started digging around the boxes, giving special attention to the items lining the wall.

This time, the digging paid off. After an hour of fruit-less, dirty perusal, Michael pulled the decaying bureau away from the wall. Behind it, he touched an item that was so amazingly familiar he reeled with excitement. Like a father adoring his newborn, Michael hoisted the item upward. Hastily, he stumbled around the boxes and Christmas tree, and exposed his find to the window. Although limited, the revealing light dashed some of Michael's original glee. This wasn't the treasure. However, it was valuable. He recognized its telltale quali-ties.

Michael would hide it under his bed until tonight, then, after Beth had settled for the evening, he would sneak it to his car and stash it with the jewelry. She would never learn of his find.

A burning sneeze punctuated his decision. The dust swirling through an overhead sunbeam seemed to applaud his find. And Michael, more determined than ever, planned to leave no item in this attic unturned.

Suddenly he heard screaming. Not screams of terror or panic or alarm. Screams of fury.

Carefully Michael deposited his find near a box, gin-gerly mounted an antique, straight-backed chair that stood under the window, and looked out.

A plump Oriental woman was running toward Beth's inn wielding a broom over her head. Her blue curlers, askew with the ongoing battle, bobbed across her forehead like great flopping antennae. Before Michael could so much as question the broom's victim, Tiffany raced away from the inn, dragging a long line of laundry behind her. Somehow, that crazy pig had escaped her pen and tangled herself in a neighbor's laundry line.

And the jaded Michael experienced something he hadn't tasted in many years. Genuine laughter.

Beth, holding the chilled sodas, looked up at Scott. Silently, he stared at her, an expectant gleam in his eyes. Beth couldn't remember the last time she had been so close to him. Once again his eyes reminded her of emeralds. Shattered emeralds, with infinite facets. As the refrigerator wafted cool air against her legs, a warm rush spread through the pit of her stomach.

Scott stood still and silent, his gaze fixed to hers like a statue carved from a block of incredulity.

And something deep within Beth responded on a level she had never before experienced. Something sweet and sensual and delicious.

Disgusted, she inwardly shook herself. This was Scott. Scott Caldwell. The brother she had never had. What was wrong with her? This stressful day must have made her lose her stability, abandon common sense, grow downright weird.

"Want a soda?" Barely recognizing her own voice, Beth tried not to dwell on images of Scott and Marilyn Douglas together. Why did that disturb her?

"Sure."

And they were back in their old routine, as if that moment when the universe tilted hadn't even existed.

"The sodas are cold. Let's not dirty any glasses, unless you want ice," Scott said cheerfully—so cheerfully it almost seemed fake.

"Okay." Beth grabbed some paper plates, forcing herself to act normal. And suddenly, she couldn't even remember what "normal" was. All she wanted to do was run home, away from this person who seemed bent on throwing her into a perpetual hurricane of confusion. She had just relaxed with him for the first time in weeks. Then . . . Beth didn't even want to consider what she had felt. The emotions were too disgusting to even acknowledge. She could only hope he didn't suspect.

Refusing to acknowledge Scott's stare, which she felt penetrating the top of her head, Beth concentrated on separating the paper plates. The phone's ringing ended her task. *Please be for me,* she pleaded inwardly, wanting to escape Scott's disconcerting presence.

"Yes, she's here," Scott said into the receiver, then turned to hand Beth the cordless phone.

"Beth, I've got some really bad news," Sheila said.

She caught her breath at her receptionist's strained voice.

"Your pig has somehow escaped the backyard and is dragging your neighbor's laundry all over the neighborhood."

A groan. "Which neighbor is it? Please tell me it isn't Mr. Juarez."

"Unless he's married to an overweight Oriental woman with red lipstick and blue curlers—"

Relief, the kind that weakens, drained Beth of her last vestiges of energy. She steeled herself against collapsing into the nearest chair. "That's Mrs. Chang from the pink house next door." Mrs. Chang was the only neighbor Tiffany had yet to assault.

"Well, Mrs. Chang is chasing the pig all over your yard and hers, trying to retrieve her laundry. She's got a broom, and things don't look so hot for the pig right now."

Mrs. Chang, their church treasurer. Mrs. Chang, one of the sweetest women Beth had ever met. Mrs. Chang, who loved to dry her sheets outside to achieve that fresh smell. Would Mrs. Chang annihilate Tiffany before Beth could save her?

"I'll be home in five minutes."

"Better make it three."

"Right." She hung up the cordless phone.

"What's going on?"

"Tiffany. She's dragging Mrs. Chang's laundry around the neighborhood." Beth rushed for her shoulder bag.

Scott's laughter only heightened Beth's tension. Without thinking, she turned on him. "Listen, this is not funny! It's the very last thing I needed today! If Tiffany keeps this up, the neighborhood is going to put a bounty on her head—and mine!"

"Have you thought of giving her away? Or—or making pork chops?"

"Very funny!" She rushed for the door. "You know how Aunt Naomi felt about Tiffany. On her deathbed, she all but made me promise to love, honor, and cherish—" Whipping open the door, she encountered the pizza delivery boy. "I'm gone," she snapped over her shoulder as Scott's hilarity died.

"Are you coming back?" he called.

The tone of his voice almost stopped Beth in her tracks. He sounded positively forlorn. Could Scott value her company that much? Despite her earlier thoughts of escaping him, Beth found she could not deny his request.

"Yes. As soon as I calm Mrs. Chang and cage Tiffany."

Within thirty minutes, Beth had done exactly that. Mrs. Chang, satisfied with Beth's offer to buy new sheets, had even apologized for growing so angry with the pig. As Beth drove back to Scott's, she wondered how long Tiffany would survive. Too many more escapades like that one, and somebody in the neighborhood would mysteriously acquire a surplus of pork sausage.

Sixteen

A week later Beth stared in horror at the calendar on her roll-top desk. The words "Scott's game, 7:00" glared back at her in bold, black letters.

The basketball game. She had promised Scott she would attend the game between the high school staff and local clergy. Last week, after smoothing over the embarrassing fiasco with Mrs. Chang and Tiffany, she helped Scott with the game's final details. Scott planned the whole thing, like the two charity games before this one, and received a showering of praise from a myriad of sources, including the Chamber of Commerce.

And Beth? Beth completely forgot about it. She told Michael she would go with him to one of the family music shows in Eureka Springs.

"Nuts," she muttered. "Now what?" She checked her watch. Six o'clock. She was supposed to meet Michael downstairs in half an hour.

She glanced toward the portrait of her aunt, which

hung over the bed. The woman who languidly stared back was in her early thirties, blond, rosy-cheeked. Even though the portrait was expertly rendered, there was something about it that Beth disliked. The look in her aunt's eyes. Was it guilt? Whatever, those half-closed brown orbs weren't the peaceful eyes she remembered.

"What should I do?" Beth asked the painting. And all the while, she knew what she would do. There had never really been a choice. *I can't let Scott down. This means so much to him.* Sure the game would bore Michael, Beth prepared to attend by herself.

But Michael had other plans. "That sounds like fun," he said when Beth explained her previous commitment. "I'll go to the game with you."

Surprised, she bit her lip, thinking of Scott's reaction if she showed up with Michael. "No, no, I wouldn't expect you to sacrifice your evening for me."

"Sacrifice?" His brows rose incredulously. "Believe me, Beth, any time with you is no sacrifice. What time does it start?"

"Well, seven." *Scott will never forgive me for this.*

"Good. We won't be too early, then. Let's go."

"Are you sure?" Without being rude, Beth desperately wished to say something—anything—that would deter Michael. "It's just a little community game. Nothing fancy. You'd probably have a much better time at the—"

"Beth, if I didn't know any better, I'd say you didn't want me to go." He turned from the door and peered into her eyes as if searching for her true motive.

"Well, I just assumed you'd be bored. I mean, you're probably used to—to—"

"I didn't come to Eureka Springs for what I'm used to." A flirting wink. "Now come on. We'll have a great time."

A cold rock settled in Beth's stomach. Scott was not going to be happy.

He hadn't contacted her since last week. But then, Beth hadn't contacted him either. After that episode by the refrigerator, Beth pledged to avoid Scott Caldwell for a while. Somehow their relationship seemed to be stationed on a new fault line subject to repeated earthquakes. Beth wasn't even sure how to act around him anymore. Even though their pizza and game planning session went peacefully, their conversation had been shallow and strained.

She hoped he wouldn't say something hateful to her and Michael at the game. But, he was coaching the faculty team, and probably wouldn't have the chance.

Sitting on the hard bleacher and staring across the crowded gym, Beth clenched and unclenched her teeth as Marilyn Douglas, smiling sweetly, cheered for Scott's team. Why had she even worried about bringing Michael? Scott hadn't so much as glanced across the crowd for her. His every spare moment, from before the game to half-time to the third quarter, had been shared with Marilyn.

Suddenly Beth saw with vivid clarity the reason she hadn't heard from Scott all week. He had been busy elsewhere. Last week, she hadn't wanted to admit the effect Scott's new friendship with Marilyn had on her. But now, Beth couldn't deny the emotion. Regardless of how ugly it seemed, she didn't like the idea of Scott—*her Scott*—being with Marilyn.

"Are you okay?" Michael's warm breath fanned her right ear.

"Fine. I'm fine," she said, tearing her attention from the striking couple to glance toward Michael. Her mind, though, didn't see him. It still saw Scott and Marilyn. Scott and Marilyn. Scott and Marilyn. His dark hair and skin so dashing against her fairness.

Taking in the smells of popcorn and hamburgers and basketballs, Beth desperately wished to be alone, alone to wallow in her misery. Or was this jealousy? Blinking, she blocked the very idea from her mind. Scott deserved a girlfriend, a wife. Beth should be thrilled for him.

"Michael, would you mind getting me some popcorn?" she asked quickly, trying to deny the constricting hand that squeezed her heart. Why did she care whom Scott Caldwell dated?

"Happy to." He patted her knee. "But when the game is over, I expect payment." A cheer went up from the crowd as Scott's team finished the third quarter ahead by ten points. Then Michael was gone, and Beth couldn't answer his quip.

Exactly what did he have in mind? Maybe the kiss she still hesitated to bestow. And why was she hesitating, anyway? Something about Scott, about not wanting to disappoint him. All week she had held Michael at a distance, despite their frequent excursions. Another glance toward Marilyn, who focused on Scott rather than the game, and Beth scoffed at her earlier hesitation.

But what about your hesitation because of God? Bristling, Beth wondered why that persistent voice was so opposed to her happiness.

Drowning in misery, Beth watched Scott. He was at his best. Wearing a dark suit. Hands on hips. Scrutinizing every move on the court. Pacing the sidelines. Giving rapid instructions to a player entering the game. Scott Caldwell ate, drank, and slept basketball. That was the reason the high school team had made it to state playoffs and planned to win state next year.

How long would he be content with high school coaching? Before leaving New York, Scott mentioned going back for his master's and coaching at a college. Did he still possess that dream?

The thought of his leaving Eureka Springs again plummeted Beth to the depths of loneliness; a loneliness that had engulfed her heart during the last week of his absence.

After a quick pep talk between quarters, Scott discreetly scanned the crowd for the third time. Still no sign of Beth. If she were here, Scott was sure she would have made herself known. When Beth attended his games, she usually sat behind him and cheered him on.

Disappointment dripped from his soul like wax from a spent candle. Even though he avoided Beth lately, Scott prayed she would make the game. At a distance, he was safe with her. Up close, he no longer trusted himself.

Last week when she turned around at his refrigerator and practically fell into his arms, Scott experienced a primeval urge to kiss her senseless. The only thing that stopped him was not being sure of her reaction. Even though he thought he saw a glimmer of attraction in her eyes, he couldn't be certain he hadn't imagined it. So he purposed to keep his distance until he could get a grip on himself. After she left, Scott hadn't called her or seen her. Not that he wasn't driven to spend every minute with her . . . but he was uncertain of her reactions and his.

A couple of times last week, he shared lunch with Marilyn, more as a means to break the loneliness than anything else. And frankly, he wasn't so sure that Marilyn didn't have the same motive. Because they had been seen out together, Scott feared he and Marilyn were becoming an "item" around their small town. Right now, their relationship remained platonic. Scott hadn't even held her hand. Something wouldn't let him. But Beth's absence seemed to weaken that "something."

"Time!" he yelled, placing the fingertips of one hand

against the palm of the other. The clergy team was in a hot scoring drive. Scott needed to concentrate on the game and save thoughts of Beth for later.

After the game, Scott deposited Marilyn in his car and sped toward her parents' home.

"You were wonderful," she said, a smile in her voice.

"Thanks."

"I've never seen you in action before. I had no idea—"

"I guess it's just in my blood."

"You know, if you got into coaching college, you might be able to work your way up into the NBA."

"Do you really think so?" Scott couldn't deny the flush of pleasure the admiration in her voice gave him.

"I do."

"Well, I have toyed with a dream or two. But right now, I'm content where I am. I enjoy the kids. And, I don't know, I guess I kinda see coaching high school as a ministry. Sometimes those boys will tell their coach stuff they wouldn't say to other teachers. By the end of the year, the principal is usually sending me a few kids for counseling." Thoughtfully, Scott paused as he turned onto Marilyn's street. "I'm not sure I'd get the same fulfillment out of college or the professional league. The money would be better, but I think maybe influencing teens is more important."

"I like the way you think."

If only Beth did.

"Want to come in for a Coke? Mom and Dad said be sure to ask you. I think you made a conquest last week when you met them."

"I'd love to," Scott said hesitantly, his thoughts still with Beth. "But it's late, and I guess I better not. Maybe another time."

Perhaps Beth was still awake. Not that he didn't find Marilyn attractive. But he really wanted to see Beth. Scott and she often shared a movie and popcorn after one of his games. Even though she hadn't made the game, she might be expecting him.

A silent question posed itself between them, and Scott didn't quite know how to escape the awkward moment. No matter what he did, he would feel guilty. If he spent the rest of the evening with Marilyn, he would worry that Beth was awaiting him. But at the same time, he frowned on the idea of leaving Marilyn at her doorstep and going to see Beth.

Scott had never been the Casanova type. Even before he found the Lord, he treated his girlfriends fairly. Because of his father's escapades, Scott had vowed to cherish his acquaintances of the opposite sex. For the first time, he felt as if he were somehow breaking that vow. But some force drove him to see Beth. See her tonight.

Finally, Marilyn graciously said goodnight, and Scott walked her to the door.

Within minutes, Scott stood on Beth's porch, ready to ring the bell. Perhaps Beth wasn't feeling well and there was a logical excuse for her absence.

The porch light wasn't burning. That sometimes meant she was in her room for the night. And it sometimes meant she simply forgot to turn on the light.

"It's a lovely night," came Beth's voice from down the driveway.

"Not half as lovely as you," a familiar male voice replied.

So she didn't come to Scott's game because she had been out with the jerk. They must have rounded off their "lovely" evening with a nocturnal stroll.

It figures.

Scott felt like a complete fool. How long would he keep putting himself in these miserable positions? Either God had a really twisted sense of humor, or He was trying to use Scott as interference between Beth and Michael. Whatever the reason, Scott wasn't exactly elated to see the happy couple. *Again.*

As they approached the porch, he instinctively stepped behind one of the massive pillars and sniffed the one odor he was allergic to. Geraniums.

Marilyn's invitation to visit with her parents replayed in his mind. As Michael and Beth stopped mere inches away, Scott saw he should have accepted that invitation. When would he ever learn?

The spicy smell of Beth's geraniums, mixing with the scent of Michael's expensive aftershave, seemed to incite

Scott to forget Beth, to admit his defeat, to focus on Marilyn. Then he remembered God's promise, and new frustration bubbled within. *Lord, are You going to follow through?*

"I would like nothing more than to kiss you, Beth," Michael murmured, his hands on her shoulders.

Scott suppressed the primitive yell roaring from his soul. This was some cruel twist of fate. The one thing Scott didn't want to witness unfolded before him like a dreaded nightmare.

Beth. Her eyes staring up into Michael's as if she were begging him to fulfill his request. Michael. Caressing her cheek with his thumb. Beth. Leaning ever so gently toward him. Michael's lips descending to hers.

Scott tried not to sniffle against the overwhelming geranium odor wafting from the shadows. If Beth ever discovered he had eavesdropped, much less at such a close range and at such a moment, she would never speak to him again.

Then, as Michael's lips were mere centimeters from Beth's, the sniffle would no longer be denied. Scott let loose with a resounding, tingling sneeze.

Beth's compulsive scream accompanied Michael's startled shout, and the neighbor's dog chimed in with a surprised "Wuff."

"It's just me," Scott said, stepping from the shadows, a satisfied smirk forcing itself on his lips despite his efforts to keep a straight face.

"Scott Caldwell!" Beth placed a flattened hand

against her chest. "You scared me to death."

"Me too," Michael said.

"Afraid you were going to have to act like a man and fight?" Scott challenged, not sure why he couldn't control the caustic remarks in Michael's presence.

Lord, please help me keep my mouth shut.

All his life, Scott strove to be the gentleman his mother had wished his father were. In Michael's presence, though, Scott saw streaks of his father within himself.

"That was uncalled for," Beth said stiffly.

"Oh? And I guess what I was about to witness *was* called for?"

Her silence attested to what the shadows hid. Only at her most furious did Beth grow deathly quiet.

"Excuse me, Michael, but I would like to talk with Scott alone," she said through clamped teeth.

"Certainly," he replied, his voice that of a satisfied panther who had just outwitted a rabbit. He obviously knew what Scott suspected.

This time, Scott had gone too far. This time, Beth wouldn't let him forget his mistake.

Michael left them.

"How dare you spy on me?" she hissed, her eyes thin, shadowed slits.

"I wasn't—"

"What did you do, sneak up here and wait for me?"

"No! I always come over after a game. What's the matter? Have you forgotten?"

Silence. Scott knew he had scored a point.

"Besides," he added, "if you had looked at the curb you would have seen my car. Isn't that proof—"

She glanced toward the street. "It's not proof of anything."

"You were too focused on Mr. Wonderful!" Scott shot back.

"Don't talk to me about being focused on somebody," she whispered. "I saw you with Marilyn Douglas tonight. As much time as you spent looking at her, I was surprised you had time to coach!"

"So you *did* grace us with your presence at the game! I thought you'd forgotten it in the face of Blondie's charm." The sarcastic twist in his voice was his father's. His father's voice. His father's words.

But somehow Scott couldn't stop. "What's the matter with you, Beth? It looks as if you've decided to throw all your Christian values to the wind!"

The silence settled between them like a massive, uncrossable chasm.

Then she spoke, slowly, deliberately, through gritted teeth. "Since when are you my spiritual guardian?"

"Since you started acting like you don't care anymore."

"And I guess you've been the perfect Christian example?" She stabbed her index finger against the center of his chest.

"A lot better than you!"

"Listen to me, you . . . you turkey!"

"No! You listen to me!" He grabbed her arms and

resisted the urge to try to shake some sense into her. "You're making a fool of yourself with this guy. Do you hear me? This is even worse than the time you wouldn't listen to me in high school. Do I have to crown you homecoming queen to get you to listen?"

"Stop it! Just stop it!"

The shattered little girl cry in her voice made Scott feel as low as his father. Why had he dragged up the past, the very incident he knew would hurt her the worst?

Because he wanted to hurt her. Wanted to hurt her as badly as she had hurt him. Well, he knew he had done exactly that, and the feeling wasn't a pretty one.

"I—I'm sorry, Beth," he muttered, reaching to stroke her cheek.

"Don't you touch me!" She stumbled backward toward the porch stairs.

"Beth," he gasped as she teetered on the top step and grasped at the air. Scott reached for her flailing arms to jerk her back into balance. That only pulled her next to him, next to his expectant heart, into his waiting arms.

Seventeen

ichael wasted no time. This was the perfect chance for him to search the attic again. His earlier find only served to whet his appetite. He knew the prize was there; it must be. He entered his room, grabbed his penlight, and was up the stairs within minutes of Beth's polite dismissal.

Before heading for the attic, he rushed to Beth's bedroom and tried the knob. Locked. Of course, she was extremely cautious. Michael couldn't say that he blamed her, but he needed to investigate every bedroom in the mansion. During the last week, he had managed to discreetly search the remainder of the mansion, including the kitchen and the storage building. He lacked only the bedrooms.

The false identification he received two days ago had provided him an escape route and fueled his bravado. He only felt a pang of remorse when Beth handed him the manila envelope, not knowing that the mail she extended him would enable him to take advantage of her.

His pulse raced. Soon—very soon—he would find his prize.

A glance over his shoulder, and he hurried into the attic. This time, as the last, Michael would be meticulously careful. The rise and fall of Beth and Scott's voices accompanied the padding of his loafers against the dust-laden floor. As long as they were talking, he knew he had time.

Pointing his light toward the east wall, Michael noticed a door he previously overlooked. Did it open to a closet? Yet another room? He stepped over a mound of magazines, his pulse quickening with greed.

Beth gasped as Scott's arms wrapped around her and pulled her against him.

"Are you okay?" he asked, his breath fanning her temple.

Her hands trembled against the lapel of his suit, and she relived the second when she had almost fallen down the mansion's steps. She could have broken a leg or arm.

"Fine. I'm fine," she said, tilting her head to look up into his face, so near, so caring. "Thanks."

Only seconds ago, they had been arguing. Now, with Scott close, his eyes seeming to peer into her very soul, Beth momentarily forgot the cause of their angry words.

Her mind replayed that moment by his refrigerator. That same something warm spread through the pit of her stomach.

His heart quickened beneath her hand as his gaze trailed to her lips. "Beth?"

Despite the tingles sprouting where his hands touched her spine, Beth remembered. Scott said she was making a fool of herself, brought up that horrible incident that still caused her pain. Not since she was seventeen had she felt such injury. And the fury of only seconds before resurfaced in a cloud of fire as she pushed against his chest.

"Let me go! Get your hands off me."

He released her, and Beth stumbled toward the door, her mind reeling in confusion and anger.

"Beth, I'm sorry. I'm sorry for the way I've been acting. I'm sorry for what I said a few minutes ago."

"No, you're not," she snarled, her eyes filling with tears.

The years rolled away. She was seventeen. Scott had warned her not to trust that pack of girls, but Beth ignored him. She wanted so desperately to be part of the "in" crowd. It was like a dream come true when she was actually nominated for homecoming queen. Those girls convinced her that she would win, advised her about her dress and hair, built up her hopes and let her think she was one of them. And then, the night of homecoming, the same girls who pretended to be her friends laughed at her.

"Didn't you know it was a joke? Did you seriously think anyone would vote for you?"

Scott, furious beyond reason, overheard them, stepped in, and sent those girls running. "Beth," he said, "you did get real votes. It wasn't a joke to have you running for homecoming queen." But Beth could never believe him. The girls' cruel words had wounded her deeply and, to her amazement, the wound still festered after all the intervening time.

"How could you?" she yelled, fumbling for the door. "How could you bring that up again after all these years?"

Wanting to lash out at him, to return the wound he had so skillfully dealt, she swiveled to stare into his searching eyes. "You're acting just like your father," she blurted. "You're nothing but another version of him." Then she rushed through the door and slammed it behind her.

Chest heaving, Beth stared at the blurry stairwell and listened. Listened as Scott eventually left the porch. Listened as his car's engine came to life. Listened as he sped away. Her mind spinning in confusion, she let the scalding tears spill freely to her cheeks and run to the corners of her mouth in salty accusation. Her words seemed the perfect trump to play. Now, they settled around her shoulders like a rotting albatross.

She ran for the stairs as if to flee those words' constricting hold. Words, words said in haste, to end a lifetime friendship, to mar what once was. Beth knew her relationship with Scott would never be the same, would perhaps not even exist. Why had they dealt so cruelly with each other after two decades of loyalty?

As she closed and locked her bedroom door, her heart seemed to shatter into a thousand fragments. She collapsed against her bed and sobbed.

His hands covered in grit, Michael straightened from his perusal of the closet. Beth's bedroom door. He thought he heard it open, then close. Tensing, he listened for the rise and fall of Beth and Scott's voices on the porch, but all he heard were a woman's muffled sobs.

A bitter curse. He had been so engrossed with digging through the layers of moth-eaten curtains in the closet that he failed to listen for Beth. Now she was in her room, and he was stuck in the attic. *Be calm,* a voice soothed. *You can always sneak out.* But the last time he tried sneaking into the attic with her nearby, she caught him. Michael didn't believe she would swallow another sleepwalking story.

So he silently seated himself beside the closet, clicked off the penlight, and waited. Waited while Beth expelled sob after sob. Waited while his heart, despite himself, was moved by her sadness. What had that Caldwell fellow said, anyway?

How often had Michael, as a child, heard his mother's

similar weeping, and longed to comfort her? At the time, he hadn't understood why his mother was crying. As an adult, he understood all too well.

Anger. An anger that had lain dormant for ages pushed through the hardened layers of Michael's rocky heart and exploded like a pent-up geyser. His hand shook. His throat tightened. His upper lip beaded in perspiration. He fought an overwhelming urge to hunt down Scott Caldwell and pummel his face.

At the same time, Michael felt a need for some answers from his own father. Answers he should have demanded before the old man died. How could Edgar Alexander have deserted his wife and son for months on end?

Gritting his teeth, Michael steeled himself against becoming involved. After all, if he achieved his goal he would probably hurt Beth as much, or more, than Scott Caldwell had. How odd, that he should grow angry with Scott. As the treasure loomed in his mind, Michael refused to allow himself to contemplate the irony of his wanting to protect Beth. The very idea defied all common sense.

The last tears draining from her eyes, Beth rolled onto her back and stared at the crystal light fixture hanging from the ceiling. She took one last shuddering breath and with that breath, smelled Scott's sandalwood cologne lingering on her white lacy blouse.

Scott held her in his arms. But had he looked into her eyes, longed for her lips, spoken her name on tremulous tongue? Or did Beth imagine it all? Whether it was real or imagined, Beth reacted as she reacted at the refrigerator last week, only more intensely. A reaction that made her attraction to Michael seem infantile. Even now, she tingled at the very thought of Scott's arms around her.

She sat straight up, her mind whirling with the implications of her foreign feelings. Once again, she reminded herself that Scott had always been the brother she never had. And that left her reaction in a sphere so distasteful she wanted to purge it from her thoughts. A warm rush of blood heated her face. What would he think if he knew?

Her thoughts danced around the room like taunting demons, bent on tormenting her. Beth jumped from the bed to rush from the room, only pausing to lock her bedroom door as she always did. A warm cup of herbal tea would soothe her raw nerves and help her put the evening into perspective.

As she hurried toward the kitchen, Beth passed Michael's closed door. Pausing, she instinctively wondered what Michael must think of her. Of Scott. Of her relationship with Scott.

Yet a certain anxiety replaced these concerns. Something akin to caution stirred her stomach, and Scott's warnings about Michael surfaced in her mind. But after her recent encounters with Scott, Beth was no longer sure if she should give ear to his opinions.

She went down to the kitchen, and as she picked up the teakettle the phone rang. She automatically turned to answer it, then stopped.

What if it were Scott?

The phone rang again. She certainly didn't want to speak with him. Or did she? A film of cold sweat covered her palms.

"Aren't you going to get your phone?" Michael asked from the kitchen doorway.

Jumping, Beth gripped the teakettle and glanced toward Michael and his careless grin.

"Here, I'll get it for you. Your hands are full." He turned for the wall phone and picked up the receiver. "Hello . . . hello?"

Beth licked her lips, knowing in her soul who was on the phone.

Then Michael replaced the receiver. "Whoever it was apparently didn't want to talk."

"He hung up," Beth muttered, imagining Scott's reaction to Michael's voice. Her hands shook. Why should she care? Scott just said the most hateful things to her.

But you were hateful too.

Despite what Scott said, Beth wished she could erase those words about his being like his father. They weren't true.

"You've been crying," Michael said softly, diminishing the distance between them.

"Oh, it's nothing." Beth turned to the sink.

"If it's enough for you to cry over, it's something," he said from close behind.

Biting her lips, Beth turned on the water and watched the teakettle slowly fill.

"It's that Scott fellow, isn't it? He's been unkind to you." His breath fanned her cheek.

She shrank from the idea of sharing her problems with Michael. Somehow, sharing with Michael seemed traitorous to Scott. "Want some tea?" Beth glanced up, smiling brightly, hoping he would take the hint and change the topic.

"I would love some. But first . . ." He moved closer, reaching to caress her upper arm.

Sidestepping him, Beth placed the kettle on the stove, turned on the flame, and grabbed two mugs. "Cream or sugar?" she asked, averting her eyes.

"I was hoping for sugar."

His obvious double meaning left her biting her lip.

Then he stroked her cheek. "Beth, you have to feel it between us. Please don't shut me out any longer. I won't let Scott abuse you anymore. I promise. Whatever he said, I'll make him apologize. I cannot stand to see you so distraught."

She looked up into his gray eyes and felt as if she were falling into their smoky depths. If there were times when Beth had questioned Michael's sincerity, she couldn't question it now. She also couldn't question that he wanted to kiss her. Only minutes ago, she almost allowed him that privilege. Why couldn't she let him kiss her now? Hadn't she decided from their first meeting that he might be Mr. Right? Shouldn't she throw all caution aside as she had vowed to do?

Then Scott's repeated warnings mingled with her parents' voices from her childhood along with that same quiet voice that wouldn't leave her.

He's not a Christian. Remember, make sure when you grow up that you marry a Christian. Don't be unequally yoked. He's not a Christian. Don't you care that he's not a Christian? Unequally yoked.

"Beth?" he breathed, leaning forward.

"I—the water's almost ready." And she turned toward the steaming teakettle.

Scott hung up the phone and stared blankly out the living room window at his lighted basketball court. He called Beth and didn't even know why, but Michael answered the phone. Scott imagined Beth in Blondie's arms that very moment, spilling out her hurt feelings to his waiting ears.

His stomach knotted.

Why had Scott mentioned that horrible homecoming incident? Any hope, any chance of winning Beth's heart had been annihilated with his angry words. She would never forgive him.

He turned from his living room of southwest decor

and toward his bedroom. When he moved back to Eureka Springs to be with his father, Scott never dreamed he would keep his childhood home. He originally intended to sell it. At the time, though, the house seemed his last link to his mother, and Scott couldn't part with it. He thought that completely remodeling it would erase his father while allowing him to hang onto the few good childhood memories he still possessed. Tonight, however, he could only feel his father's presence.

Beth was right. He was just like his father.

Lord, I am more confused than I have ever been. I thought—I thought I was maturing as a Christian. I thought I was beyond my father's influence and the way I acted tonight. Please forgive me. Please heal me. Please, Lord, don't let Beth hate me.

Scott stripped and fumbled through his oak dresser drawers for a pair of shorts and a T-shirt. That's when he saw the black velvet ring box. A disillusioned grimace, and he opened the box to stare at the diamond winking with a bluish-white fire. The stone seemed to say, "You've thrown your money and your heart away."

Scott knew the mocking words were right.

The jeweler told him he could return the ring within thirty days for a full refund. Mentally, Scott deposited the refund into his savings account as he dropped the ring box into the drawer.

At one time, he thought of expunging Beth from his mind by spending more time with Marilyn. Maybe the time had arrived to stop reaching for the stars and start facing reality.

Perhaps God's promise of a godly wife wasn't about Beth at all. Maybe Scott, in his human weakness, had believed God was pointing him to Beth, when actually Marilyn was the answer to his prayers.

Eighteen

ichael slumped on his bed. Over the past two days he'd had perfect windows of time to explore . . . but a thorough perusal of the attic revealed no new finds. He was starting to worry. He'd been so sure of the prize's presence at McAllister's Bed and Breakfast, but every new turn denied his assurance. What if he searched each room, including Beth's, and still didn't find it?

Work. Work. Work. The word beckoned to him like the remnants of a terrifying nightmare. Even though the jewelry and the attic find would support him awhile, they couldn't provide long-term financial solvency.

His fingers nervously beat out a tattoo against the bed's blue comforter, and another plan entered his mind. Beth McAllister owned a flourishing business. She also liked Michael. Even though she kept resisting him, Michael sensed her resolve weakening. If he couldn't find the treasure, perhaps he could settle here, convince

Beth to marry him, and live "happily ever after." Immediately he stood, aghast at his own thoughts.

What had this woman done to him? With an ironic twist of his mouth, Michael chuckled at the incongruity of his emotions. He came here to take advantage of Beth, and within weeks of his stay he was angry with someone who made her cry. After hearing her sob the other night, Michael spent several hours angry with Scott Caldwell. As if Michael really cared for Beth. Perhaps his anger was an overflow of the anger he felt toward his father and nothing more. Perhaps . . . but then . . .

He must find the treasure and leave. As soon as possible. Otherwise, Beth would turn him into a mere shadow of the hardened bachelor he was upon arrival.

With new resolve, Michael walked down the hallway to the room two doors from his. Yesterday, he overheard Beth telling the maid that the room was vacant and needed a thorough cleaning. It also cried for a thorough search.

"Good morning," Lauren called from the front door.

"Morning!" Beth, carrying a tray laden with fruit and sweet rolls, exited the kitchen with Tiffany, as usual, on her heels. Most of her guests retrieved their complimentary continental breakfast to enjoy it in their rooms. Not Michael. He usually ate with Beth and Tiffany.

"Mmm, cinnamon rolls," Lauren said, rolling her eyes.

"Want to join me?" Beth asked hesitantly. They hadn't talked since their last conflict at the restaurant. Each time Beth thought about calling Lauren, she talked herself out of it.

"Thought you'd never ask. I haven't seen you out and about for a few days, so I thought I'd drop by. How are things between you and Tom Cruise?"

"Very funny."

"Has he kissed you?"

"No." Beth set the tray on the registration desk. Since she skillfully avoided him two nights ago, Michael had acted the consummate gentleman. She was relieved.

"You're kidding! What's he waiting for?"

Shrugging, Beth concentrated on arranging the strawberries and cantaloupe.

"Oh," Lauren said meaningfully. "Better not give him too many cold shoulders. He's likely to go elsewhere."

Beth swallowed, knowing Lauren was right. Perhaps the time had come to let Michael move closer, but is that what she really wanted?

"He's not a Christian, you know."

"Well, that can be remedied. Have you witnessed to him?"

"It's not that easy," Beth replied, not wanting to admit that Michael wasn't interested. "You have a lot to learn, Little Sis."

Unequally yoked . . . unequally yoked . . . The words were

Debra White Smith

beginning to pound out a slow, monotonous torture in Beth's mind.

She thought about the lesson she taught to her senior high Sunday school class a couple months ago outlining the complications of a Christian dating and marrying a non-Christian. Beth had been proud of her conclusion at the time, a conclusion that now seemed trite and simplistic: "I know the temptations you face every day. You are surrounded by potential boyfriends and girlfriends who aren't Christians, so you have to make up your mind to follow this biblical standard and date only Christians." She closed in a prayer asking God to empower those young people to seek His will in all they did, including their choice of friends.

Suppressing an ironic snort, Beth knew she was failing miserably at practicing what she preached. She also knew she possessed no idea about the intensity of the temptations those young people were facing.

Not until now.

Suddenly, Beth fervently hoped none of her Sunday school class had seen her out with Michael. What would they think if they learned the truth?

What about your reputation as a Christian? Scott's words once again taunted her.

"Have you heard the latest about our dear Scott?" Lauren popped a strawberry into her mouth.

"What about him?" Beth snapped. She hadn't seen or heard from the man in two days, and the very mention of his name evoked a flood of pain, confusion, shame.

198

"Touchy, touchy, touchy."

Silently, Beth went into the kitchen to retrieve the waiting pot of coffee. After Scott followed her to the Crescent Hotel, Beth wondered if he were experiencing some emotional problems because of his traumatic childhood and his father's recent death. When she found him spying on her by her own front door she was even more certain that he was unwell. Perhaps she should forget their argument, forget his slicing words, and concentrate on helping him heal. But her aching heart told her to concentrate on her own wounds.

She'd had nightmares the last two nights, nightmares in which a dozen laughing teenage girls, all dressed in formal wear, were mocking her . . . mocking . . . mocking.

"Scott and Marilyn Douglas were at the restaurant yesterday for lunch," Lauren said as Beth returned to the front desk. "Rumor has it they're a hot item." Lauren helped herself to two cinnamon rolls.

"I wouldn't know." Beth tried to keep the waspish tone from her voice as she thought of Marilyn smiling at Scott during the basketball game. The waspish tone won. "He hasn't been here in days."

The coffee pot blurred, and Beth blinked against the tears burning her eyes.

"My, my, my, aren't we in a mood?"

"No, we're not."

"If I didn't know any better, I'd say you were jealous."

Beth placed her fists on her hips. "Jealous? Of whom?"

Thoughtfully chewing, Lauren gazed into Beth's eyes. "Everybody knows it but you," she muttered.

"What?"

A calculating smile. "Oh nothing. Just something Dad said that didn't make sense at the time." She reached for the coffee pot and a cup. "Are all your rooms still full?"

"One vacancy. I had a couple check out last night."

"Oh well, you have no worries." A sip of hot coffee. "If only we all were so lucky."

"What's that supposed to mean?" Beth asked, her irritation moving from Scott to her sister. Why didn't Lauren let the inheritance issue die? Beth was ready to forget Aunt Naomi's mistake and move on. Why couldn't her sister?

Lauren toyed with the hem of her Penn State T-shirt, then set her mouth in a firm line. "You inherited all of this." She waved her hand across the Victorian living room. "If we were all as lucky as you are—"

"As I am? Lauren, when are you going to wake up?" Beth snapped her fingers in front of Lauren's nose. The pressure of worrying about Scott, about Lauren, about Michael, found release as Beth vented her frustrations over Lauren's blindness. "Look at me! I'm overweight. I'm short. I'm far from pretty. And look at you," she accused. "You're perfect. Your hair, your teeth, your figure. And Mom and Dad are giving you an opportunity I never had. I worked the whole time I was in college. You have the privilege of all the extracurricular activities and dating that I had to say no to. Don't you think any of that may have played a part in Aunt Naomi's decision to leave me this?"

Lauren blinked, then stared at Beth in stunned silence. The silence lasted only seconds. "Well, when are you going to wake up?" Lauren repeated Beth's spiteful finger snapping. "You've always been everybody's favorite. Anybody who knows us can't stop singing your praises. Do you know what it was like trying to go through high school with all your old teachers? I never measured up to your perfect grade point average. All my life, I've felt inferior to you! Do you have any idea what it's been like to grow up in your shadow?"

"My shadow?" Beth gasped, hardly able to comprehend Lauren's words.

"Yes! You might have had to work through college, but don't you see, Beth, it would kill my grades to have to work like you did. You could hold down a full-time job and full-time college and still graduate with honors! I may have nice packaging, but packaging isn't everything. You got the brains. You got the personality. And you—you got Aunt Naomi's love!"

The two sisters stared at each other as their words hung between them like bitter betrayal.

Beth's heart constricted with regret. She had never spoken so severely to her baby sister; Lauren had never spoken so severely with her. Could either of them truly mean it?

Lauren set her cup on the desk and raced from the house, slamming the door behind her.

Cold, heavy silence cloaked Beth as she stared at the closed door. What had made her say those words? What had made Lauren respond so cruelly?

Beth groaned to herself, wondering how she could survive the summer. So far, her two best friends were alienated from her. Why did her life seem to be shattering at her feet?

Healing . . . emotional healing . . . The words haunted her as Beth recognized the source for all her turmoil.

She needed to be healed.

But even with that recognition, she couldn't fathom how. She told Scott the Holy Spirit could work miracles.

"Well, Lord," she muttered to the God who seemed to daily inch farther from her, "I need a miracle."

Stifling her tears, Beth trudged up the stairs to start her usual round of chores. To her surprise, she stepped into the hallway just as Michael stepped out of a room—but not his room.

He stopped, his eyes rounded in alarm. "Beth!"

"Michael? Is there something I can get for you?"

Scott's warning once again floated across her consciousness as her spine prickled in suspicion. Why was Michael coming out of the green room?

"No." A sheepish smile. "I—um—" Another smile. "I hated to say anything, but the air conditioner in my room hasn't been as cool as it should be." Slipping a hand into the pocket of his khaki shorts, he shrugged. "I guess I was snooping, but I wanted to see if the air conditioner in this room is any better."

"Oh." Her suspicion melted, and Beth felt as if Scott had caused her unnecessary paranoia. Just one more thing to fuel her agitation. "If you'd like, we could move you into the green room. The unit in the blue room is showing some wear; I've thought of replacing it."

"Would you mind? I'm terribly hot natured."

"I don't mind a bit." Beth grinned politely, and this time her heart didn't flutter with his sassy wink.

"What's on the agenda for today?" he asked, walking toward the stairs.

"The usual. Work, work, work. I have a maid three days a week, and sometimes we work together the days she's here."

"All work and no play makes Beth a boring girl."

"Do I bore you?" she asked absently.

"Of course not." He grabbed her hand. "I was just trying to convince you to come out with me today. I thought I'd drive into the mountains and take in the scenery. Want to come?"

Hesitating, she thought of the mound of bed linens she planned to wash, the living room windows she planned to clean, the front flower beds she planned to weed. Then she remembered her musings from only moments before. She had considered letting Michael move closer. Wouldn't this be the perfect opportunity?

"Let me think about it," she said.

Unequally yoked . . . unequally yoked.

"Oh, come on." He pulled her fingers to his lips. "Please."

She deliberated over her decision, suddenly dreading more time with him. Time with Michael tired her, emotionally and spiritually.

"I'll tell you what," she started, knowing he would never agree to her proposal. "If you'll help me clean up after breakfast and change the bed linens, I'll go. The maid can see to the rest and watch the desk while I'm gone. But I have to be home by three. Tiffany's yearly checkup is at four."

"It's a deal."

Beth hid her surprise as her heart sank with disappointment.

His fingers pressed her palm, and he pulled her toward the staircase. "Come on. The sooner we get through cleaning up, the sooner we can have fun."

With a sigh, she pasted a grin on her face and tried to act congenial. Oh well, maybe going out for a drive would do her good. Perhaps when she got back, she could try again to talk with Lauren. Maybe she would even call Scott.

Nineteen

For the third time in fifteen minutes, Scott drove down Beth's street. Two days. Two whole days since their argument. Or had it been two years since he'd seen her? Since he'd held her. Since he'd almost kissed her.

After his initial self-incrimination over his thoughtless words, Scott began to wonder if Beth suspected his desires during the minutes she was in his arms. Had she known he wanted to feel her lips against his?

Rubbing his tense neck, he slowed the car as her house came into view. Should he stop? His heart ached to see her gorgeous blue eyes and sunny smile, but he didn't know if she would even speak to him. He rubbed his neck again, his head aching as it only did when he hadn't slept.

He thought of Marilyn and his brief consideration that God might have meant for him to become involved with her. A derisive chuckle. That was definitely not going to work. The whole time he was with her, all he could think of, all he could see, was Beth. Before Marilyn got too attached to him, Scott knew he had to break it off. Otherwise, he would be using her—something his father had been good at, something Scott despised.

Applying the brakes, Scott made up his mind to stop at Beth's inn.

That's when he saw them. Michael and Beth, walking toward the Mercedes.

Beth laughed at something Michael said and turned her face up to his. Michael took full advantage of her position and bestowed a kiss on her forehead while casually draping an arm around her shoulders.

Grinding his teeth, Scott reversed his decision. He wouldn't stop. Why had he ever thought of dropping by in the first place?

Without another glance he pressed the accelerator. Just as his car picked up speed, he noticed a flash of something brown near the curb. Then a sickening thud. A squeal. And Beth's horror-filled cries.

He pulled sharply into the next driveway, turned around, and stopped at to the curb in front of the Beth's house.

She stood there motionless, staring at the lifeless form of her pet.

🐉🎶

Tiffany lay on her side in the street. How had she

escaped the fence this time? A warm rush of nausea, and Beth hoped this was a nightmare.

Suddenly there was Scott, leaning over Tiffany. Scott, looking up at Beth. Scott's eyes imploring her forgiveness. Scott, gingerly picking up the pig.

"Is she—is she—" Beth rushed forward.

"No. She's still breathing."

Hot tears filled Beth's eyes as she took in the lax angle of Tiffany's neck. The poor little creature. Beth spent more time agitated with her than anything else. Now, Tiffany's crimes seemed minuscule, and Beth wished she had been more understanding.

"We need to take her to the vet," Scott said. "Here. You get in the back seat with her."

"But your car . . ." Beth said, recalling how proud Scott was of the leather interior.

"Hang my car." His eyes full of anxiety, Scott glanced toward Michael nearby. "Would you call the vet and tell her we're coming?"

"It's Dr. Ginger Lovelady," Beth said, looking at the nonplused Michael. She opened the car's back door and slid onto the seat. "There's a phone book on the front desk. And would you also please tell Mrs. Spencer where I've gone?"

"I'll be glad to," Michael said. "Will you be all right?"

"Fine. I'm fine," Beth said as Scott placed the unconscious pig beside her. She stroked a limp ear.

Then Scott closed the door, and they were racing toward the veterinarian.

"I'm so sorry, Bet." Scott looked at her in the rearview mirror, his tired eyes showing signs of insomnia. "I just didn't see her."

"I know, I know." She swallowed against the lump in her throat. "She shouldn't have been out in the first place."

Beth looked at the pitiful form lying beside her. "The poor thing. It seemed she was always into something, and I—I—"

"Don't lambaste yourself. If it's any consolation, she was—is—probably the luckiest pig in the nation. You spoil her rotten."

A tremulous smile through threatening tears. "I just hope—"

"I'm sure she's going to be fine."

Why didn't he sound sure? Beth had a terrible feeling in the pit of her stomach that Tiffany had met her demise.

Her suspicions were confirmed in the examining room when the veterinarian helplessly shook her head.

"I'm terribly sorry," Dr. Lovelady said, staring at Tiffany, who struggled to breathe. "But she has extensive internal injuries. The best thing is to put her to sleep."

Her heart pounding in sorrow, Beth gripped Scott's hand as he let out a slow, defeated sigh. "Okay," she croaked, watching her pet on the examination table. "But I don't want to watch."

"That's fine." The veterinarian smiled in sympathy. "If you'll just wait out front, I can take care of it. Would you like to leave her with me, or—"

"No. I'll take her home." Beth gulped. "I have a special place for her."

"Okay. I think I've got a box just big enough for you to carry her home in."

In brotherly comfort, Scott draped a consoling arm around Beth's shoulders as they walked toward the waiting room. "I'm so sorry," he breathed, his voice laden with guilt.

"It's not your fault." Taking in the smells of animals and antiseptic, Beth glanced up at his stricken face. "It—it was Tiffany's fault."

"I don't know how she got out," Scott said. "I made sure that gate latch was sturdy."

Numb, Beth sat in the first chair she came to, and Scott took the seat next to hers. "She probably rooted under the fence."

"Knowing Tiffany, she might have climbed it."

Beth giggled, then sniffled against a tear. "Oh Scott," she said, leaning her head against his shoulder. "I know she's only a pig. I'm probably being silly, but—"

"No, no," he soothed, stroking her hair. "It's only natural to mourn her loss. She was a part of your life that's gone now. I'll tell you something if you promise not to tell anyone."

"Okay." Another sniffle as she stared at a selection of dry dog food in red and green bags.

"Remember when my parrot died last fall?"

"Yes."

"Well, I shed a tear or two myself."

"Did you?"

"Uh huh. And I still miss him. He woke me up every morning with, 'Get up, you lazy bum.'"

As the companionable silence stretched, and Beth realized where her mourning had led her, her spine stiffened. Her head was on Scott's shoulder. His arm around her. Her hand against his chest. And that moment only two nights ago when he pulled her into his arms flashed through her mind. Then she recalled their heated, hateful words, and her anger resurfaced, as did her pride.

She pulled away to make a big job of searching her purse for a tissue. "Were you stopping by the house for something?" she asked, her voice sounding strained even to her own ears.

"Well . . . yes," he said, glancing out the window.

More silence.

"Actually . . ."

She felt his glance and, preparing herself for an apology, kept her focus on the dog food.

"I wanted to ask you a favor."

"Oh?" she responded, surprised that he had the audacity to ask a favor after their argument.

"Yes. I'm having company tomorrow night, and I wondered if you could whip up an apple pie for me."

"Doesn't Marilyn do pies?" Not sure what prompted that petty remark, she darted him a spiteful glance.

"Marilyn?" he asked as if the name were foreign to him.

"Well, hello," a voice said from the hallway.

Beth turned to see the very topic of their conversation, and her cheeks warmed. Had she heard anything they had said?

"Oh hi," Scott said with a familiar smile. "Marilyn, do you remember Beth?"

"Of course I do," Marilyn said, her brown eyes smiling into Beth's. "Dr. Lovelady just told me about your pet, Beth. I'm so sorry."

"Thanks."

"I was in the back doing some cleaning," Marilyn said.

"Dr. Lovelady just hired Marilyn as her part-time receptionist—"

"And assistant, and general go-for," Marilyn supplied through a friendly chuckle. "I think I'm going to like it."

"How nice," Beth said, wishing she could simply get her pet and leave.

"Tiffany is ready now," Dr. Lovelady said reverently as she entered the waiting room. "I went ahead and placed her in the box and covered her with a cloth."

"Thank you," Beth said, her emotions wilting.

"I'll put her in the car." Scott stood. "And you can send the bill to me."

"But—" Beth began.

"No," he said firmly. "This was my fault. I'm paying."

"Well . . . okay."

"Don't forget, Mom's fixing a roast for you tonight," Marilyn said, laying a possessive hand on Scott's arm.

Beth, her heart constricting, reached for her over-sized handbag and busied herself with nothing. Marilyn was a kind and beautiful woman, and even in high school, she had been firm about her belief in Christ. Beth should be happy for Scott. But how could she be happy for him and angry with him at the same time? Or was this the jealousy Lauren mentioned?

Michael, glancing over his shoulder, applied the screwdriver to the locked door. Beth called this the yellow room, and its occupants were out sightseeing or doing whatever tourists did in this sorry excuse for a town. With a jiggle and a quick turn of the wrist, the ancient knob gave, and the door swung open with a wheeze of its hinges.

Michael walked in to hungrily peer around the neat room. He had to find his prize.

Beth nearly caught him examining the green room that morning. Luckily, he thought of the failing air conditioner as an excuse and got himself out of another tight spot. She was so naive. She would probably believe him if he told her he was a space alien visiting from Mars.

And he had to continue playing her naiveté. Keep her thinking *she* was his interest.

Something in his midsection twisted uncomfortably. He thought of Beth's candid blue eyes, cheery smile, and trusting spirit. Taking advantage of her was growing more and more difficult. He even felt sorry for her when she whisked that stupid pig away to the veterinarian.

What was wrong with him?

Compressing his lips in determination, Michael strode to the closet, whipped open the door, and pulled the string to click on the light. He shoved aside the jeans and T-shirts and ran his hands over the wooden panels lining the closet. He would leave no possibility unturned. Old houses were notorious for hidden rooms. And hidden treasures.

Once he found that treasure, regardless of his feelings for Beth McAllister, Michael would leave and never look back.

In Beth's backyard, Scott placed the last shovelful of dirt on Tiffany's grave near a huge oak. At the grave's head, Beth put a large, oblong stone she removed from her flower bed.

If it weren't for Beth's stricken expression, Scott would have laughed. He never dreamed he would be attending a funeral for a pig. Just that morning he ate sausage! But at the same time, he did feel sorry for Beth, and he would probably even miss the ornery animal.

"I'm so sorry," he said again, his heart pulsating with regret. "I just didn't see her."

"I know. But as I've already said, it wasn't your fault. You saw where she dug out from under the fence." Those were the only words she had voiced since their arrival, and they were strained.

Nodding, Scott looked past Beth and toward a squirrel frolicking in the oak's full branches. He didn't trust himself to look into Beth's eyes. If he did, Scott might not be responsible for his actions.

For a moment at the vet's office, he and Beth were like the buddies they had always been. Then she remembered. He felt her very thoughts when her body stiffened, and knew she was remembering those horrible words he threw at her two nights ago. Could she ever forgive him?

He chanced a guarded glance toward her. "The apple pie wasn't the only reason I was going to stop by today."

"Oh?" Her right brow peaked in interest despite her bland expression.

"I, um, I also wanted to apologize for the way I've been acting lately and the things I said a couple of nights ago. They were uncalled for. I—" He cleared his dry throat, feeling as if he were exposing his very soul. "I don't know what got into me. I shouldn't have ever brought up that homecoming incident—"

"I don't want to talk about it."

"Beth, you've been saying that since it happened. One day, you're going to have to talk about it. How can you expect to heal—"

"I forgive you for bringing it up," she said, skillfully cutting him off. "I guess I owe you an apology, too." A cautious glance his way. "You aren't anything at all like your father."

"Thanks." He extended his hand. "Friends again?"

With a smile, she placed her hand in his. "Friends."

"Maybe the rest of the summer will go smoother."

"Scott," she said, pulling her warm hand from his.

Did she suspect that he wanted more than a hand-shake?

"I know you've already said you're handling your father's death, but don't you think it would be a good idea to talk with our pastor, just to make sure? With all frankness, you just aren't acting like yourself. It's not like you to—"

"No," he snapped. Why did she have to insist that there was something wrong with him? Couldn't she see— no, she couldn't. And that exasperated him all the more. Would she ever see him as more than a brother?

Lord, are You up there? he demanded. *Can't You do something?*

"You never said whether or not you would make the pie," Scott said, changing the subject.

Her eyes clouded with an emotion Scott couldn't define.

How strange.

Beth's eyes had never been anything but honest. That was one of the things he so admired about her.

"Sorry," she said as the invisible barrier once again erected itself. "But I don't have time."

"You don't have time?" he asked incredulously, his irritation sprouting anew. If he didn't know any better, he would say Beth was playing some kind of game. Maybe she was the one who needed counseling. This wasn't the first time he asked her to bake for him, and she always cheerfully agreed. She knew he couldn't cook worth a flip.

"I have a business to run, you know, and I'm behind on the laundry and windows and—"

"Beth, there you are," Michael called as he opened the back door and walked toward them. "I was beginning to wonder if you would make it back in time for our drive. Are you still planning to go?"

"Yes."

"What happened with Tif—?" Michael spotted the grave and stopped. "Oh, no," he said with regret.

"Yes, I'm afraid so." Beth's voice dripped with sadness.

Scott stepped away from Beth as Michael draped a proprietary arm over her shoulders. Their words dissolved into unintelligible murmuring.

Beth had plenty of time to take a drive with Michael, but she didn't have time to make one measly pie for Scott. Repressing the urge to pull out his and her hair, Scott turned on his heel and marched to his car.

Twenty

*B*eth watched as Scott stomped away.

    Buddy, if you think I'm going to bake a pie for your girlfriend, you're crazy, she thought as Michael steered her toward the house.

Scott hadn't said the pie was for Marilyn, but it didn't take a rocket scientist to deduce that his "company" tomorrow night would be she. Although Beth often baked for him, she didn't feel inclined to assist him in wooing a woman. The very thought made her feel used. So what if he got mad. He had been mad before, and he could get over it.

Besides, she really didn't have the time. This drive with Michael was going to force her to stay up until midnight catching up on her chores, and tomorrow would be just as busy.

Without analyzing the situation further, Beth concentrated on Michael's words. She could use a drive in the country; anything to get her mind off of Scott and

Lauren and the deceased Tiffany.

"Do you know what I would really enjoy?" Michael asked.

"What?"

Unequally yoked . . . unequally yoked.

As they walked into her country kitchen, Beth wished Michael would remove his arm from her shoulders. Earlier, he took advantage of their close proximity and kissed her on the forehead, something which surprised, then flattered, then irritated her.

"This mansion is so quaint and so full of antiques, I'd love a grand tour of the whole house. I was just admiring the Victorian settee in your living room and then the sleigh bed in the green room. I thought that if you didn't mind I'd take a few photos. I might do a write-up on McAllister's Bed and Breakfast and possibly sell it to a travel magazine. It would be free advertising."

"That would be great," Beth said, thrilling at the possibility. "Give me a day or two to get everything shipshape, and we'll do it."

"Great." That same sassy wink. "Are you about ready to go?"

"I'll be ready in fifteen minutes." Beth trotted toward the stairs to freshen up.

But as she changed from her soiled jeans to linen shorts, touched up her makeup, and sprayed a light touch of the rose perfume, Beth's mind wasn't on the coming drive with Michael. She thought instead of Scott. His crestfallen face when he had heard her agree to go on the ride with Michael. His lips set firmly before he turned for his car. His spine stiff as he walked from her yard.

Scott. They had been a pair since she could remember. They had shared friendship and secrets and dreams. Why did it seem that with each passing day their friendship deteriorated into a nightmare?

After burying poor Tiffany, Beth thought they called a truce. Then she made the mistake of suggesting counseling again, Scott snapped at her, and the bickering was back. Trying to force him from her mind, Beth grabbed her shoulder bag and walked for the door.

Pushing her mane of hair over her shoulder, she paused at the door and, out of habit, glanced back to her answering machine. The light blinked to indicate a message. Beth stopped to hit the play button, and her mother's clear voice floated into the room.

"Beth, I just talked with Lauren and wanted to tell you what I told her. My sister and I didn't speak for three years over a diamond bracelet. See ya."

Beth blinked at the abrupt message. Knowing her mother, she would probably never mention it again, but her meaning came through loud and clear. With a sigh, Beth turned from the machine to stare at the guilty-eyed portrait of her aunt over the bed.

"Why did you do it, Aunt Naomi?" she asked the smiling young woman who barely resembled the beloved, wrinkled aunt who had passed away. "Now I'm the one who has to deal with Lauren's anger."

But as she once again turned for the door, Beth knew Aunt Naomi had never intended to cause a rift. She also knew Aunt Naomi wasn't the only one responsible for Lauren's anger. Beth herself said words that should never have been said. Beth allowed unhealthy envy to soil her attitude toward Lauren. And Lauren had apparently envied too; envied for a long while.

Tonight. Tonight Beth would call her sister and begin the healing. She certainly didn't want to emulate her mother and aunt with a three-year silence.

"Ready to go?" Michael asked as she entered the living room.

"Sure," Beth said, her heart still chasing Scott. "I'm going to have to move my car first, though. It's in the driveway behind yours."

"Oh yeah, I forgot. You were just about to do that when poor Tiffany caught it."

Biting her lip, Beth nodded.

"I'm sorry. I shouldn't have brought it up."

"It's okay. Let's just concentrate on enjoying our drive."

Unequally yoked . . . unequally yoked.

"Sounds good to me."

But as she tried to crank her worn Camaro and the engine refused to turn over, she wondered if Scott had somehow orchestrated her motor's demise to prohibit her from taking the drive with Michael.

"It won't crank," Beth said, looking to Michael through the open door. "Do you know—"

With an impotent shrug, he shook his head. "Don't look to me, my dear. When it comes to cars, I'm illiterate."

"Nuts. I'll have to call—" Beth stopped herself. She had been about to say she would have to call Scott. Why was he always her first thought when she needed help? "I'll have to call the garage," she finished. "There's no telling what it will cost."

FREE KITTENS. Scott slowed his car when he saw the sign in the yard three houses from his. A lanky boy sat in a lawn chair beside a box.

A cat. The perfect replacement for Tiffany. Would Beth take the gift? Last week he would have been certain of her acceptance, but it seemed he could no longer predict her response. With a resigned sigh, he pulled into the driveway.

Maybe a cute, cuddly kitten would open Beth's door to him once more. And once her door was open, she would be in for a surprise. Scott was tired of silently standing by while his heart felt as if it were being ripped from his chest. He was tired of watching Michael circle her like a hungry tomcat stalking an injured robin. He was tired of her assuming something was dreadfully wrong with him, when what was "wrong" amounted to thwarted love.

Beth's father told Scott of the eye-opening kiss that awakened his love. That's what Scott would do. Maybe he could catch Beth before she went for that drive. The time had come to take action. And if taking action resulted in Scott's losing her forever, then so let it be. Anything was better than the limbo he was in.

After phoning the mechanic, Beth walked onto the porch and sat beside Michael in one of the wicker chairs.

"Sorry," she said lamely, wondering why her feelings didn't match her words. If she were honest, she would say she really didn't care whether she went for a drive with Michael or not. How ironic. A couple weeks ago, she wondered if he were Mr. Right. But for some reason he was losing his appeal. Perhaps it was that insistent voice that wouldn't cease when she was with him.

"It's quite all right. We still have time."

"I don't think so. The mechanic said it would be at least two hours before the tow truck comes to pick it up, and I really do have some chores to finish. I guess we'll have to wait until tomorrow."

"That's fine." He reached for her hand. "I'm in no rush." His eyes spoke a double message.

Beth pulled her hand from his, sure of only one thing. She never wanted him to touch her again. She could no longer wrestle against that persistent voice within, that voice which was causing her more spiritual misery than she had ever experienced. The voice of God.

Okay, Lord, You win, she prayed, feeling relief for the first time in weeks. *Scott was right. You were right. I cannot become romantically involved with him and stay strong in You.*

As warm peace flooded her heart, Beth turned for the door. She reveled in the release, which left her feeling as if a load of misery had been taken from her shoulders.

If You don't ever want me to marry, I won't. Just give me the strength to accept Your will.

"Well, I guess I'll go change into my work clothes and get busy," she said absently, her mind roaming to Scott, to the way he had abruptly left less than an hour ago. He would be relieved to know Michael no longer influenced her. Silently she stood, scanned the street, turned to go into the house, only to stop.

A green Chevrolet cruised down the road and halted at the curb: Scott's green Chevrolet.

Before he went inside, Michael said something. Something Beth ignored. And she swallowed against a throat, suddenly dry. Why had Scott come back?

Twenty-one

“Excuse me," a hesitant feminine voice said.

Beth turned around toward her guest, who stepped onto the porch. The Bennetts checked into the yellow room last week. Honeymooners, they kept to themselves, and Beth caught only periodic glimpses of them.

"Is there something I can help you with?" she asked as the petite, gray-haired lady closed the inn's front door.

"Yes. We've debated mentioning it because we don't want you to think we aren't enjoying our stay, but there's been a bit of a problem. I finally decided to, well, to just tell you." Her hazel eyes clouding with indecision, Mrs. Bennett twisted her fingers.

"Is it something I've done? You're room—is it—"

"No, no, dear." She laid a reassuring hand on Beth's arm. "It's nothing like that. We're truly enjoying our stay. It's just that I think we've had a prowler."

"A prowler?"

"Yes. I didn't notice anything amiss until I opened the closet. And well, I always leave my clothes hanging just so. After I iron them, I hang them so that none of the hangers touch. That way, they don't get crushed against each other. When we came back from shopping this morning, my clothes were all pushed together, and a pair of pants had fallen to the floor."

Mrs. Bennett's worried frown looked like that of a woman who has experienced the worst of traumas.

"Oh," Beth said, thinking of her own cluttered closet. Should she take Mrs. Bennett's claim seriously? She noticed when the Bennetts checked in that the burly Mr. Bennett looked far less meticulous than his new bride. Perhaps he mussed her clothing.

"I didn't notice anything wrong when I changed your linens. Was anything missing?" Beth asked as Scott walked up behind her.

"No. We double-checked our things to make sure, but we don't know about *your* things. That's the main reason I wanted to tell you."

"Thanks." An image of Michael leaving the green room that morning flashed through Beth's memory, but she immediately dismissed the thought. "Would you mind if I took a look?" she asked, more as a comfort to her guest than as an admission of a prowler. If there was nothing missing, then Beth suspected Mr. Bennett didn't want to admit that he had disturbed his bride's clothing.

"I don't mind in the least. We're about to leave again and won't be back until tonight."

An assuring smile. "All right. I still haven't distributed fresh towels for the day. When I do, I'll thoroughly check your room. I normally have the towels out by now, but I've had a . . ." Beth thought of Tiffany's lifeless form, and her throat tightened. ". . . A hectic morning."

"That's fine dear. And I would feel so much better if you would check your things. You do have such nice things. Adam says it's nothing to worry about, but it still bothers me."

"I appreciate your concern."

As Mrs. Bennett stepped back into the mansion, Beth turned to face a smiling Scott extending his hands, in which was nestled a golden striped kitten.

"Hi," Scott said, smiling in boyish appeal. "I've got something for you. I thought he might be a nice replacement for Tiffany."

The old Scott was back. Just as if they hadn't shared those tense words. Just as if all were well between them. Why did he repeatedly do this? One minute he made her want to punch him. The next minute, he made her want to welcome him with open arms.

Warm pleasure chased Mrs. Bennett and her problem from Beth's mind. Speechless, she reached for the fearful feline, all claws and whiskers. "Thanks," she said as the cat nosed his way between her hair and neck and produced a distressed meow. "Hey there, little guy, it's okay."

Reveling in delight, Beth rubbed her cheek against the velvet-soft fur while her heart warmed with Scott's thoughtfulness. "This is so sweet of you."

He smiled his pleasure. "It's the least I could do, don't you think?" A moment of hesitation. "Beth—" He stepped toward her, only to pause.

Cuddling the kitten in the crook of her arm, she raised her brows. "Yes?"

"Um . . . would it be okay if I sat down?"

"Of course." Scott had never asked permission to sprawl on her furniture. Why now?

"I wondered if I would catch you still home," he said as if they were polite strangers. "I thought you and Michael were going for a drive." Scott deposited his lanky, jeans-clad form on the settee.

"We were." Sitting, Beth stroked the kitten. "But my car wouldn't crank, and it's blocking his car. The only way he could have gotten out was to drive across the flower beds." Oops. She just told Scott of her car trouble. Would he be offended that she hadn't called him to fix it? The old Scott would. But this was a different Scott.

"What's wrong with your car?"

"I—I don't know." Beth bit her lip and chanced a glance his way.

"Do you want me to take a look at it?"

"Well, I already called the garage."

"Oh."

The crestfallen look in his green eyes, the wilt of his white-toothed smile cloaked Beth in guilt. An hour ago, she refused to bake a measly pie for him. In response he brought her a kitten and was stricken that she hadn't asked him to fix her car. What did it matter to her whom he fed the pie to? Why had she been so petty?

"I hated to bother you," she rushed, trying to cover her chagrin. "I mean—you're so busy, and have already done so much this summer—"

"Do you mind if I take a look at it?"

"No—no, of course not." She smiled, hoping to ease his disappointment.

"What did it do when you tried to crank it?" he asked, standing.

"Nothing." Beth followed him.

"Sounds like the starter."

Soon Scott was peering under the hood of her car as he had ever since she owned a car. After a moment of silent contemplation, he said, "You know, Bet, there comes a time when you just need to buy a new car. It happens to the best of us. A hundred and fifty thousand is a lot of miles."

"I know," she said, snuggling the kitten. "I should have done that a long time ago. But I like this car. It's like one of the family. And besides, cars are expensive. I've got to replace the inn's roof before it starts leaking. Maybe by the end of the summer I'll have the cash for a good used car."

Scott listened to her, his gaze roaming over her features.

Beth's stomach quivered as his eyes seemed to pin her to the spot. Had he always been this handsome? This masculine? This charming? She blinked. She licked her lips. She took several quick breaths.

His thick ebony hair was casually too long. Just the right length for danger. Dark, heavy brows. A proud, prominent nose. A square jaw line and firm lips. Only the small white scar above his right brow marred his looks; a scar he received twenty years ago when he and Beth crashed their bicycles.

Other than that, Scott Caldwell was what Lauren would call a hunk. No wonder Marilyn Douglas was after him. Beth had known he was attractive, as any sister would know if her brother were attractive. But this was something different. Something on a deeper, even scary level. It was as if she were seeing Scott for the first time. As if she were taking a terrifying dive off a jagged cliff into the icy, heaving ocean. Or into his glittering, emerald eyes.

That same delicious, sensual sweetness rushed through Beth's midsection; a rush that propelled her forward.

"Beth?" Scott said uncertainly.

She stumbled backward, trying to break the magnetic force that pulled her toward him. What would he think if he knew her thoughts? Her face heated. Scott Caldwell, who could probably have any single woman in Eureka Springs, would laugh her to scorn. What did she, plain, plump Beth, have to offer the likes of him? Friendship. That was all. Friends were all they had ever been, would ever be.

"Um . . . how much do you think it will cost?" she rushed, hoping her words hid her embarrassment.

"What?"

"The starter," she said breathlessly.

"The starter."

He turned back to the engine. "Not much. A whole lot less than a car." And his mischievous grin created twin endearing dimples. "I'll run to the parts store and be back in two shakes of a lamb's tail. Why don't you go call the mechanic and tell him not to come?"

"Okay." Still cuddling the kitten, she turned for the porch, glad for a reason to distance herself from him.

"Oh, and Beth?"

"Yes?" Pivoting back, she stroked the cat's ears, clinging to any contact with reality.

"I . . ." He hesitated. "I meant to ask you something earlier and didn't. If you were a woman—no, I mean—" He took a deep breath and floundered for words as if he were an adolescent. "If—how would you recommend that I tell a certain woman I'm in love with her?" Then the words poured out. "I'm afraid it's going to be a terrible shock, and I was wondering how you think it would be best for me to break the ice."

Marilyn.

The name sliced through Beth's heart like a razor. He was in love with Marilyn Douglas. Of course it would be a shock. They hadn't been dating long. But then, they had known each other for years, and if Beth remembered right, Scott silently adored her in high school. He probably wanted to marry her. The mental image of the pair walking down the aisle made her stomach turn upside down, and Beth wanted to lash out in pain. *If you were a woman,* he said, as if she weren't; as if he could never see her as anything but his pal.

"If I were a woman," she said sarcastically.

"Now Bet, that's not what I meant."

"Exactly what did you mean?" she said, trying not to shout, trying to comprehend the turbulent emotions churning through her.

"Nothing," he clipped, his lips set in a firm line. "Just forget it. I'll be back with your starter."

And he was in his car, driving away.

Twenty-two

*M*ichael was losing influence with Beth. The thought struck him as odd and challenging. In a reflective daze, he sank to the edge of his bed. From the start, Beth acted less than thrilled at the prospect of their going for a drive. When her car wouldn't crank, her eyes even registered relief.

Perhaps Michael had been too cautious in approaching her. Perhaps he should have come on stronger. Perhaps she was losing interest in him because she feared he wasn't interested in her.

With a calculating smile, Michael plotted to alter his plans. He still needed to search three of the guest rooms and Beth's room as well. If he were to accomplish his purpose, he must keep Beth hooked. As yet, she thwarted his every attempt to kiss her, unless you could call a brush of his lips against her forehead a kiss. If he were to kiss her, and properly, perhaps her original interest would awaken.

Thoughts of how to keep a female involved with him

were so foreign that Michael suppressed perverse laughter. In the past, he had been the one who broke off relationships. Like his father before him, he couldn't remember all the faces, let alone the names, of the women to whom he waved good-bye.

With thoughts of his father came memories of his mother and all the nights Michael heard her crying. Then another foreign thought: had the women he dumped shed any tears over him? Michael never considered their feelings.

Why was he doing it now?

Because of Beth McAllister. Somehow, she had charmed her way past Michael's tough shell and planted doubts regarding his former behavior. Michael resented his father for all his absences, for his calloused use and abuse of women, especially of Michael's mother. And the very behavior that instigated Michael's bitterness was mirrored in his own life.

If he did what was right, Michael would leave McAllister's Bed and Breakfast, leave the treasure wherever it was, and earn a living the honest way. If he did what was right . . . but when had that ever been?

New resolve settling in his gut, Michael stood. No more thinking. He had arrived here with a goal. He would accomplish that goal. If exploiting Beth McAllister was the means to the end, he would do it and stop at nothing.

Beth gave the kitten some milk and found a box for his home. Then she phoned the mechanic, canceled her order for a tow truck, and hung up.

Turning from the desk phone, she collapsed onto the Victorian sofa and, staring out the window, earnestly sought the Lord for the first time in weeks.

Father, she began awkwardly, not knowing exactly what to say. *I'm so sorry. I—I don't know why I was so taken with Michael, unless it was because—because I've never felt like I quite measured up, and he represents everything I've wanted to measure up to. Please . . . please help me sort out what's going on inside me. I don't understand why, after all these years, I'm starting to hurt over what happened in high school. I thought it was buried and gone and—and I feel that perhaps my wanting to be with Michael has something to do with the past, but I don't know how. If You could only show me—*

"I couldn't help but overhear your phone call."

Beth opened her eyes and turned to see Michael walking down the stairs.

"Is Mr. Caldwell going to fix your car?" he said with a cocky grin.

"Yes. He thinks it's the starter." Something in the assured tilt of Michael's chin set off an alarm in Beth's mind.

"You know, if I didn't know you two any better, I'd say you were married." Michael, concentrating on her mouth, walked toward her.

Nervously Beth flipped her hair over her shoulder and stood to back away from his approach. "No, just good friends." *Or we used to be.*

"Well, that's good to hear." Swiftly Michael closed the distance between them, reached for her hand, and kissed her fingers. "I was beginning to get worried."

He was determined to kiss her. Beth could see it in his eyes, could feel it between them like a glistening challenge, but she no longer wanted him near. Stiffly she pulled her hand from his.

He moved closer.

A river of alarm washed up from her knotting stomach.

"Beth . . ." he said hoarsely.

"Michael, I—there's something I want to talk with you about."

"Haven't we talked enough?" A step forward.

Two steps backward. "No, no, we—we haven't," she said, walking behind the green velvet wing-backed chair.

He followed. "You've kept me at a distance long enough, don't you think?"

As he reached to stroke her cheek, Beth backed into a corner near the mahogany grandfather clock. "Michael," she said firmly. "I don't want you to kiss me. I don't want you near me. I—I—"

Ignoring her, Michael placed a hand on either side of her to trap her in the corner.

"This is not the time or the place for kiss—kissing. A

guest might come in and—and—see." Like a captive squirrel, Beth tried to dodge one way, then the other as she struggled to escape his encircling arms. "Let me go." Her voice rising, she prepared to drive the heel of her sandal against his foot.

Suddenly Scott loomed behind Michael, grabbed his shoulder, and jerked him away from Beth. Michael, yelping with surprise, toppled backward to strike his head against the massive registration desk, then collapse onto the crimson Oriental rug.

Scott hovered over the smaller man, who squirmed like a rodent. "If I ever catch you near her again, I'll . . ."

When Michael tried to sit up, Scott pushed him back to the floor. Beth had never seen her friend so riled. Growling, he grabbed Michael's shirt and hauled him to his feet.

"Stop it!" She rushed forward, pulling at Scott's arm. While she was glad he rescued her, she didn't want any violence. Her chest heaving, she gritted her teeth and from sheer willpower forced Scott to look at her. "Nobody asked you to beat up my customers."

Why did Scott Caldwell think he had the right to charge into her life and turn into Superman anyway? In a matter of months, he would probably marry Marilyn and leave Beth forever to fend for herself. Anger replaced her relief.

"Beat him up? All I did was save you."

Michael, taking advantage of Scott's distraction, stumbled toward the staircase. "I could have you arrested for assault," he said, not sounding quite as confident as usual.

"Assault! Since when is rescuing a lady in distress assault?"

"Don't exaggerate," Beth scoffed, not sure why she was playing devil's advocate. Perhaps she wanted to needle Scott just as his relationship with Marilyn needled her. "He was just trying to kiss me."

"Just trying to kiss you? When I walked in, you weren't quite as casual about it, Bet. What did you expect me to do? Sit down and wait to see if you got free?"

"No." Her eyes narrowing, she clamped her teeth. And her fury with Michael redirected itself to Scott. "I'm not the passive weakling you seem to think I am."

"Ha!" His lips curved into a sarcastic smirk. "You think you're any kind of a match for him?"

She heard Michael's hasty retreat up the squeaking stairs, and Beth sensed he was scared. A coward at heart. The thought made her even more angry; angry with herself for ever being attracted to him.

As that anger grew, so did her anger with Scott. He was abandoning her. All these years, even when he was in New York, Scott had been there for her. Now, with Marilyn on the horizon, he would no longer have time for Beth. Well, she might as well sever the ties now, before he had to. It would be much less humiliating.

Her confusion and aggravation over the past few weeks erupted in a torrent of scalding words. "Why don't you just go home, Scott Caldwell? I don't want you fixing my car. I don't want you mowing my yard. I don't want you eating my pies. I want you out of my life!"

His eyes widening, Scott flinched with the impact of her words.

Her heart raced. Her legs shook. And more emotional words poured out. "I've already told you once, I have a business to run! I can't have you pushing around my customers every time they don't suit you. Now leave!" She pointed toward the front door.

"Beth," he ground out, his chin set in a determined line, "If I leave, you won't see me for a long, long time."

"I think that will be for the best." Her words held a finality akin to death, a death that seemed to settle over the room like a thin film of stifling dust. No sooner had they left her lips than a part of Beth wanted to retract them.

But she didn't. For a different part of her, a more stubborn part, believed she meant it.

Without another word, without another glance her way, Scott squared his shoulders, stomped through the front door, slammed it, walked to his car, and drove out of Beth's life.

Then came the tears. They gushed like a never-ending river of grief to sting her cheeks, to drive her toward the haven of her room. And for the second time in three days, she threw herself onto her bed to cry over Scott. What had gotten into the man? What had turned him into the monster who replaced her loyal friend?

Don't leave, Scott, her heart called. *I don't want you out of my life. Please say you care for me, not Marilyn.*

A tentative knock on the door ended her pleading.

"Yes?" Beth said through a sniffle, trying to force her voice into its normal tones. She failed.

"Beth?" It was Michael.

Her heart drumming in dread, she didn't answer. Had he come to pursue her once more? Regardless of her brave words to Scott, doubt still lurked within. Beth knew she had no choice but to ask Michael to check out.

"I—I heard you crying and wanted to apologize," he said through the door in a soft, regretful voice.

Biting her lip, she glanced up at the guilty-eyed portrait of her aunt as if the woman could instruct her.

"Also, I was wondering if you could make me an ice pack. I have a knot on my head."

She sighed with relief. *An ice pack. All he wants is an ice pack.* The phone's ringing bolstered her courage, and a glance at the blinking light told her the call was on her private line. "Okay. I'll be down in a minute."

"Thanks."

Beth picked up the receiver. "Hello."

"Are you all right?" Lauren's voice floated over the line. "You sound like you've been crying."

Only Lauren could detect tears after one word. Lauren, and perhaps Scott. The thought of him, of his stricken expression when she told him to get out of her life, brought on a new onslaught of threatening tears.

"Can you come over—*now?*" Beth asked, grabbing at any form of buffer between herself and Michael.

"Sure, what's up?"

"I'll explain when you get here."

"Okay. See ya in five minutes."

In five minutes, Beth could touch up her makeup, brush her hair, and put on a professional facade. She started to stand, then stopped.

Lauren. Lauren called as if nothing had happened this morning, as if they never exchanged those hasty words. Perhaps Beth should have been the one to call first, but time had not allowed that. Maybe Lauren's call meant they could finally discuss their problems.

Lord, help us mend our relationship. Help me to explain. . . .

Beth wasn't exactly sure what she was supposed to explain. She hadn't sorted through it all herself, but her Lord would help her; the same Lord whose sweet peace was spreading to Beth's very fingertips. Even in the face of hers and Scott's problems, Beth felt a certainty that all would be well.

Twenty-three

*W*ith a curse, Michael collapsed onto his sleigh bed and fingered the knot forming on the back of his head. He made a terrible mistake. His main objective in staying at McAllister's was to find the treasure. Now, he might have ruined every chance of getting his hands on it.

Why had he become so carried away? He should have taken Beth's hints, but Michael had hoped that the closer he got, the more her resolve would weaken.

Ironically, the closer he got, the more his resolve to kiss her increased. Once again he pondered the amazing power Beth seemed to have over him. Perhaps because she was so unaware of her beauty. Perhaps because she was simply unattainable. Whatever the reason, Michael lost his head. What would his friend Gaylon think if he knew?

Gaylon would laugh you to scorn.

Exasperated, Michael thought of his life as a "working

man." The more mistakes he made, the smaller his chances of attaining the prize. Up until this moment, Michael presumed he would find the treasure. Now he wasn't so sure. His head throbbed with every heartbeat, and his pulse escalated to a panicked tattoo.

He must get the treasure. It rightfully belonged to him. He must somehow find a way into Beth's bedroom. It had to be in there. He would see if she was still willing to give him the grand tour she promised only that morning.

When he spotted the treasure, Michael would make her an offer. If she declined, he would be forced to treat her to a couple of his little green gel caps and steal the piece. He knew from experience that one gel cap would make her sleep; two would knock her out for many hours. As much as he hated to drug Beth, the time had come for action.

Michael was beyond caring now; beyond caring, and thrown headlong into desperation. He would have his treasure. And with the false identification and passport Gaylon had mailed him, Michael and the treasure would be safely out of the country before Beth ever woke up.

Fleetingly, he thought of Beth's charming vulnerability, of the way she readily trusted him. At first, he congratulated himself on finding Beth so naive. Now, with an unexpected onslaught of guilt marring his plans, he wished she had been more scheming. Filled with ulterior motives. Less like his mother. More like himself.

After he maneuvered his way into Beth's bedroom, if

he still didn't find the prize, Michael would assume that Naomi McAllister had sold it. He would take the jewelry and the other item, cut his losses, and go.

When his trust fund dwindled to the point of embarrassment, Michael would find a wealthy, older woman who would enjoy his company enough to overlook his philandering.

Beth glimpsed Lauren's white Volkswagen out the window, cautiously opened her door, and stepped into the carpeted hallway. No sign of Michael. Sighing with relief, she locked her bedroom door and silently hurried for the stairs.

Holding her breath, she slowed her pace to peer around the staircase wall. No Michael. His door was closed, so Beth tiptoed past as if she were a cat burglar, then hurried down the steps.

"Hi. What's going on?" Lauren asked as soon as Beth entered the foyer.

Beth glanced over her shoulder, up the stairs. Still no Michael. "It's a long story, but boy, am I glad you're here." Impulsively she drew her younger sister into her arms and gave her a warm hug.

At first Lauren stiffened, and Beth thought she would pull away. Then she clung to Beth as if they hadn't seen one another in a decade. Beth heard a muffled sob. And suddenly, having barely abated her crying after Scott's exit, Beth was unable to stop a new onslaught of tears.

Earlier, Lauren opened a door in her heart, revealing the pain Beth never knew existed. For the first time since Aunt Naomi's death, Beth understood why Lauren behaved so strangely. Without ever intending to, Beth somehow made Lauren feel as if she didn't measure up. Aunt Naomi only intensified the feelings. How well Beth could relate to Lauren's emotions. Strange that, in her own pain, Beth had been unable to recognize Lauren's.

"I—I'm sorry," Beth choked, as Lauren's Chanel No. 5 permeated her senses. "I don't know what got into me. I shouldn't have—"

"It's okay. It's just that—" Lauren pulled away. "I guess I shouldn't have said what I did either, but it was—it is the way I feel." Guiltily, she glanced down.

"Is there anything I can do to change that?"

"I don't know." Lauren shrugged helplessly.

Immediately, Beth wanted to crush the barrier, which even now seemed to be destroying her relationship with her sister. "What if I sold the inn and split the money with you? Would that—"

"It's bigger than that. Can't you see?"

At once Beth did see. For some reason, Lauren had never really accepted herself the way she was. Somehow, she had rejected what God created and longed for what she couldn't be. The idea struck Beth as crazy. Lauren the beautiful. Lauren the witty. Lauren with the perfect figure. Lauren represented what many women only dreamed of being. How could she question her worth?

The same way you could question your worth. The thought took her so off guard that Beth almost stumbled backward with its power.

"I understand, Lauren," she rasped. "I've been there. I am there."

Like a child, Lauren scrubbed at her diminishing tears. "Where do we go from here?"

"I'm not sure." For the first time Beth saw Lauren as an adult rather than her baby sister. It took a lot of guts for Lauren to call after their heated words of the morning. Beth knew they still had a struggle, but at least they were now working together.

Thanks for this miracle, Lord, Beth prayed as she hugged her sister once more.

"Excuse me," Michael said from behind. "I was wondering about that ice pack?"

With a questioning glance, Lauren stepped aside as Beth walked toward the kitchen, not daring to look at her client.

"Beth." Michael's restraining hand on her arm compelled her to stop.

She glanced into regretful eyes.

"I'm really sorry." Michael gingerly fingered the back of his head.

Lauren cleared her throat in discreet curiosity.

"It's okay," Beth replied, feeling infinitely foolish but not knowing what else to say.

"If it's any consolation, I plan to check out today."

Relief flooded through her. "Let's just get the ice pack and put today behind us."

"Okay."

With Lauren and Michael close behind, Beth walked into the kitchen.

"Oh! It's a little kitty," Lauren crooned, bending over the box.

Beth completely forgot about that cuddly scrap of life. The kitten had snuggled into the corner and buried his nose in the stuffed bear she put in for company. And he had drunk every drop of his milk.

Now he responded to Lauren's attention with a toothy yawn and a pathetic meow.

"Where'd you get it, Beth?" Lauren scooped the kitten into her arms.

"Scott," Beth said as she filled a plastic sandwich bag with ice. The very mention of his name seemed to stifle her. "He brought it by this afternoon." Beth wrapped the ice pack in a blue cloth and handed it to a subdued Michael.

"I imagine Tiffany is not a happy camper. She's so jealous!"

"Tiffany . . ." Beth glanced to Michael, and her eyes began to sting anew. Too much had happened today.

"Scott ran over Tiffany," Michael said discreetly as he placed the ice pack against his head.

"Oh, no." Lauren's shoulders sagged.

"We buried her in the backyard, under the big oak," Beth choked out, thankful that somebody else, even if it had to be Michael, broke the news. She wished for the hundredth time that she had been more patient with the ornery pig.

"I know it doesn't help," Lauren said, "but it's amazing that she lasted as long as she did. She was always getting out."

"You're right." Beth reached to stroke the purring kitten. "Maybe this little guy'll last longer. Cats have a way of surviving."

"Yeah. And you don't have to worry about keeping him inside the fence. What are you going to name him?"

Continually conscious of Michael's scrutiny, Beth chewed her lip and watched the cat. Why didn't he leave now? His presence, his obvious attraction for her, made Beth more and more uncomfortable. She couldn't think for trying to predict his next move. It was almost as if he were trying to read her mind, as if she could feel him peering into her very thoughts.

"I know what you could name him," Lauren said, a glimmer in her eyes.

"What?"

"Sweetheart." A teasing laugh.

"Oh," Beth said, nonplused. What was Lauren getting at?

"Er, if you ladies will excuse me," Michael said. "I'm going to my room to lie down for a while."

"Would you like something for your headache?" Beth asked, feeling only a trace of sympathy for him.

"Yes. A simple aspirin would be fine." His smile

reminded her of a serpent hiding behind a lamb's mask.

Beth immediately regretted her offer. The aspirin was upstairs in her bathroom. She didn't want to take Michael to her room. At the same time she didn't want to leave him alone with her sister. Beth no longer trusted him. She could send Lauren up for the medicine, but Beth didn't want to be alone with him either.

"Lauren," she said, hoping she sounded more natural to them than she did to herself. "I'm going to have to go to my room for the aspirin. Why don't you bring, um, Sweetheart and come with me? That way, you can see my new . . . um . . ." What had she recently purchased? "My new quilt. The one I bought at the quilt shop downtown to use as a bedspread," she rushed, knowing that the quilt was six weeks old and Lauren had already seen it. "I wanted your opinion on what color curtains I should put with it."

"But I've already—"

Beth gripped Lauren's upper arm and pushed her toward the kitchen stairway. "They've got a set of curtains that exactly matches the quilt. I don't know whether to buy those or a solid color," she said through clamped teeth, and it was the absolute truth.

"Okay, okay, I'll take a look," Lauren muttered.

"We'll be right back, Michael," Beth called, glancing over her shoulder.

But Michael was gone.

"Would you please tell me what's going on?" Lauren hissed as they ascended the steep stairs to the third floor. "What happened to Michael's head?"

"He tried to kiss me. I tried to get away. Scott came in, and to make a long story short, Scott got, um, forceful, and Michael bumped his head on the registration desk."

Lauren's laugh filled the hallway.

"It isn't funny. Michael is one of my guests. I have a professional image to keep up. What will happen to my business if word gets out that my friend roughed up a customer?"

"So did you and Scott argue?" Lauren asked, her eyes brimming with mirth.

"You bet we argued, and I told him to get out of my life and stay out." Icy chills spiraled through her heart.

"Oh, Beth," Lauren gasped. "How could you?"

They halted outside Beth's bedroom door, and Beth turned to her sister. "Lauren, the man is driving me nuts. He's been acting crazy ever since summer started. You don't know what he's been like."

"I think Scott's just jealous. Jealousy will make you crazy, you know."

"Jealous?" Beth gave a bitter laugh. "Why would he be jealous? That puts the icing on this whole day. It's been weird from the start."

"Oh well, think what you like." Lauren shrugged, stroked the kitten, and peered into Beth's eyes. "But Dad says—" She clamped her mouth shut as if the words were battling to jump out. "Never mind."

"Dad says what?" Beth demanded, her hand on the cool knob as she inserted the key.

"Nothing. It's nothing. Just a passing thought,"

Lauren promptly changed the subject. "So why did you really want me up here? You know I'm useless when it comes to decorating."

"No, you aren't. You just think you are. I really want your opinion, but that's not the only reason I asked you. You're the lawyer; what's the matter with your deductive reasoning?" Beth chided, pushing open the door. "Can't you figure out that I didn't want to leave you downstairs with Michael? I don't even want to be by myself with him. I don't trust him."

"Thanks for looking out for me, but I don't think I'd be in danger. The man's in too much pain." Still stroking the sleepy-eyed kitten, Lauren aimlessly walked toward the front window.

Beth strode into her bathroom, an extension of her bedroom. She opened her mirrored medicine cabinet and removed a bottle of aspirin.

"So what do you think?" she asked, turning back to the bedroom. "Should I buy the floral curtains to match the comforter or get a solid color?"

"Er, excuse me," said a voice from the doorway.

Startled, Beth turned to Michael, who still held the ice pack against his head. Uninvited, he had followed her upstairs.

"I just thought I'd save you the trip all the way back to the kitchen." But Michael's gaze was not on Beth. It lingered on the guilty-eyed painting of Aunt Naomi hanging over the bed. Beth thought she detected a flash of shock, then excitement flickering in his eyes. But when he looked at her, his bland expression defied her supposition.

Twenty-four

Nice painting," Michael said, walking toward the bed.

Beth nervously eyed him. "Thanks. It's of my aunt when she was younger."

"She owned this place," Lauren said, turning from the window.

"Would you mind if I got a closer look? I'm a collector, and I'm always interested in good paintings."

Beth watched as Michael placed his knee on her bed and closely peered at the work. Slowly he lowered the ice pack and with his free hand touched the canvas.

"I've never really cared for that painting," Beth chattered. "It just doesn't look like the aunt I knew. There's something about her eyes I don't like." Staring into those brown, guilt-ridden orbs, Beth wondered why she was telling Michael all this.

"Have you ever thought of selling it?" he asked.

"Well . . ." Beth glanced at Lauren, who shrugged.

"As I said, I collect fine paintings. I could pay . . . I don't know . . ." Michael turned down the corners of his mouth as if in deep thought. "Maybe ten thousand dollars."

Ten thousand dollars! Beth had no idea the painting was worth that much.

"Ten thousand?" Lauren gasped.

Michael's chuckle dripped with satisfaction.

Beth thought about her need for a new car. Ten thousand would put a large dent in the price. Then she hesitated. She wasn't an art expert, but she hadn't earned an M.B.A. without knowing about business. If Michael was willing to offer a quick ten thousand, it was probably worth even more. Maybe double or triple that. She should get an appraisal first.

"I'm not sure I want to sell it, actually. And if I did, I would have it appraised first."

"Oh." He glanced at her, and a hardened gleam entered Michael's gray eyes, turning them into relentless flint.

A chill chased down Beth's spine. When would Michael ever leave? How could she have been attracted to him in the first place? She handed him the aspirin.

"Thanks."

The silence descending between them seemed an uncrossable gulf.

Lauren nervously cleared her throat.

"I'm going to my room to pack now." Michael quirked one brow. "You don't have to say it. I know you're glad."

Beth opened her mouth to politely protest, then shut it. She couldn't lie. "I hope you've enjoyed your stay," she said instead.

"Oh, I've enjoyed it. I've enjoyed it greatly." Without another word, Michael Alexander left the room.

"I'm sorry I sent him over here." Lauren plopped onto the edge of Beth's bed and released the kitten.

"It's not your fault, Lauren. He saw my brochure." A deep sigh. Beth joined Lauren on the bed and stroked the kitten as it playfully rolled onto its back. "I'll just be glad when he's gone."

"Yeah, and he knows it, too."

"Good."

A mutual snicker. Then expectant silence. Beth wanted to broach the subject of the rift between herself and Lauren, but didn't quite know how to introduce it. Perhaps it would take time, but Beth desperately wanted to work toward healing their relationship. Being estranged from Scott taxed her enough. Adding Lauren's problems to the list almost overwhelmed her.

Lord, she prayed silently, *give me the right words.*

"You know," Beth said, watching the kitten. "I've experienced some of the same feelings you shared with me earlier."

"You mean feeling like you don't quite measure up?"

"No. I mean feeling like I don't measure up big time." There. Beth said it. She finally admitted her feelings of inferiority, and somehow the act of expressing how she felt began to release the tension deep within. "I guess that's part of the reason I was so blown away by Michael, even though I knew he wasn't a Christian. He represents every person I've ever wanted approval from. You know, the people who seem to have it all—looks, personality, money."

"Do you know what it's like to have people love you for your looks alone?" Lauren asked.

"No. I've never had that problem."

"Well, I've never had *your* problem either."

"What's that?"

"What I've already said, Beth. When people love you, they love you for who you are, not for how you look. Do you know how many times I've wanted to stand up in a crowd and scream, 'Listen, people! There's more to me than the way I look!'"

Silently, Beth traced her finger along the seams in the quilt. And words began to spill forth that she never planned to say. "Listen to us, Lauren. I've rejected myself because I'm not as beautiful as you. And you've rejected yourself because you aren't as—as—"

"As smart—"

"Whatever—as I am."

"Do you think this is something our parents did to us?" Lauren asked.

"I can't imagine how, if they did. I never felt pressure from them to be like you."

"I never did either."

"Perhaps it's just something we all have to deal with at one time or another. I mean, society has a way of dumping people into molds. I've never thought about it before, but I guess being beautiful can have its drawbacks just like being plump and brainy can."

"You talk about yourself as though you're ugly, Beth," Lauren said incredulously.

"Oh come on, Lauren. I've got a mirror."

"Yes, and everybody says I look a lot like you. You just said I was beautiful."

Beth rolled her eyes. "But you don't know the kind of stuff I put up with most of my childhood. I'm beginning to wonder if I'll ever get over it."

"You mean stuff like the homecoming incident?" Lauren asked gently.

"Who told you about that?" Beth snapped. At the time it happened, Beth was so devastated she refused to discuss it, even with her mother.

"I was nine when it happened. I remember your coming home crying. A few years later, Mom told me about it."

Beth felt somehow betrayed. "I know when she told you. It was when you got voted homecoming queen, wasn't it?"

"Yes."

"She probably told you not to talk about it a lot because—"

"She was trying to protect your feelings, Beth. That's all."

The two looked at each other in silence, and somehow the silence began the mending of their relationship.

Finally Beth spoke. "I've been praying about this—the way I feel—today. And I think there's an answer to our problem."

"You mean, like what we've been told all our lives? Like, accepting yourself for who you are in Christ and realizing you're worthy because He died for you?"

"Sometimes it's easier said than done," Beth said.

"Maybe because it isn't something we can do on our own."

"Maybe." Beth narrowed her eyes. "You know, you're a whole lot smarter than you give yourself credit for."

"And you're a whole lot more beautiful than you'll ever admit."

Beth impulsively grabbed her sister in a bear hug, and the two toppled over on the bed.

The telephone's ringing ended their revelry. "You get it," Beth said. "It's closer to you."

"McAllister's Bed and Breakfast," Lauren said into the receiver.

Beth stared up at the portrait of Aunt Naomi. Funny, that she and Lauren should have their conversation in the "presence" of the very person who had unknowingly created a rift between them.

"Okay. I'll be there in a minute," Lauren said and hung up. "They need me at the restaurant. Sherry's baby is sick, and she's taking him to the doctor."

"That means I'm here by myself with Michael."

"He said he was leaving, didn't he?"

"Yeah. But I don't know when. He could hang around

another two or three hours."

"Why don't you call Scott?"

Beth stared at her meaningfully.

"Oh yeah. I forgot. What about your maid?"

"Already left for the day."

"I could call Mom back and tell her—"

"No, no, don't do that. I'll just hang out by the phone. That way, if I have to call the police—"

"I don't think you will," Lauren said, her eyes brimming with humor. "I think he's taken the hint."

"I hope you're right."

"I'll call back in an hour or so and make sure you're okay." Lauren stroked the kitten's ears one last time and turned for the door.

"Thanks. And Lauren?"

She stopped to face Beth once more.

"I love you," Beth whispered.

"I love you too."

Michael paced his room like a man who has seen paradise dangled before his eyes only to have it snatched away. He should have offered Beth more than ten thousand. Clearly, he had underestimated the woman. Once she had the painting appraised and realized its increasing value, she would probably keep it. If he had offered a hundred thousand dollars, she probably would have accepted the offer, and he would still have gotten the painting at a fraction of its worth. Once she rejected his offer to buy, he was left only one alternative.

He glanced toward his suitcase. The false identification lay in the manila envelope on top of his clothing. Something inside him cringed at the prospect of changing his name to Douglas Silby Etheridge. Another cringe when he thought of being a fugitive of the law. But better to be a rich fugitive than an honest pauper.

His mind wandered to the painting. *Naomi's Secret.* The name taunted him like an untouchable mirage. As he grabbed the bottle of chloral hydrate from beneath the manila envelope in his suitcase, the one thought that burned through his veins, the one obsession that would not let him rest, urged him to get that painting at any cost. The inferior landscape painting he had discovered in the attic, although his father's work, did not compare to the quality of *Naomi's Secret.* The treasure was well worth the search.

He must have it. It was his own father's work. It rightfully belonged to him.

Michael would give Beth, and if need be, Lauren, two of the gel caps. He and the painting would be out of the country before they woke up.

Twenty-five

*B*eth firmly shut her bedroom door and peered at the painting of her aunt gracefully lounging in a wicker settee under a weeping willow. Dressed in a summer dress of gauze-like yellow cotton, Naomi appeared to be languidly awaiting some romantic hero. Her mysterious smile. Her half-closed eyes with the slightest gleam of guilt. Her wisps of blonde hair. The artist expertly rendered an aura of sensuality that Beth never enjoyed associating with her aunt.

She approached her bed, crawled onto the mattress, and carefully lifted the large canvas from the wall. The closer Beth brought the ivory-skinned Aunt Naomi, the more guilty those eyes became. What had the painter known to portray this marred image of such an otherwise lovely, godly woman?

Settling against the massive headboard, Beth continued to stare into those eyes. "It seems Lauren and I are working through our problems. Now if only you could tell me what to do about Scott," she muttered. As always, her dear aunt would have the perfect solution to Beth's dilemma. If only she were living.

Longing for Aunt Naomi's comforting hug, Beth blinked against stinging eyes and heard what her aunt had told her on many occasions. *Pray, child. Remember always to pray. The Lord can help you solve your toughest problem.*

"I miss you." With those words, she knew the answer to Michael's ten thousand dollar offer. This painting might not be an accurate portrayal of the aunt she remembered, but it was still an image of the aunt she loved. No. Even if Michael offered twice as much, Beth could never let him have any memory of her aunt.

With that settled, she knelt on the pillows and began the task of rehanging the painting. Tongue between teeth, she stretched the last inch to catch the nail with the hanging wire and release the portrait to its rightful place. As it settled against the wall, a piece of paper slipped from behind it to sail past the headboard and plop to the floor.

Beth retrieved a folded note with her name written across the front in her aunt's shaky scrawl. What was this? Why would Aunt Naomi resort to secretive notes? Beth and she had always been so close. Sometimes Beth felt closer to her aunt than she did to her own mother. What could this note possibly say that Aunt Naomi could not have said to her in person?

Her curiosity piqued, Beth pushed her hair over her

shoulder and unfolded the paper.

Dear Beth,

It's November, and I suspect I will not live much longer. My heart tells me that my days on earth are numbered. There are some things I wanted to talk with you about before I died, but I cannot conjure the courage or strength, so I must resort to this note. Please forgive me for being such a coward.

I placed this note behind the painting for a reason. If you are moving the portrait, you are more than likely thinking of storing or selling it. I knew you never really cared for this image of me, and neither did I. I often thought of selling it, because I suspect it has risen in value. However, I would not allow myself the pleasure because it reminds me of my moment of weakness and has kept me strong through the years.

It will come as a shock to you to know that I had a brief affair with the artist who painted this portrait. Very few people knew, and I bore the scars of my hasty decision for the rest of my life.

Beth blinked, then stared at the words in wide-eyed shock. Aunt Naomi, her Aunt Naomi, the Aunt Naomi who had served the Lord, who had shown Christ's love as none other . . . that Aunt Naomi had had a . . . a fling? Biting her lip, Beth almost toppled over with the disappointment that struck her like a punch to the face.

I was engaged to a young man you never knew. When he learned of my infidelity, he could no longer marry me. At the time, I thought it was all for the best because he seemed so predictable and somewhat boring in the face of my artist. But soon I learned my artist was married with a family of his own. I also learned he was using me as nothing more than a summer plaything on a long list of other playthings. Then I realized I had broken my fiancé's heart and ruined my own happiness.

Why am I telling you this, my dear Beth? Well, even though I know God has forgiven me, and I have totally accepted His forgiveness, I hope that maybe something good can come of my error. Perhaps you can learn something from it. You know I have taught you to always base your decisions on the Bible, not on your emotions. This is why. Your emotions can sometimes lead you down the wrong path. Remember, it is best to temper them with a good dose of common sense and a heavier dose of God's Word.

I will always love you, my dear.

Aunt Naomi

P. S. You will find in my storage closet across the hall a hatbox holding several pieces of valuable jewelry that he gave me. Also, in the attic behind the antique bureau, you will find another of his paintings. Although not his best work, I believe it, too, is valuable. Give these to Lauren with my love, and please do not tell her from whom I received them. Also, if you do sell my portrait, I want you to halve the profit with Lauren. Please understand that I wanted to tell her of *this inheritance myself before I died, but couldn't bring myself to do it.*

So Aunt Naomi had dealt fairly with Lauren. A river of relief surged through Beth's veins. She felt as if her aunt had risen from the grave, waltzed into the bedroom, and sat down for a brief chat. The sensation was the oddest and most heartwarming Beth ever encountered.

But as those feelings subsided, her initial reaction returned. Disappointment. Disillusionment. Disenchantment with the aunt whom Beth had seen as her spiritual mentor. Aunt Naomi was right. Lauren need never know.

"Why did you even have to tell me?" Beth asked the painting as she crumpled the letter. "I didn't want to know."

Her eyes stung anew as a wave of loneliness washed over her. How could you? she wanted to wail. *I've kept myself pure all these years, and you . . . you . . .*

Hands shaking, Beth studied the confession penned in black. Suddenly, she wondered about the man who had managed to do what no other man had ever done. The man who had caused Aunt Naomi to abandon her Christian principles and common sense and jeopardize her future. Beth stared at the painting's lower right corner. She had always been so disturbed by her aunt's haunting eyes, she had never stopped to decipher the artist's signature.

The scrawled name jumped out at her. "E. Alexander."

Swallowing against her tightening throat, Beth wanted to deny the implications. *It's a coincidence. There's no way Michael Alexander could be related to the man who painted this portrait.* But her churning stomach told her otherwise.

She thought of Michael at the attic door. Michael coming from the green room. Mrs. Bennett's claim of a prowler. Michael's immediately noticing the painting. His ten-thousand-dollar offer.

And it all made sense. He was after this painting. He was related to the artist. Somehow, he knew Beth possessed the portrait. Perhaps it was even more valuable than Aunt Naomi presumed.

Her heart pounding in dismay, Beth scurried from the bed, pocketing her aunt's note as she went. Scott was right. Beth had made an idiot of herself. Michael Alexander was never in the least interested in her. Humiliation, the kind that crushes, crept up her spine.

Then fury. How often Michael must have laughed at her! He came here to take advantage of her, and he almost succeeded. Beth wanted to kick him in the seat of his pants on his way out. Trying to control the rage now making her tremble, Beth marched from her bedroom.

Before she faced Michael, she needed to get control of herself. She would find the jewelry and other painting Aunt Naomi intended for Lauren. She would drink a slow cup of tea. Then she would tap on Michael's door, present him with his bill, and demand his departure.

Marilyn Douglas stared blindly at the book she was attempting to read. One of Dr. Lovelady's textbooks from school, it detailed the methods of safely handling small, frightened animals. When Dr. Lovelady left for an afternoon off, she asked Marilyn to answer the phone until five o'clock and do some educational reading.

But the words blurred. Marilyn could see nothing but alternate visions of her ex-husband and Scott Caldwell. For the first time, Marilyn realized just how many subtle similarities they shared. Although Greg was fair, Scott's eyes, like Greg's, were as green as jade. Scott was tall, like Greg. He was lean yet muscular, like Greg. He had a deep faith in God, like Greg . . . or like Greg used to have.

Looking at the quaint waiting room, Marilyn took in the clinic smells of puppies and tomcats and antiseptic. She stood and slowly walked to the back of the office to peer out the window. A curious squirrel, twitching its tail, danced up and down a massive oak.

Absently watching, Marilyn continued her musing. When she watched Dr. Gregory Thatcher drive away from the courthouse, their divorce final, she vowed never to think of him again. But not only were her dreams full of him, she was associating with a man who somehow reminded her of him on a very deep level.

When Scott told Marilyn her ex-husband was crazy for divorcing her, she felt as if Greg himself were saying he regretted leaving her. When Scott suggested she join him at the basketball game, Marilyn felt that she and Greg were dating all over again. When Scott agreed to have dinner with her family tonight, Marilyn felt as if she would be sharing a meal with Greg once more.

Why hadn't she seen it before now?

The numbness. The numbness blinded her to her true feelings. Perhaps the numbness worked as a safety device to keep her heart from exploding with pain.

As the squirrel scurried up the tree, Marilyn faced her true emotions for the first time since arriving in Eureka Springs; for the first time since Gregory left.

She still loved her husband.

Even though he cruelly rejected her, even though she had removed her wedding ring, even though she had vowed to put him from her life, Marilyn could not put him from her heart. She still loved him, and in her soul she was still married to him. That divorce decree had not changed a thing.

All those lonely nights her heart hadn't yearned for just any company. She had been yearning for Gregory.

"Oh, Greg," she whispered as silent tears trickled down the side of her nose to baptize the corners of her mouth in salty witness to her pain. "Why did you leave me? Oh Lord, why did You let him?"

Marilyn had prayed precious little since Greg's desertion. Not that she stopped believing in God, but perhaps she stopped believing in His intervention. She had also rejected any possibility of ever attending church again. Once she felt a call from God to be a pastor's wife, felt it as strongly as Greg felt his call to ministry. Now all that had changed.

Slipping her hand into the pocket of her white lab coat, she fished out a crumpled tissue and absently dabbed at her cheeks, nose, and eyes. Then her thoughts turned back to Scott. A few times, she knew he thought of taking her in his arms. But ever the gentleman, he never even held her hand. Lately Marilyn was slightly frustrated that their relationship seemed destined to forever remain platonic.

Now she was so thankful.

She probably made a big enough fool of herself without their friendship developing any more than it had. She groaned, recalling the way she practically invited herself into his house that first night. Then, after imposing, she hadn't left until two A.M. And to end the evening, she used her body language to almost beg him to kiss her.

Marilyn refused to think about the other times they had been together. A person could only handle so much embarrassment in one afternoon.

She scrubbed at her cheeks for the last time and determined to be honest with Scott. She would simply tell him . . . tell him . . . what would she tell him? Somehow, saying she was still in love with her ex-husband sounded too melodramatic. But it was the truth.

She sighed. Marilyn would simply tell Scott the truth.

She checked her sporty Bulova. 4:55. With determination, Marilyn turned for the desk and prepared to leave. She hoped Scott would be home. Her parents, having instantly fallen in love with him, invited him to dinner tonight. She knew they secretly hoped for her sake that the friendship would develop into something deeper. Before her well-meaning parents exposed Scott to any pointed hints, Marilyn needed to talk with him.

Twenty-six

Scott paced across his living room like a thwarted lion. Past the sectional sofa. Past the big screen TV. Past the rock fireplace. And he started over again.

I want you out of my life! Beth's words encircled his mind like a swarm of angry hornets. Why had she been so abrupt? Scott honestly thought he had been doing her a favor when he pulled the jerk away from her. Beth, the woman he thought he knew better than any other woman, had grown into an enigma.

Twice he almost grabbed her and kissed her, once on the porch and once by the car. Each time Scott chided himself for being a chicken. Now he was glad he hadn't followed through. She probably would have punched him in the stomach and called the police.

But for one second, after he diagnosed the problem with her car, Scott thought he saw a glimmer of something awakening in her eyes. Something akin to attraction.

No. He must have dreamed it, must have conjured his own desires in her eyes, just as he conjured her reaction at his refrigerator last week.

He stopped pacing, plopped onto the sofa, and broodingly stared out the window. A blue jay taunted the neighbors' unsuspecting poodle. Its squall became Beth's very words. *I want you out of my life . . . out of my life . . . out of my life.*

Scott knew he had a variety of choices. He could comply with her request, avoid her, ignore her. He could show up tomorrow and act as though nothing ever happened. Or he could appear on her front porch and refuse to budge until that blond sleazebag left.

Lord, give me wisdom, he prayed. As he waited, a new thought struck him. Beth had been resisting Michael's kiss. Wasn't that an improvement? Did that mean she had finally seen Michael for what he was? This new possibility made Scott's spirits skyrocket. If so, did that mean the Lord was working to fulfill His earlier promise to Scott?

The thought sent a spear of guilt through Scott's heart. He had been angry with God. Could God have been working all along? Not daring to dwell on such a wonderful possibility, Scott began to pray.

Lord, he started sheepishly, *I think I've been impatient. Please forgive me, and help me to make the right decision now. I think I see Your hand here. Help me to know what's right. Do I comply with Beth's demand and stay out of her life or what?*

His mind churned with the options. Regardless of his tough act with Beth, Scott didn't think he could bear not seeing her. And he was tired of pretending their relationship wasn't shifting. Furthermore, he did not in any way trust Michael Alexander. All this left only one choice. Tonight, Scott would deposit himself on the threshold of Beth's bedroom door and not budge until morning.

With purpose he leaned toward the oak end table, picked up his cordless phone, dialed Marilyn's home number, and awaited the answering machine's beep.

"Hello Marilyn, this is Scott. Just wanted to let you know that something unexpected has come up. I won't be able to have dinner with you and your parents tonight." A tendril of guilt started in his stomach and twined its way through his heart. He knew Marilyn would be disappointed. "I'm terribly sorry," he added, then hung up.

Soon he needed to have a long talk with Marilyn. She was too interested. In all fairness, Scott should tell her his heart belonged to another.

He marched to his bedroom, opened his closet, and grabbed his sleeping bag. "Miss Beth McAllister," he muttered through clamped teeth. "I *will* fix your car. I *will* mow your yard. And I *am going* to eat your pies. You can forget it if you think I'm ever getting out of your life."

In minutes, he had packed his duffel bag and headed for the front door, only to see Marilyn Douglas mounting his porch steps.

Michael dumped four of the chloral hydrate gel caps into his palm and deposited them in his shirt pocket. Lost in thought, he dropped the pill bottle into his suitcase, then took the false ID from the manila envelope. Reluctantly he placed the new identification in his billfold and removed his own driver's license, social security card, and credit cards. He carefully lifted the insoles from a pair of his loafers and tucked the cards snugly in the toes of his shoes, then replaced the insoles and dropped the shoes into his suitcase. He would destroy and throw away his old ID in the men's rest room at the airport. Decisively he zipped the luggage, grabbed his garment bag, and headed for the door.

He still wasn't sure how he would get the drug into Beth's mouth. If she were alone, he could hold her down and squeeze it into her mouth. If Lauren were still here, that wouldn't work. While he wrestled Beth, Lauren would be able to call the police. Perhaps he could ask them to share a cup of tea or coffee with him before his departure. But another problem posed itself. How would he place the chloral hydrate into their cups without their seeing him?

Still pondering his dilemma, Michael deposited his luggage into the trunk of his rented Mercedes. Carefully he arranged the small painting and the boxes of jewelry he had already stolen. He would place *Naomi's Secret*, frame and all, in the back seat. Once he was safely out of town, he would stop long enough to remove both paintings from their frames, roll them, and insert them into the large cardboard tube that he brought from home. He planned to dump the jewelry down the tube as well.

When he reached the Springfield, Missouri airport, he would call Gaylon. Armed with his new identification, he could carry the tube on his flight from Springfield, and no one would suspect he held items worth millions. At J.F.K. he would meet Gaylon, give him the tube, and board the next flight to Thailand. He didn't need a pre-arranged visa to enter Thailand.

He glanced across the parking area and curb. Lauren's white Volkswagen was no longer here. Her absence would greatly simplify the situation.

As Michael approached Beth's porch steps, he was simultaneously excited and burdened. Could he actually stoop to drugging Beth?

The false ID seemed to burn in his pocket. An unexpected wave of guilt. Perhaps if he offered her a hundred thousand, Beth would sell the painting without having it appraised. Michael's father had intended him to offer a price high enough to approach fairness but low enough to make a good profit. Even though the painting was worth a million, he winced at the thought of giving Beth a hundred thousand. But buying the painting wouldn't force him to escape the country under an assumed name. Beth didn't know of the jewelry and the smaller painting. Even if he gave her two hundred thousand for *Naomi's Secret*, he would still have those items as an added bonus.

Flashlight in hand, Beth picked her way through the boxes and clutter in the attic next to her room. The musty smells of old books and ancient clothing enveloped her like a gauzy cocoon. She headed for the ancient bureau sitting against the north wall. Aunt Naomi said the other painting was behind it. Planning to pull the bureau away from the wall, Beth stepped over a pile of deteriorating magazines, then stopped.

The bureau had already been moved.

She darted the flashlight beam behind the antique. Nothing was there. However, the otherwise dusty wall bore a suspicious dust-free square, as if something had been leaning against it for ages. Something the shape of a painting.

Once again, Beth pictured Michael Alexander standing at the attic door that stormy night. Even then, he must have been searching her house, looking for Aunt Naomi's portrait. Had he also known about the painting in the attic? Or did he discover it by accident? Beth felt as if she had swallowed a bucketful of lead. Not only did Michael try to swindle her, he had probably stolen from her as well.

The realization urged her to search out the jewelry Aunt Naomi left in the storage closet. As if racing from an inferno, Beth scrambled out of the attic, rushed down the hallway, and whipped open the closet door. Fingers trembling, she pulled the string hanging from the ceiling. A faint click, and the rows of stale-smelling clothing, shoes, and yesteryear's leftovers were bathed in a soft light.

Aunt Naomi said she stored the jewelry in one of the hatboxes. Beth, her mouth dry, examined the thirty or so hatboxes perching on the shelves. She needed a ladder. Without hesitation, she dropped her flashlight, raced to the library, and returned with a stepladder.

Beth ripped away the tops of each of the hatboxes. Within seconds, a mound of lids cluttered the closet floor, but she discovered only hats.

No jewelry.

Her heart pounded. Had Michael also discovered the jewelry? Desperate for another explanation, Beth stepped to the floor. She frantically rummaged through the double row of hanging clothing that circled the walk-in closet, hoping to spot another hatbox lodged in the garments. Perhaps Aunt Naomi hid the box containing the jewelry.

Her forehead, her upper lip, her spine beaded in chilling sweat. With each dress or coat or blouse Beth shoved aside, the lead in her stomach seemed to increase.

Halfway across the back wall, Beth stopped her search as if attacked by sudden paralysis. Her mind reeling, she spotted a door she never knew existed. The double rack of clothing hid it. As yet Beth had not perused the mansion's every corner, especially the closets such as this one that contained Aunt Naomi's personal possessions. Out of respect for her aunt, Beth had postponed that chore. Now, she lambasted herself.

Where did this doorway lead? Her mind racing with possibilities, she scurried under the bottom clothing rack and cautiously opened the door to view a dark, narrow stairway. She retrieved her flashlight and descended the spider-infested corridor. Her mind spinning, she barely acknowledged the eight-legged creatures that scurried from her pathway.

Once at the stairs' base, Beth stood in a short hallway that ran left to right. She envisioned the second floor and the approximate position of the stairway in relation to the guest rooms. And she knew where she stood. Smack between the yellow room and the blue room. To the left, the Bennetts resided in the yellow room. To the right, Michael Alexander had resided in the blue room.

She pointed the flashlight to the left. A piece of dry-wall barred the entrance to a doorless walkway. To prove her hypothesis about the hallway's location, Beth ducked under a spider web and discreetly listened through the plasterboard while Mrs. Bennett asked her husband his opinion on a dress. As if she were standing in the yellow room, Beth visualized the wall behind which she now stood. Yellow striped wallpaper dotted with tiny bur-gundy flowers covered the drywall. An antique, full-length mirror hung over the very spot the door would be.

Not wanting to hear anymore of the Bennetts' con-versation, Beth tiptoed toward the other doorway. What the flashlight's beam revealed left her whirling in tornadic rage. Another walkway blocked by drywall—sporting a gaping hole. And through the hole, Beth viewed the back of the ornate dresser that resided in the blue room.

A few times in the last week, Beth thought she was furious with Scott Caldwell. She had been wrong. Until now, she never knew true fury; a fury that roared through her veins; a fury that left her determined to confront Michael Alexander. Somehow, he discovered the hidden door leading into this stairway and took the jewelry.

Silently she stood at the hole and listened. Was Michael in his room? No noise. Immediately Beth decided she didn't care whether he was in there or not. If he were, seeing his shock when she arrived in the room would be a great satisfaction. Unceremoniously, Beth dashed away a spider web and stepped through the hole. With a great heave, she strained against the dresser, eventually inching it away from the wall enough to squeeze through.

No sign of Michael. All his luggage was gone. Had he left without paying his bill? Beth rushed to the window overlooking the driveway. The scarlet Mercedes still shone in the summer sun. Perhaps he was waiting to check out downstairs. But that would make no sense. Would he steal from her, then wait to pay his bill?

Decisively Beth whirled from the window to stomp toward the door. As she passed the rumpled bed, she kicked the edge of a box protruding from beneath the navy blue dust ruffle; a hatbox. Beth stared at the half-opened box. The lid askew. The contents jumbled. She dropped to her knees and grabbed a handful of notes and photos of a man who might have been Michael's clone. Hands shaking, Beth scanned one of the notes, signed with the same thin scrawl that labeled Aunt Naomi's portrait.

Edgar Alexander.

Nausea crept up her throat. This man must be Michael's father. Their resemblance was too strong to be any other relation. That only confirmed what Beth assumed. Michael Alexander came to the inn with one motive: to find his father's paintings. Somehow, Michael learned that Aunt Naomi possessed some of Edgar's work.

Beth suppressed the urge to strangle him. And once again she chided herself. *How could I have been so stupid?*

Grabbing the box, she stood. Michael may have taken advantage of her trusting nature, but he wouldn't get away without a fight.

Twenty-seven

*A*fter stepping through the inn's front door, Michael closed and locked it. This job required privacy. As he approached the receptionist's desk, Beth descended the steps, a hatbox in hand. A spider web's gauzy threads decorated her hair. Stonily, she stared at him.

"I was just in your room," she said evenly. Her eyes flashed angrily as she planted herself behind the desk and plopped the box between them.

"Oh?" Michael forced an innocent expression.

"Would you care to tell me exactly how you're related to the man who painted my aunt's portrait?"

"Why would you suppose I'm related to him?"

"You share the same last name." Her lips pressing into a firm line, she narrowed her eyes. "And . . ." She scooped up a snapshot from the box. ". . . you look exactly like him. I am not as stupid as you think."

"I never said I thought you were stupid, Beth."

Michael caressed every word, creating a nuance of regret. Feigned regret.

"You must. Otherwise you wouldn't have presumed that I wouldn't catch on to you." Beth threw the picture back into the box as if for added emphasis.

"Catch on to me?"

"Don't think I buy your act anymore, Michael. I know the only reason you came here was for that painting."

"Why would you think such a terrible thing of me? I really thought perhaps you and I—"

"No, you didn't." A red flush crept up her neck. "You'll be interested to know that I found your hole in the wall. I also know there is supposed to be some valuable jewelry in this box. Just as there's supposed to be another painting by your father in the attic behind the bureau. Would you care to tell me where those items might be?"

"I'm terribly offended." Michael faked an injured expression.

"You're also a very good actor." Beth paused, and her voice held an edge of threat when she spoke again. "I think it's time you leave. If you will hand over the painting and jewelry you've already stolen, you may leave peacefully. If you refuse to give them back . . ." She placed her hand on the desk phone. ". . . I'm calling the police."

"As I already told you, I'm planning on leaving now. There's no reason to get rude."

"Good," she ground out. "Here's your bill. As soon as

you pay it, I expect you to return my possessions. Do you understand?" Her penetrating stare dared him to disagree.

Thoughtfully Michael examined his bill, desperately trying to determine how to manipulate this situation to suit him. Then he decided to do what he most likely should have done in the first place; what his mother would no doubt applaud.

Be honest.

"I do have the jewelry and the other painting in the car," he said slowly.

Beth's eyes widened.

"Earlier, I offered you ten thousand for the painting upstairs. I will gladly give you fifty thousand for both paintings and the jewelry."

A surprised spark flickered in her eyes, only to be replaced by renewed anger. "If you will gladly give fifty thousand, they are probably worth ten times that," she mocked. "Now, I've already told you once. I want that jewelry and that other painting back. I want you to pay your bill and leave."

"A hundred thousand," he snapped, hating the thought of drugging Beth more than ever.

"No."

"Two hundred thousand."

She picked up the receiver.

"Okay. Okay." Michael reached for his billfold, and Beth slowly replaced the receiver. He had only two choices left. He could capitulate to Beth's demands or use the chloral hydrate. The latter seemed his only option. Michael would rather make Beth uncomfortable for half a day than make himself work the rest of his life.

He would be forced to slip Beth the gel caps. A half-empty mug of tea sat on the desk. Whether it was hers or not couldn't be determined. Besides, the tea looked as if it had been there a while. The harder Michael reasoned, the more his head pounded from the blow he had received in his tangle with Scott. Then genius struck.

"Would you make me another ice pack before I go?" Michael pulled a stack of one-hundred-dollar bills from his billfold and awaited his change. "My head is still giving me a bit of trouble."

"If you think I'm stupid enough to fall for that one, you're crazy. I'm not letting you out of my sight for one second, buddy."

"Fine." He pocketed his change. "Then I'll make it myself." Without waiting for her permission, Michael whipped around the desk and headed for the kitchen.

"Stop right there," she demanded.

Michael, ignoring her, hid a triumphant smirk as he heard her enraged footsteps behind him. Earlier, he wondered if perhaps he should force the gel caps directly into her mouth. At the time, Michael had been worried about Lauren's presence. But Lauren wasn't here. Immediately, he imagined Beth's struggle and the likelihood of his bruising her. Michael flinched. Really, he didn't want a mess. He just wanted his painting.

As he entered the kitchen, the block of butcher

knives on the counter answered his dilemma. Before he could form another thought, he stepped forward, grabbed the biggest one, and turned on Beth.

A gasp. She glanced from his face to the knife and back to his face. Her cheeks drained of all color.

The silver blade glistened in the sunlight pouring through the window, and Michael hoped his acting abilities included playing the role of murderer. If only the poor girl knew he would never use a knife on her; he simply wanted that painting. But she didn't know, and that was his advantage.

"Now, if you'll just cooperate with me, Beth, no one will get hurt."

She backed against the oven and licked her lips.

"I've got a couple of pills I want you to take," he said evenly.

"I'm not taking anything," she croaked.

"I think you would be better off to cooperate. I wanted to slip them into your tea, but that seems to work only in the movies." He fished the four green gel caps from his pocket.

Terror blazed through her eyes as she scrutinized the pills.

"It's just chloral hydrate. They won't harm you. I take one every night. They're going to make you sleep, that's all. When you wake up, you'll be as good as new."

"If you don't put down that knife and leave, I'll scream my lungs out."

"Who'll hear you?"

"The Bennetts are here. I heard them talking when I discovered the hidden stairway."

Michael narrowed his eyes. "If you scream, I'll stab you." He added an extra growl to his voice to create a convincing edge.

The effort paid off, for her eyes widened with renewed fear. "I'm not taking those pills."

"You have two choices, Beth. You can either swallow two of them on your own, or I'll force all four of them down your throat." Michael frowned menacingly. "I'm not exactly sure the effect four of them will have on you. I know from experience that two of them will simply induce a deep sleep."

Again she looked from his eyes to the pills and back to him. "Why?"

"I'll let you figure that one out. I'm pretty sure you already know." Slowly he approached her.

"You've been a fake from the start," she said through clamped teeth.

Suddenly Michael flashed back to a night when he was ten. His father arrived home from one of his "excursions," and Michael awakened in his room to the eruption between his parents. "You're nothing but a fake," his mother screamed through a torrent of tears. "A fake father and a fake husband. Can't you see we need the *real* you?"

Michael heard no more, for he had covered his ears and cried himself to sleep. He had been the richest kid of all his acquaintances. The richest, and the poorest.

As an adult, he became nothing more than a clone of the father he resented. Michael thought that by copying his dad, he could win the fatherly approval he never felt. Looking back, he didn't think anything would have gained his father's approval.

Beth's fear-filled eyes penetrated his reverie. She had called him a fake. The very suggestion disgusted him . . . because it was true.

But another more pressing truth involved his trust fund. As bad as he hated to continue this charade, Michael couldn't ignore his own financial demise.

"Here are the pills," he said flatly, opening his palm. "I want you to slowly fill a cup with water, then swallow both of them." As an added threat, Michael nudged the knife's point against her ribcage.

Mutely Beth picked up two of the gel caps. "Before I take these, I want to know how you knew those paintings and jewelry were here."

"I discovered the painting in the attic and the jewelry on my own. But before he died, my father told me about the portrait of your aunt. He wanted me to buy it and maybe resell it. You rejected my offer. That left me only one choice." He pushed her toward the sink. "Now. Nice and slowly, I want you to get a cup of water and swallow those pills like a good girl."

"Why do I feel as if these are going to kill me?" She walked to the cabinet, took out a black mug, and filled it with water.

"You'll just have to take my word for it. These pills are

the lesser of the two evils."

Hesitating, Beth placed the gel caps into her mouth, drank the water, and deposited the cup into the sink.

"Now we wait. In about fifteen minutes you'll go to sleep. By the time you wake up, the painting and I will be long gone. I'll let you sit on your couch in the den." Michael jerked his head toward the cozy room just next to the kitchen. "That way, when you fall over, you'll have a comfortable spot to land."

"Thanks a lot," Beth said sarcastically.

"Ladies first." Michael waved his hand toward the doorway. Renewed pressure of the knife against her ribcage prompted her hasty compliance. She settled on the sofa. Michael chose the wicker chair nearby, the knife strategically pointing her way.

With satisfaction, he watched. As each minute passed, Beth's eyelids grew heavier and heavier. Her admirable attempts to hold them open soon failed, and she slumped sideways.

A final onslaught of guilt forced Michael to swing Beth's feet onto the couch and place a pillow under her head. No sense in her getting a cramp in her neck over this. Losing an heirloom was enough.

Gently, he brushed his lips against her flawless cheek, and his gut twisted with the attraction he long ago failed to suppress. Another time, another place, and who knew what could have transpired between them?

Slamming the door on those desires, Michael rushed up the back stairway.

"Hi," Marilyn said, with uncertain smile.

"Hello there," Scott said. "I just left a message on your machine at home."

"Oh?" She glanced at the sleeping bag and duffel bag he carried. "I guess you aren't going to be able to make it to dinner then?"

"No. I—something has come up."

Marilyn seemed to wilt with relief, and Scott didn't know whether to be relieved himself or offended. Surely his company wasn't that burdensome.

"Care to come in for a Coke or something?" he asked, not sounding half as congenial as he intended. Thoughts of what might be happening at Beth's outweighed his present conversation.

"No. I would like to sit down on your swing for a minute. Do you have time to talk?"

"Uh, yeah." *No!* his mind urged. Dropping his bags, he joined Marilyn on the porch swing. Perhaps he could speed their conversation along without seeming rude. Earlier, he planned to have a chat with Marilyn regarding his love for Beth. Now would be a good opportunity. But that would probably take more time than Scott wanted to spare.

Marilyn nervously toyed with the hem of her lab coat, and an awkward silence wrapped its stifling arms around them. She cast him an indecisive glance, her doe-brown eyes almost pleading for him to read her mind.

Scott looked back, nonplused. He couldn't figure out what Beth McAllister was thinking, and he had known her his whole life. How did Marilyn think he was going to read her mind?

"Nice weather today," he said absently. "Not too terribly hot. But warm enough."

"Yes."

"Nice, cool breeze."

"Uh-huh."

Out of habit, Scott checked his Timex. Just after five. He had been away from Beth long enough.

"Are you late for an appointment?" Marilyn asked.

"Yes," he said without thinking. "I mean no—not an appointment. It's just—"

"You're in a hurry?"

"I'm worried about Beth. Believe me, it's a long story." Scott hesitated, not wanting to hurt Marilyn's feelings, but some force urged him to Beth's. Something must be wrong. Dreadfully wrong. "I really need to get to her house."

Marilyn thoughtfully peered at him. "You're in love with her, aren't you?"

"Why would you think that?" Scott snapped, irritated with himself. If Beth's dad could see it, and Marilyn could see it, the whole town must know of his feelings. Was Scott that transparent?

"Actually, I haven't thought it before. But when you were in the clinic earlier today, I noticed something. It just didn't click until now."

With a resigned sigh, Scott smiled in self-mockery. "I was worried about how I was going to tell you. Please don't think I was trying to use you, Marilyn. I think you're—"

"Oh, I wouldn't think that in a million years," she rushed, her eyes rounded in relief.

Scott had the uneasy feeling Marilyn planned to break their friendship but didn't quite know how to do it. He shared in her relief, but at the same time he was a bit perturbed. After all, no man enjoyed rejection.

"I was trying to think of a way to tell you that I—I— think the reason I like you so much is because there are some things about you that remind me of Gregory."

"Your ex-husband?"

Marilyn nodded, and her unshed tears momentarily shifted Scott's attention from Beth to her.

"You really loved him, didn't you?" Scott placed a consoling hand on her shoulder.

Another nod. "As much as I hate to admit it, I still do." Stubbornly, Marilyn brushed at the tears. "Do you have any suggestions on how to force yourself to stop loving somebody?"

He snorted. "Believe me, I've tried a dozen times to talk myself out of loving Beth. I kept hoping your beautiful face might joust me out of my feelings for her." As if they were two chums, Scott wrapped his arm around Marilyn's shoulder and gave her a sideways hug.

Marilyn placed her head on his shoulder and

released a muffled sob.

"Hey," Scott said, stroking her shoulder in brotherly comfort. "There's no need to cry. It's going to be okay."

"Why do I doubt that?" She sniffled against the tears. "I feel like my heart has been ripped out. Greg and I had a life together. We had a daughter. We had a min—min—ministry."

"I know. I know," he soothed. "And I'm so, so sorry."

Softly, she wept for several minutes.

Scott let her. Poor woman. He had never been rejected by a spouse. But at a very tender age, Scott had been rejected by his father. Witnessing Marilyn's pain was like reliving his own.

"My father verbally abused me," he said, absently stroking her hair. "I'm sure you probably suspected that since we attended the same school. It's been a hard journey to forgiveness, and some days I still want to sob with the pain of some of the stuff he said to me.

"But God can help you with your pain, Marilyn. There are all kinds of healing, you know. There's physical healing, but then there's also emotional and spiritual healing. Those miracles are just as amazing as any physical healing." Thoughtfully, Scott blinked, wondering where those words of wisdom had come from. "I'm not sure I'm completely healed yet, myself," he muttered. "It's a process, I guess. A long process. But I know God has been faithful to hold my hand and comfort me through the whole ordeal—or, should I say, miracle."

Marilyn stiffened. "If God is so interested in miracles,

why didn't he miraculously convince Gregory to stay in our marriage? I would have been willing to work through our problems. I would have forgiven him for the affair and even gone to a counselor, if God had just given me the chance."

Scott stared at the ferns hanging from the eaves and prayed that the Lord would give him something to say. Then the answer struck him. "God isn't going to force somebody to do what's right, Marilyn. Greg had to be willing to turn to the Lord."

She pulled away from him. "Thanks." And the subject was closed. "I didn't intend to come over here and blubber all over you." Marilyn fished a tissue from her pocket.

"I'm glad you came. I think we both needed to clear the air."

"I hope Beth McAllister understands what a lucky woman she is." A wobbly, tear-filled smile.

"Well, you just remember what I've already told you. Gregory Thatcher was crazy. And I'm sure God will provide you with another mate." Like a fond brother, Scott brushed his lips against her damp cheek. He experienced no reaction, and knew Marilyn didn't either. But hopefully, the gesture comforted her.

"This is all assuming I want another mate," she said sarcastically. "I think I can cheerfully live without the risk of more heartache."

"I can see why you would feel that way."

Abruptly, she stood. "I've taken enough of your time. I didn't intend to stay this long. Brooke and my parents will wonder what's happened to me."

"You're very fortunate to have your parents' support."

"Yes. That's one thing in all this mess I can be thankful for."

"I'm sure there will be more, if you'll just look."

Scott, amazed at his own words, watched Marilyn drive away. The irony of the whole conversation was that Scott actually needed someone to tell him some of the things he told Marilyn. He had to admit he wasn't terribly thankful himself regarding his own situation with Beth.

Their relationship had plummeted him to the depths of despair. Only a miracle would sweep away their conflict and restore their friendship, or what was left of it. Scott hadn't been terribly conscientious in praying for his own miracle. He had been more focused on venting his frustrations to God. Perhaps the time had come for him to take his own medicine.

For the second time that day, he began a sheepish prayer. *Lord, I need a miracle. I'm heading over to Beth's, now. Please prepare the way before me. And, um, is there any way You could make her fall in love with me?*

Twenty-eight

$\mathcal{B}$eth peeked between her lashes to watch Michael rush from the den and head for the back stairway. She took a risk when she spit the green pills into the mug of water rather than swallowing them. Michael Alexander grossly underestimated her. If he thought she would passively swallow some strange pills, he was wrong.

Now all she could do was wait. Wait until he went to her room and took the painting. Wait until he exited the inn. Wait until he drove away. Then, she would call the police.

She toyed with the thought of trying to stop Michael, but the memory of the knife's menacing gleam ended that consideration. Beth would rather have her life than a painting, regardless of its value. Only when she saw Michael pulling from her driveway would she believe that he wasn't coming back.

She heard a muted bump as if he were kicking in her

locked bedroom door. Then she heard him rushing down the stairs. The front door opened. Closed. He was gone.

Losing no time, Beth sat straight up. Cautiously, she tiptoed from the den into the kitchen, through the dining room, and to the front desk. As she had suspected, the red Mercedes was speeding over her front yard, through the flower bed, and up the street.

Mrs. Bennett descended the stairs, eyes wide. "Is something the matter, dear? Mr. Bennett told me not to interfere, but I simply could not stay in that room another minute."

"Yes. One of my guests just stole something."

Still shaking, Beth picked up the telephone and dialed 911. After clipping out the necessary information, she hung up and dialed Mrs. Spencer's number.

"Is there anything I can do?" Mrs. Bennett offered anxiously.

"Yes. You can stay by the front desk until Sheila comes. She's my part-time receptionist."

"Of course, dear, anything to help."

Beth bounded up the stairs. Until the police caught up with Michael, she would follow him at a distance. She ran into her room to retrieve her car keys. Out of the corner of her eye, she saw the empty space on the wall where Aunt Naomi's portrait had hung. As long as the painting had been there, Beth felt as if apart of her aunt were still alive. Losing the painting was almost like losing Aunt Naomi all over again.

Scott was right all along about Michael Alexander. *How could I have been so stupid?*

Swallowing against her tightened throat, Beth rushed down the stairs to the front door. Only when she placed her hand on the doorknob did she remember her car was debilitated. She groaned and pounded her fist against the door frame.

Just then a green Chevrolet turned into the driveway, and Beth almost shouted. *Scott!* He hadn't listened to her demand to stay away. "Thank You, Lord," she whispered, barely aware of Mrs. Bennett's curious appraisal.

Beth threw open the front door, raced down the porch steps, and, as Scott was stepping from his car, greeted him with a bear hug. "You have no idea how glad I am to see you!"

"Now that's the kind of greeting I can live with," he said, his arms tightening around her waist. "The last thing I remember, you wanted me out of your life—"

"We don't have time to discuss any of that right now." She pulled away. "Michael stole the painting of Aunt Naomi from over my bed."

"What? How did he get out with it in broad daylight?"

"It's a long story." Beth rounded the car. "I'll tell you on the way." She plopped into the passenger seat.

"On the way?" Scott sat behind the steering wheel.

"Yeah. We're gonna chase him. He went that way." She pointed to the left.

"Have you called the police?"

"Yes. But I thought we could follow him at a distance

until they showed up. I don't want him to get away. Now get a move on it!" She snapped her fingers at the steering wheel.

"Yes ma'am!" Deftly, Scott cranked the car and sped from the driveway.

"You were right about Michael," Beth said, hating to take such bitter medicine.

She had been duped. How could she have been so gullible? Scott warned her. The Holy Spirit warned her. But did Beth listen?

She was too enamored with Michael's movie star looks, his charming smile, his obvious wealth, his blatant attraction to her. But now she knew. That "blatant attraction" was nothing but an act to get to the painting. How Michael must have laughed at her.

"You were right," she said again, clicking her seat belt into place. "I've acted like an idiot."

"Don't, Beth—"

"No." She raised her hand in humiliating admission. "It's the truth. There's no sense in avoiding it. And he was worse than even you imagined. Do you know he held me at knife point?"

"What?" Scott yelled, turning his widened eyes to Beth.

"Watch the road!" she screamed as they approached a hairpin curve in the wrong lane.

Scott steered the car back into his own lane. "Did he hurt you?" he growled. "Because if he did—"

"No, no, no. He got one of my butcher knives and

tried to force me to swallow some sleeping pills."

"Why—"

"He wanted to knock me out so he could take the painting and make a clean getaway. He figured that by the time I woke up, he would be long gone."

"How in the world did you get out of taking them?"

Beth briefed him on the whole story.

"They'll charge him with robbery and threatening your life. I can't wait to see his face when he sees you awake." Thoughtful silence. "Beth, I don't know what I would have done if he'd killed you."

If she didn't know any better, if this were not Scott, Beth would say he was trying to tell her how much she meant to him. She glanced away, not really sure what she thought. But that twisting in the pit of her stomach returned.

The last week had left her confused at best. This turbulence with Scott, this tingling in her midsection, made her feel as if she were spinning, spinning, spinning in a whirlwind of emotions.

Then she caught a glimpse of red several blocks away and, pointing, leaned forward in her excitement. "Oh, oh, oh! There he is! Turning onto this street!"

"I see him! I see him!" Scott wrapped his hand around hers. "Just calm down," he said, not removing his hand. "I bet you my life's savings he's gotten turned around on these hillside roads. We'll catch up with him."

"But he's got Aunt Naomi, and . . . and . . ." She sputtered to a halt as an explosion of sensation spiderwebbed from his fingers into her hand and up her arm. Was this Scott holding her hand in brotherly concern? Scott? Or a stranger she had never before known, never before seen until this summer?

As casually as possible, Beth removed her hand from his loose grasp to place it in her lap. The painting. She must concentrate on retrieving the painting. These other thoughts would lead her nowhere. Scott was in love with Marilyn.

A siren's loud shrill seemed to punctuate that thought.

"Look, Bet." He pointed toward the Mercedes. "Just like I figured. He's so lost he's turning up Crescent Drive. He's going toward the hotel." With those words Scott slowed, and the patrol car passed them to pursue the thief.

Crescent Drive. The very street on which she and Michael had taken that carriage ride the night of his arrival. How he must have laughed at her even then. A new shower of shame taunted her.

As if she were in a dream, Beth watched another police car, lights flashing, roll to a stop in front of the Mercedes. Michael was caught. In a matter of minutes, the officials read Michael his rights, then searched the Mercedes.

After removing the paintings from the car, a familiar policeman approached them.

Scott rolled down the window. "Hello, Darryl."

Beth wiggled her fingers at Scott's neighbor. The

good thing about such a small town was that everybody knew everybody.

"Beth, you called the station about one painting, but we've discovered two paintings and several pieces of jewelry. Are you missing those items as well?"

"Yes. I was so unnerved when I called that I didn't mention the rest." Nausea crept up her throat.

"Okay," Darryl said. "We're going to need you at the station to press charges."

"I'll be there," Beth said emphatically.

"There was more?" Scott asked as Darryl turned to leave.

"Yes." Beth, wallowing in more humiliation, told Scott about the note from Aunt Naomi, the missing painting in the attic, and the secret stairway. Only one thought saved her from dying in an inferno of embarrassment. More than likely, Beth wasn't the first woman Michael had manipulated. He was simply too accomplished at the art.

And suddenly, Beth experienced the need to face him. "I'll be back." She unfastened her seat belt.

"Where are you going?" Scott asked.

Beth opened the car door. "I've got a message to deliver." Fists clamped at her sides, she marched toward the police car.

Just as the policeman was about to deposit Michael into the seat, Beth cleared her throat. "Excuse me."

Michael and the policeman both looked at her.

She ignored the policeman. "Michael, you might have outsmarted me in the beginning, but in the end, I won. If you thought I was stupid enough to swallow those pills, you're crazy. I spit them back in the cup and faked it. And I was the one who called the police."

Silently he appraised her, the cocky tilt of his chin replaced by the stunned expression of a thwarted weasel.

Beth, daring him to speak, held his gaze. Michael Alexander had finally met his match, and Beth wanted to make sure he remembered this moment a long, long time.

"Have you said all you wanted to say?" Michael asked, his tone flat.

"No. But I've said all I need to say." Beth turned on her heel and stalked back to Scott's car.

Michael slumped into the patrol car's backseat. Numb. He was numb. When he pulled away from the inn, he had been sure he succeeded. Now he saw his mistake. He should have been less a gentleman and forced the chloral hydrate down Beth's throat. He probably faced charges of threatening her life as well as larceny. And there was no denying it. His fingerprints were all over the butcher knife he stashed under the car seat. He had planned to trash the knife at the airport when he destroyed and discarded his true ID.

The only thought that sustained him was his mother's loyalty. Michael knew from his adolescent skirmish with drugs that she would spare no costs in hiring the best defense attorney money could buy. Michael also knew that the overwhelming evidence would almost guarantee him a spot in prison. The question was going to be how long. He propped his head against the window, stunned that his well-laid plan had been foiled by one woman.

He watched as Beth, her cheeks still flushed, climbed back into the green Chevrolet. Michael couldn't deny the way she stirred his pulse, even after she had discovered his motives. Poetic justice had been served. The only woman who truly affected him wouldn't have him. Certainly not now.

Twenty-nine

I owe you an apology, Scott," Beth said imploringly as they watched the police cars drive away. "You tried to tell me about Michael."

The green eyes she had seen dance with mirth, pool with tears, fill with disappointment, seemed to caress her every feature. "It's okay. I understand, I guess."

"Well, I'm not sure I do," she said. "I guess I just got carried away because I thought he might be Mr. Right. You know, my last chance at happiness."

"Come on, don't be so fatalistic."

"I'm not. Look at me, Scott. Just look at me. I'm twenty-eight, plump, plain, and still single, without a prospect in sight."

"Beth McAllister, what is the matter with your eyes? You are maybe ten pounds overweight! I wouldn't call that plump. And—"

"But compared to Lauren—and—and—" She averted her eyes to stare at the surrounding pines. Her talk with

Lauren somehow freed her to express her true feelings. Lauren reminded her about accepting oneself as worthy because of Christ's love. Beth, ready to embrace that truth, wasn't sure just how to comprehend it in her soul. "And I've always been fat, Scott. Don't you remember my nickname in high school? Fatty!"

"But you're much thinner than you were in high school."

His claim went unheard as Beth's pain spewed forth. "And when those girls . . . set me up at homecoming . . . I know you haven't forgotten, Scott." Her tears gushed out like heated, angry rivulets. And with every tear, with every sob, she relived the scornful laughter that haunted her emotions, tortured her mind.

"Ah, Beth, come here," he muttered, his warm arms encircling her. "It's going to be okay. Just cry it out."

As sobs racked her body, Beth gripped the front of Scott's shirt, desperately clinging to any scrap of sanity she could grasp. She had wondered what road her emotional healing would take, but never dreamed it would be this painful. Beth was seventeen once more, and the pain of a seventeen-year-old ravaged her soul. *Oh, Lord, help me. Heal me!*

"Why were they so mean?" she wailed as the sobs abated to sniffles.

"I think they were just jealous."

"Jealous?" The word, so unexpected, caused Beth to raise her head. So close was she to Scott, their noses nearly touched, but Beth was too entwined in her own pain to contemplate the implications teasing her thoughts. "Jealous of me? Why?"

"Beth . . ." He sighed and shook his head. "Who won the math award her senior year? Who won the science award? Who won the award for literature and was the class valedictorian?"

"Me, but—"

"Can't you see, Beth? You were—are—smarter than all of those girls put together. You tutored most of their boyfriends, and they hated it! One of those girls didn't finish college because she couldn't pass algebra. She tried at four different schools. When did you ever struggle with algebra, Beth?"

"But look at me!"

Grasping her upper arms, Scott gently shook her. "I have looked at you for years, and there's nothing wrong with your appearance!"

"But compared to Lauren—"

"Why do you compare yourself to Lauren?"

Biting her lip in contemplation, Beth stared at a cardinal flitting from one oak to another. In those brief seconds, she searched every corridor of her mind, but couldn't answer Scott's question. "I have no idea," she finally said as the black cloak that had snugly shrouded her emotions loosened, and Scott slowly released his hold.

The lack of his warmth, of his nearness, made Beth aware of how close they had been, and she awkwardly shifted away from him.

"The irony of the whole thing is that Lauren has always compared herself to me. Believe it or not, she feels inferior too. That was part of the reason she was so upset over Aunt Naomi's will."

Scott propped his elbow on the console between them.

"That just blows my mind, Scott. She's so beautiful. I'm sure nobody has ever made fun of her."

"No, but she's confided in me some, Beth, and I know for a fact that looking the way she does has its drawbacks. Men like her for her looks, not for who she is, and sometimes women are so jealous they hate her for her looks."

"Yeah, she mentioned some of that."

"I know what those girls did hurt you, but it in no way was a reflection of your worth. It was a reflection of their cruelty and insecurities. And I think bottling it up all these years probably hurt you just as much as the original incident."

"I just never felt as though I could talk about it. I was so ashamed. I felt as if I had done something to deserve their treatment, that maybe—"

"That maybe you were a lesser person because of it?" he asked softly.

"Exactly. How did you know?"

"Because . . ." Scott turned to gently look into her eyes. ". . . I felt the same way about my father's abuse. It took me years to realize that I did nothing to deserve the things he said to me. The problem was his, not mine. Once I got to that place, the Holy Spirit could start His work—the healing." He turned to stare out the window. "And to tell you the truth, He's still working. I had a—a bad memory from childhood not long ago. Dad used to let my cereal soak in the milk until it was soggy before he would let me eat it."

"How awful! Why?"

"I have no idea. Meanness, I guess. He blamed me for Mom's death. Sometimes he would tell me that the stress of raising me caused her cancer."

Beth's heart beat in sympathy for the little boy who often came to school in dirty clothing. What evils he must have endured.

"Anyway, I had completely forgotten about it, I guess out of self-preservation. Then last week, I was pouring myself a bowl of cereal, and whammy, I remembered the whole thing," he said, his voice thickening.

"Oh, Scott." Beth placed a consoling hand on his shoulder. While he pressed his hands against his eyes for several silent seconds, Beth's own problems seemed miniscule compared to his.

"So, like I said, I've had to ask the Holy Spirit to heal this memory too. I guess we're just going to work on one memory at a time.

"I honestly thought I had worked through all the bitterness I held toward Dad. When I came back to be with him while he was dying, I led him to the Lord. Then he realized what he'd done and apologized over and over and over again. It was a healing for both of us. I thought it was over, but maybe it's just begun."

Thoughtfully, he lifted her hand from his shoulder and covered it with his hand. "Two nights ago, I dreamed Captain Crunch was chasing me with a bowl of milk." A soft chuckle. "I woke up all sweaty, or should I say, soggy!"

Beth giggled and pulled her hand from his to press unsteady fingers against her lips and hopefully suppress the laughter welling up within.

"One night I dreamed that those girls were chasing me and they all were dressed like clowns—overalls, big red noses, the whole nine yards. Then I was flying, and I landed in a beautiful field of flowers where I was the homecoming queen."

Scott turned contemplative eyes to her. "Interesting, don't you think? After all, those girls tried to convince you that you were the clown when, in reality, they were the ones who came off looking bad."

Beth nodded. "I've wondered if the Lord was trying to tell me something to that effect."

"Maybe He was. You know, Beth, I told you when all this happened that they lied to you, and you wouldn't listen to me."

"Oh?"

"Yes. Those girls might have convinced you to run for homecoming queen as a cruel joke, but they had no control over your making it into the finals. Think about it. They wouldn't have sacrificed their own votes for you. You made it into the finals because people liked you."

The very truth that Beth couldn't accept eleven years before now made perfect sense. She silently contemplated

Scott's words as her heart continued its mending.

"There's a Scripture that has been the only thing that has kept me going some days," Scott said. 'Cast all your cares upon Him, for He cares for you.' Maybe that's what the Lord was trying to help you see with that dream. Maybe He wants you to give this pain to Him so the Holy Spirit can lift you above it. As you told me not long ago, it's amazing how He can heal. And believe me, do I know."

"If you think about it, you have done remarkably well for someone with such a traumatic past."

"It's all the Lord's work, Beth. Anything I am, I owe to Him. He's taught me to base my self-worth not on who my father was or how I was treated, but on my being a child of God. Wow! Just think about it! Jesus Christ died for me! But I'm sure you've already thought all this through. After all, you're the one who introduced me to Him. You've been a Christian much longer than I have."

"But I never saw until now," she muttered, marveling in the spiritual wisdom Scott had gained. And she saw; she saw for the first time how she allowed her past to discolor her present and taint her future.

Father, here it is. Here's the pain. Please take it, and—and make me new.

As this prayer left her thoughts, so her heart, her emotions were released from the binding cords that once constricted her growth. A gurgling stream seemed to bubble through her heart, cleansing her of those feelings of inferiority that had been her bedfellow, her tormentor.

"Are you going to be all right?" Scott asked.

"Yeah." Nodding her head, she turned a tremulous smile to him. "Thanks."

"Now if I can just get Captain Crunch off my back."

Feeling as if she were in a weightless air balloon, Beth joined in his light laughter. "It sounds to me like you're halfway there."

"Actually, I'm almost all the way there. Just the fact that I can laugh about it means a lot."

"But there's still some pain."

"Yes. Still some pain, but I've given it to the Lord. I know that over time that pain will turn to joy, as He promised. Some wounds take longer to heal than others."

"I'll pray for a quick recovery."

"Thanks. And just for the record, you're a very attractive woman, Bet. And you have a lot to offer any man. Take my word for it, you'll find Mr. Right."

"I hope you're right." *I wish you were Mr. Right.* But Beth knew Scott was Marilyn's Mr. Right.

"I guess we need to get to the police station," she said, trying to cleanse her mind of those futile thoughts.

Thirty

Scott opened the door for Beth, and she preceded him from the police station.

"Do you want to grab a hamburger before I take you home?" He scanned the streets of the busy tourist town, dotted with fast food restaurants and country music theaters.

"No. I really need to get back to the inn. Sheila was sweet to come and tend the desk at such short notice, but I know she's got things to do."

"Okay. Just make sure you don't skip dinner altogether," Scott admonished with brotherly affection.

"Believe me, I could stand to miss a meal or two."

He opened the car door for her. "I thought we were through with that kind of talk."

"Sorry." She dimpled up at him as she slid into the seat.

Silently, Scott shook his index finger at her and feigned a stern expression.

Beth giggled, a relieved giggle that sounded like the gurgle of a happy brook.

Resisting the urge to plant a kiss on her cheek, he shut her door instead. Desperately, Scott wished to tell her of his love. But was this the right time or place? He rounded the car, unlocked his door, and scooted behind the wheel.

"My head is killing me," she said. "Do you have an aspirin?"

"Yeah. In the glove box." *By the way, I love you.*

While she rummaged through papers, Scott cranked the car and started toward the inn.

"I guess I'll need you to fix the hole in the wall in Michael's room—I mean the blue room—as soon as you can." Taking a sip of the diet soda they had given her in the police station, Beth swallowed two aspirins.

"Sure." *I'll do anything you need me to do, Beth, any time, because I love you.*

"I wonder if perhaps that stairway was placed between those two rooms so a mother could have easy access to her children's rooms. Instead of going all the way down the end of the hallway for the main staircase, she could just trot down those stairs as soon as she heard their cries."

Probably." *Do you want children, Beth? I hope so. I'd love for us to have a big family.*

Beth massaged her forehead. "It might be good to reopen the hallway and attach doors there. I could close off the stairway. That way, if a family came, they could have the option of two rooms connected."

"Yes."

As silence settled between them. Scott gripped the steering wheel. Even though this probably wasn't the best time or place to tell Beth of his feelings, he could hardly suppress his words.

"You're certainly the conversationalist," she said.

Slowing to a halt for the stop sign two blocks from the inn, he turned to stare into her eyes. Eyes full of questions. Tired eyes with dark circles under them.

He opened his mouth to blurt his love, then stopped himself. Poor Beth. She had been through so much today. How could he add to her stress with news of his true feelings? That would be nothing but Scott acting in self-interest. He should save his news until she was rested. Maybe tomorrow.

"I guess I'm just as tired as you must be," he said, turning his attention back to the road. "This has been a difficult day for both of us, hasn't it? After all, I did run over Tiffany this morning." Even to his own ears, he sounded strained. How she must wonder at his change of tone.

"I—I haven't thanked you yet for coming back and helping me chase Michael, even after I told you to leave—"

"Don't worry about it." Scott guided the car into the inn's driveway and parked it. "I certainly didn't, did I?" With an assuring smile, he turned to her once more. "I think we've both said and done some pretty weird things lately." *Especially me, because I love you.* "We'll just chalk it up to temporary strangeness." *Except for me. There's nothing temporary about the way I feel. Is there any way that I could convince you to love me, Beth?*

Kiss her, a voice urged as their gaze lengthened. And Scott couldn't deny that this time there was a tiny flicker of something in Beth's eyes. The same something he noticed in his kitchen. The same something he saw earlier today while examining her car. And he sensed that she probably wouldn't pull away if he were to take her in his arms. *Kiss her,* that obstinate voice urged again.

But Scott forced himself to get out of the car. If he stayed cooped up with her much longer, he wouldn't be responsible for his words or actions. When he told Beth he loved her, when he took her in his arms, Scott wanted to be sure that her response wasn't tainted by stress or exhaustion. Whether she responded positively or negatively, Scott desired an honest reaction. He didn't want to take advantage of her weakened emotions. And after such a day, what woman wouldn't need a hug? Or a shoulder to cry on? Scott simply couldn't be that shoulder today. Not if tomorrow Beth would regret her hasty impulse.

"I'm going to go ahead and fix your car," he said as she got out. "I'll look at the wall in the blue room tomorrow, if that's okay with you."

"That's fine."

And a barrier erected itself between them. In distancing himself from her, Scott must have given the wrong impression. She must think that he was ready to leave. If only she knew the very opposite were true.

Scott could contain his words no longer. The perfect time to tell her might never come. He might as well take his chances now. As she stepped toward the mansion, her head bent, her shoulders sagging, Scott placed a hand on her shoulder.

"Beth, there's something we need to discuss—"

"Good. You're home," Sheila called from the doorway. "There's a couple on the phone who want to know if you can give them two rooms starting tomorrow night. I couldn't find your reservation book and didn't know what to tell them."

"Thanks, Sheila," Beth said, hurrying up the porch steps. "I left the reservation book in the den this morning and forgot to return it to the desk."

And she was gone.

❧

Late that night Beth removed Scott's fragrant apple pie from the oven. Its flaky crust was baked to golden perfection, and she knew Scott would be both elated and surprised. For all he had done, he deserved the requested pie. During the arrest, filing the police report, and facing Michael, Scott stood firmly beside her. Beth didn't know what she would have done without him. He even replaced the starter on her car as he promised.

As long as Scott had been there, Beth smothered herself in work, some of which could have been postponed until the next day. Now her shoulders ached with fatigue. Earlier, Scott seemed distant, and Beth didn't want to make him feel as if he had to stay with her. When they took Tiffany to the clinic, Marilyn mentioned his eating dinner with her and her folks that night. Beth didn't want to interrupt his life.

With a hint of guilt, she recalled her morning refusal to bake for him. Actually, whether Beth took the drive with Michael or not, she didn't have time for extra baking. But in the face of Scott's afternoon support, Beth knew she must make time. She still hated the thought that Marilyn would eat the pie she slaved over, but Beth could no longer withhold the favor from Scott. He had done too much for her.

As she carefully placed the dessert on the cooling rack, the front door opened, and Beth knew her folks and Lauren had arrived. She asked them to come over after they closed the restaurant but didn't explain why. Beth needed to share parts of Aunt Naomi's note with them.

"Anybody home?" Don McAllister called.

Removing her green checked apron, Beth walked toward the lobby. "You guys come back to the den. I've got some herbal tea ready."

"Great," Lauren said, her eyes droopy with exhaustion. "I could use a pick-me-up."

"I guess it was another busy evening?"

Frances McAllister nodded. "You would think the

whole population of Eureka Springs was starving to death. But . . ." She cast an expectant glance toward her husband. ". . . Lauren and I had time to run to the library once the dinner crowd thinned out."

"Yeah," Lauren said, plopping onto the sofa. "We checked on the paintings."

"And?" Beth asked, distributing mugs of steaming cinnamon tea.

"And—" her mom said as if she were awaiting a drum roll.

"Well, tell the poor girl," Don said, his eyes sparkling.

"And . . ." Beth said, her interest soaring. She phoned her mother and Lauren to request they consult the local librarian, Mrs. Pauly, about the painting. She was the town art expert. Beth held her breath as she recalled Michael's offer of two-hundred-thousand dollars.

"Mrs. Pauly knew exactly the artist we were talking about. She produced a print of one of his works and a book on contemporary American artists, with a whole chapter about him. Anyway, Edgar Alexander recently passed away, and the value of all his paintings has gone through the ceiling. Mrs. Pauly says Naomi's portrait could be worth nearly a million and the smaller painting a quarter or half of that. The jewelry will be worth a good bit more than its market value just because it's accompanied by cards with his signature on it."

Beth's stomach felt as if she had plummeted down a steep hill. Compulsively, she gulped her tea. *"Millions?"*

"Can you believe it?" Lauren asked. "You're rich!"

"No, *you're* rich," Beth said, sinking to the sofa next to her sister. "I found a note from Aunt Naomi, Lauren. It was tucked behind the painting on the wall. There was something confidential in it, but there was also something she wanted me to tell you."

"Really?" Lauren asked, her eyes full of the pain Beth now recognized as a legitimate wound. "I can't imagine—"

"Well, imagine this, Lauren. Aunt Naomi wanted you to have the smaller painting, all the jewelry, and half the value of the portrait."

"What?" Lauren shrieked, spilling her tea on her jeans.

"Yes. It was her way of evening up the inheritance between us."

"Why didn't she say that in the will?" Lauren asked. "Or just give them to me before she died? Then I would have never felt like—like—"

"Like she didn't love you as much as she loved me?"

"Yes. Exactly."

Beth exchanged a furtive glance with her parents. Their knowing expressions attested to their understanding Aunt Naomi's motives all too well. Even though they didn't comprehend the value of the paintings, they must have known of her affair at the time it happened. "Well, there's a story behind the paintings and jewelry I can't share. Even though she's dead, Lauren, I can't break Aunt Naomi's confidence. I can understand why she didn't want to dig the items out of storage and just give them to you. I can also understand why she didn't want to mention them in the will. That will was read by her attorney and his secretaries, and I don't think Aunt Naomi wanted her name associated with that artist under any circumstances. I do feel that I can tell you that there was something Aunt Naomi was ashamed of, and she simply didn't want to face it again."

"She had an affair with that painter, didn't she?" Lauren asked, disillusionment in her voice.

Beth stared at her sister.

"It doesn't take Sherlock Holmes to figure it out, Beth." Lauren counted off the clues on her fingers. "He gave her jewelry. He painted her portrait. Aunt Naomi was ashamed of something. An affair makes perfect sense."

Beth remained silent. Admitting Lauren's valid points would mean betraying her aunt's confidence. Denying her assumptions would mean lying. One thing was certain, Lauren was going to make a bang-up lawyer.

"Well, sounds like we've gotten to the bottom of everything," Don McAllister said, skillfully changing the subject. "Is that apple pie I smell?"

"You can't be hungry!" his wife chided.

"It's for Scott anyway," Beth said.

"For Scott, huh?" Don's brows arched as if he were the possessor of a particularly juicy secret.

"I guess you've decided to let Scott back into your life then?" Lauren picked up the kitten as it awakened from its nap in the corner of the sofa.

"You could say that," Beth muttered, her face uncomfortably warm. "Or you could say he decided to ignore me when I told him to get out. It's a long story."

"My, my, my, aren't we secretive of late." Lauren's mischievous smile mirrored her father's.

Beth grew even more disconcerted.

"I think we need to get home and hit the hay." Frances stood.

"Me too," her husband agreed. "Tomorrow is another long day. We're going to be interviewing potential managers for the restaurant."

"So you've finally decided to take it a bit easier?" Beth asked, glad of the change of subject.

"It's time they did, don't you think?" Lauren lagged behind as her parents went out the front door.

The small talk ended in warm hugs and calls of goodnight. Beth turned to bid Lauren good-bye as well, but she clung to Beth in a tight hug. "I'm so sorry. I've acted despicably."

"Aunt Naomi wasn't unfair after all, was she?"

"No, but this apology doesn't have anything to do with what Aunt Naomi did with her stuff. I was going to stop by here again even before Michael pulled his stunt. Our talk today helped me a lot. Even though I was still hurt because I felt like Aunt Naomi didn't care that much for me, our talk made me see that I had no right to feel resentment toward you, Beth. None of this was your fault."

"Thanks." The camaraderie Beth and Lauren once knew wrapped its arms around them.

"Quite frankly, I'm not really sure I want the money

from the painting and jewelry."

"What? Why on earth not?"

Lauren shrugged. "Dad and Mom could use the money to travel as they've always dreamed of doing. And you know, lots of children are hungry or even blind. Maybe I could donate to Christian Blind Mission or someone like them . . . " she trailed off thoughtfully. "Anyway, there are a lot of things in life worth much more than equal inheritance."

At that moment, if Beth could have gathered every star into one corner of the universe, their light would have paled in comparison to her glowing pride in Lauren.

"Do you think we should sell the portrait?" Lauren asked.

"I don't know. It's like selling Aunt Naomi." But Beth recalled the circumstances that surrounded the painting's creation, and she shrank from her original intentions of keeping it. That painting was a continuing reminder of Aunt Naomi's sin; the sin that had dashed Beth's respect for the woman she revered. The same question that began when Beth read Aunt Naomi's letter once again plagued her mind. *How could you?*

"I think Aunt Naomi would understand if we did." Lauren's words left the clear impression that she shared in Beth's feelings.

"You're probably right." Why had Aunt Naomi even told her about the affair? Beth could cheerfully have gone through life without ever learning of her aunt's past. "Besides, I'm with you. I'd rather see part of the money the portrait brings go to help someone in need."

After another hug, Lauren bid adieu and sped away in her Volkswagen.

Beth turned to enter her quiet inn. Even if she did have to spend her life alone, at least she would be set financially. Now she could afford a car and a new roof, and she could even hire more staff to help run the inn if she chose.

Deep in thought, she climbed the stairs to her room, ready to exchange her rumpled shorts for pajamas. Only hours ago she wished she had never seen Michael Alexander. Now, Beth was glad he came after the painting. Otherwise, she would not have learned of its value. Also, she might not have seen how she had based her self-worth on the injuries from her past rather than the God of her present.

Nor would she have awakened to how much she leaned on Scott. Speculatively, she eyed the phone in her room. Should she call him to once again express her appreciation for his support that day? Should she tell him how much she . . . How much she what? How much she cared? Or was this love?

Blinking, her throat tightening, Beth forced herself to climb into bed. She steeled herself against doing something she would later regret, something that would lead to her lasting embarrassment.

Tomorrow. Tomorrow she would take Scott the pie. That would be sufficient demonstration of her appreciation.

❦

Scott pounded the basketball against his outdoor court, jumped into the air, took a long shot, and waited as the ball sank through the net. Absently, he jogged toward the ball, retrieved it, and headed indoors to shower.

All evening, Scott debated whether to go back to Beth's. At the inn, she had been swamped in work, so he quietly fixed her car and took his leave. He wanted to hang around and wait for an opportunity to talk with her, but she was too busy, too busy and too tired.

Scott toweled himself dry and glanced at the digital clock on his night stand. Almost ten. Should he call her tonight?

An onslaught of chilling fear slithered through his veins, and Scott's palms grew clammy. What if he told her how he felt and she rejected him? What if his love revolted her?

Their relationship would be annihilated. Scott couldn't imagine not seeing her. At least as things stood, she was approachable. But what if he revealed his heart's desire, and she in turn crushed that desire?

Scott had no close family. His mother, his father both were gone. Beth was the closest thing to family he had. If she too were out of his life, his life would be a lonely existence indeed.

He donned a clean pair of gym shorts and stared blindly out the window. For weeks he had grumbled at

God for not answering his prayers concerning Beth and Michael. Now that those prayers were answered, Scott was failing to keep up his end of the deal.

A coward. That's what he had been today. He passed up four excellent opportunities to tell Beth how he felt: when he gave her the kitten, when he looked at her car's engine, when they followed Michael, and after filing the police report. He let each opportunity slip through his fingers. Each time he used what seemed to be a valid excuse, but, looking back, Scott wondered if his real reason was cowardice.

Lord, what are You going to do with me? I was angry with You because I didn't think You were holding up Your end of our bargain. Now, I don't seem to be able to hold up my end.

But what if she rejects me? His stomach twisted in response. *The woman is making me a nervous wreck.* Perhaps because he had known her his whole life. Somehow, that alone added an uncertain dimension to their relationship. Seemingly, everybody knew he loved Beth except her. Sooner or later, she would figure it out. Better that he tell her and face rejection than have her feeling sorry for him if she learned on her own.

Turning from the window, Scott made his decision. With determination, he removed the velvet box from his dresser drawer. Tomorrow morning, he would make a special trip to visit Beth McAllister. A trip with a definite purpose.

Thirty-one

*B*eth stood in front of her full-length mirror, examining her appearance in the morning light. The royal blue rayon pantsuit, the exact color of her eyes, set her mahogany hair afire with red highlights. Pivoting, Beth scrutinized the reflection as if seeing herself for the first time. And for the first time, she felt good about what she saw. Scott had been right, she was attractive, not super-model material, but definitely not an ugly duckling either. Smiling triumphantly, she thrilled in the new feelings of worthiness that pulsed through her very being.

"Thank You, Lord," she breathed, reveling in the emotional transformation only God Himself could render.

"Well, Aunt Naomi," she began practically, "I'm going to see Scott this morning—" But she stopped in mid-sentence as her eyes encountered the blank wall over her bed. She momentarily forgot that Aunt Naomi's portrait now resided at the police station.

With thoughts of her aunt came the same feelings of disappointment, of disillusionment. As if to run from those emotions, Beth grabbed her handbag and rushed out the door. She planned an early, quick trip to deliver Scott's pie, then it was back to the inn to prepare the usual continental breakfast. But as she closed her bedroom door, Beth glimpsed her aunt's crumpled letter where she tossed it the night before. If God could forgive Aunt Naomi, why couldn't she? It sounded simple, but it just wasn't that easy.

In a few minutes she tentatively knocked on Scott's front door, her legs trembling in an aggravating way. "Hello," Beth said awkwardly as Scott opened the door.

"Hi! I wasn't expecting you." His eyes widened in surprise. "Especially not so early and not all dressed up. What's the occasion?"

Beth's cheeks grew warm. Scott made a disheveled, although attractive picture after his usual morning jog. Never had she felt so disconcerted in his presence.

On impulse, she donned the new pantsuit, French braided her hair, and added an extra touch of makeup. At the time, she hadn't analyzed her motives. Now, she wished she had. How was she going to explain her appearance to him when she didn't fully understand it?

"I—I just had an urge to dress up." A nonchalant shrug. At least that was the truth.

"You should get these urges more often." His eyes hinted of appreciation, but Beth couldn't be sure.

That uncertainty alone sent a tremor through her stomach. No. This was not the Scott she had known all her life. He had changed. But then, so had she.

"I brought you a pie." Beth hesitantly extended it. "You asked me to bake it for you yesterday."

"Oh. That's for me? I mean—why don't you come in?"

She nervously cleared her throat and started to refuse his offer, but her mouth had other plans. "I could, if you—if you aren't busy."

"Busy? You know I'm never too busy for you, Bet." His smile said he meant it.

And Beth's heart stepped up its pace. That smile. Scott had filled her life with that smile, and she hadn't realized until lately how empty her life would be without it. *Dear Lord, is there any way You could make Scott fall in love with me?* she pleaded.

Weeks ago, she told Scott he would make somebody a good husband. As she stepped through his doorway, her feelings from the previous evening were confirmed. She wanted him be a good husband for *her*. How would he react if he learned of these longings, so new to her?

"Here, I'll take the pie," he said as she passed. "And have a seat. I'll put this in the kitchen and be right back."

Like a woman in a daze, Beth plopped onto the southwest sectional sofa to watch him walk into the kitchen.

Then he turned back to her. "I just remembered something I need to do right quick, Bet," he said, his smile uncertain. "Help yourself to a soda, if you like. I'll be right out."

"Okay."

He wore his usual jogging attire. Floppy knee shorts and a sweaty T-shirt. Definitely not clothing to evoke romantic notions. But to Beth, seeing him dressed so was like coming home. This was the Scott she knew, had always known, had always depended upon. Those faded knee shorts were suddenly as dear to her as his tousled hair, ever in need of a trim.

When did this happen? When had she fallen in love with her best friend? Beth thought of his near-constant presence in the last year. Of her supporting him through his father's gradual demise, and ultimately through the funeral. Of his sending flowers to her after it was all over. Of her thrill at his thoughtfulness. Of Scott being her on-call handyman, Scott raving over her cooking, Scott sitting beside her in church.

Scott. Scott. Scott.

And Beth knew she had been in love with him for months. That was the reason she had been so hurt when she saw him with Marilyn. That was the reason she kept Michael at arm's length. Because of Scott. Scott, and his spiritual warnings. Scott, and her love for him. Like a child marveling over a butterfly escaping its cocoon, Beth marveled over the love bursting from her heart to splendidly expose itself.

In love.

The ramifications sent her rigid with apprehension.

Beth stared at the rock fireplace's mantel, absent of decor. Finally she saw the whole situation, and what she saw made her shiver in fear. Scott, the brother she had always known, would probably laugh if he knew. At all costs she must not let him see.

Frantic, she stood to flee. He said he would be gone a few minutes. How long had Beth been sitting there in that trance-like state? Perhaps she could leave before he returned. Leave, and never come back.

She was gripping the front doorknob when he called to her.

"Beth? You aren't going, are you?" he said, a disappointed wilt to his voice.

"Well, I thought, I just thought . . ." She glanced over her shoulder, and the words faded from her mind.

He had changed into black jeans, a crisp white shirt, and those loafers Tiffany chewed. And his hair was damp as if he had taken a quick shower. The effect left her speechless. Except for the faint white scar across his right brow, he looked like something out of a magazine.

Beth McAllister, you have been blind. For years, you haven't really seen him.

As the silence stretched into an ache, Beth grappled with words, any words to fill the canyon between them. But her whole vocabulary seemed to have vanished.

"I just thought I'd do a quick change." Placing a hand into his jeans pocket, he shrugged. "I'd been out jogging and was sweaty. And well, you were all dressed up, so I decided . . ." Another shrug. And although he looked nonplused, his eyes begged her to stay.

"Oh."

"Did you get tired of waiting?"

Two strangers. They sounded like two strangers on a blind date.

"No, um, yes, um, I—I just thought perhaps you might need some privacy or something." *Nuts.* Had she taken leave of all of her senses? They had parted company only yesterday evening, and Beth, like a woman with some intelligence, had warmly thanked him for all his support. Now, she couldn't pair two intelligent words in one sentence.

As he closed the space between them and took her hand, she breathed deeply in an attempt to still her nerves. But that breath took in the full body of his sandalwood scent, and her stomach knotted anew.

"Come back to the couch," he muttered. "We need to talk."

"Uh, I really think I should leave now," she rushed, pulling her hand from his as the fire leapt from his palm to hers. If she stayed much longer, he might suspect her feelings. That would be the ultimate humiliation. Michael Alexander spent the summer laughing at her, and Beth did not want to add Scott Caldwell to the list.

Blindly, she grasped for the doorknob.

"Bet, please don't leave."

He was close now, so close his breath brushed her neck, exposed by her braid. Her heart pounded. She gulped for her every breath. With him so close, with his body's warmth seeping into her back, she feared that any second her emotions would overrule her common sense. Any second she would throw herself into his arms. Any second she would display her love.

Then she remembered Aunt Naomi's warning. *Temper your heart's desire with common sense.* And Beth, gritting her teeth, knew she must be strong, must hide her feelings, must never do anything to embarrass Scott. *Lord, please get me out of this with my new self-esteem intact.*

"I really just came over to leave the pie. I'm sure your company tonight will enjoy it." Amazed at her voice's cool tones, she schooled her features into a bland mask and exposed him to an equally cool gaze. If only he knew an inferno burned within.

"I'm sure he will too."

"He?"

"Yes. Didn't I tell you my cousin from Nebraska is coming for a visit?"

"No, you didn't. I thought Marilyn was coming," she blurted as a spring of joy bubbled within. So she hadn't baked for Scott's girlfriend after all.

"Marilyn?" His eyes narrowed as if the name were foreign. Then a dawning light. "Is *that* the reason you didn't want to bake it for me? Because you thought it was for—"

Beth bit her lips, her mind filling with the horror that he suspected her jealousy and, subsequently, her love. "Well, I—I really didn't have any extra time. The inn has kept me so busy. Honestly, I didn't get to cook it until last night."

"Oh." He knew. He knew a lack of time wasn't the only reason. Beth saw it in the faint twist of his mouth, in the humorous light of his eyes, in the tilt of his right brow, in the brush of her cheek with the back of his lean fingers.

That contact, that mere touch, was enough to still Beth into motionless wonder. The tender line of Scott's lips, the softness of his touch. Perhaps he *did* care for her. Beth's spirits soared with the possibility.

Then his arms inched to her waist, and his lips were descending to hers. "Beth," he whispered, "Oh, Beth."

As if pulled by a river's engulfing current, Beth leaned toward him, her hands sliding up the crisp cotton of his Oxford shirt. His lips brushed hers in a caress, ever so gentle, ever so dear. Then the caress deepened and spoke of promises that Beth had never dared hope.

Scott only lifted his mouth to place a trail of kisses to her ear. "Oh, Beth," he whispered again, but the soft knock on the door stopped any more words. With a flustered growl, he opened the door.

"Hello," Marilyn said, glancing at the peachy lipstick smudging Scott's mouth, then pointedly looking to Beth. "Oh, I'm sorry. I didn't mean to interrupt." An embarrassed smile. "I just wanted to drop your sweater off, Scott." More glances: to Beth, then Scott, then Beth again. "Remember, I borrowed it the night it had been raining. I meant to return it before now. I didn't mean to interrupt . . ." she said again, looking as clumsy as Beth felt.

"You didn't," Beth said, averting her eyes. "I was just leaving." *Run! Run! Run!* a frantic voice urged. For in the face of Marilyn's polished perfection, Beth felt as if she were competing in a game she would never win.

"Beth!" Scott called, trying to grab her arm. "Beth, don't leave." But his attempts to stop her were useless. She was gone.

As her car's engine came to life, the noise seemed to slice into Scott's very soul, a soul that was withering like a weathered prune. He blew it. In his nervousness, in his eagerness to do the right thing, he came on too strong. Would she ever give him a second chance?

"I am *so sorry*," Marilyn whispered.

Marilyn. Scott had completely forgotten about her. Embarrassed, he turned to her. "It's okay." He scrubbed his fingers through his damp hair but felt like pulling it out by the roots. "Actually, I don't think your arriving changed anything." An apologetic smile. "It looks like I'm in the same boat with you. Sometimes the ones we love don't love us back." Dejectedly, Scott took the sweater.

"You're kidding?" Marilyn gasped, her eyes rounded in shock.

"Nope."

She glanced at his lips again.

"Yeah, I kissed her." Scott scrubbed away the peach-colored lipstick.

"And she didn't like it?" Marilyn asked.

"Well, maybe." Scott thought of the way Beth readily leaned against him and slipped her arms around his neck. "Yeah—I guess."

"So why are you so disappointed?"

"You saw the way she ran."

"Well, did—does she know you and I have been—um—seen around town?" Marilyn smiled mischievously.

"Yes."

"Enough said." She playfully punched him in the arm. "Now, I'm going to be late for work if I don't get out of here. See ya!"

Thoughtfully, Scott watched Marilyn get into her Toyota and cruise away. Marilyn did have a point. Why did Scott feel like a total dunce in this whole thing with Beth? Somehow, his love had blinded him to the simplest explanations. Perhaps he was just too close to see anything in proper perspective.

Watching a neighborhood cat dash along the sidewalk, Scott experienced a new perspective over the last few weeks. Upon the heels of God's promise, Michael Alexander marched into Beth's life. Scott had assumed Michael's presence was a detrimental force. Now he suspected Michael was a part of God's grand scheme. He awakened Beth to her erroneous feelings of inferiority. Her experience with Michael taught her to stop measuring her worth based on the acceptance of others.

Furthermore, the episode with Michael taught Scott to wait on God; really wait on God.

Lord, I see Your hand in everything now. I've been impatient and immature. Please give me the patience to woo Beth. Help me to learn Your timing, not mine. Turning to go back into the house, he added one more plea. *And Lord? Be with Marilyn. Heal her as You're continuing to heal me and Beth.*

Thirty-two

Seven hours. Seven hours had dragged by since Beth last saw Scott. She punched the bed pillow and stared unseeing at the black print on the pages of the mystery novel that once enthralled her. The last seven hours seemed like seven days.

Laying the book aside, she sat up from her afternoon reverie and dangled her legs off the bed. Her sleeping kitten rolled to his back and stretched in feline languish.

"I wish I could sleep like you do," Beth said, rubbing the kitten's ear and thinking of Scott's eyes when he replaced Tiffany with Sweetheart. Those endearing eyes had prohibited her from taking an afternoon siesta, something she needed in the face of her continual work.

Staring at the phone, she debated for the hundredth time whether or not to call him. She desperately wished to hear his voice, had hoped perhaps he would call her. *Probably too busy with Marilyn.* And that thought, as it had done all morning, put an end to calling him. She most certainly didn't want him to feel sorry for her.

But perhaps you overreacted when you saw Marilyn, a doubtful voice whispered. *Scott has never kissed you. Maybe that kiss meant more than you know.* Licking her lips, Beth contemplated the possibility. Her nerves had been raw with Michael's recent escapade. Could she have been too hasty in assuming Scott's attachment to Marilyn? Scott wasn't the kind of man to kiss one woman while involved with another. Beth glanced once more at the phone, but she knew it was hopeless. There was no way they could resume a normal friendship. Not after that kiss.

Oh Lord, help me to know Your will. I don't want to go against You again, as I did with Michael. I don't ever again want to come close to making a mistake like Aunt Naomi's.

Restless, Beth flopped to her stomach only to have the final words of her prayer reverberate through her mind. *A mistake like Aunt Naomi's.* The implications made her bolt upright. Beth, like Aunt Naomi, fell for a non-Christian man, the son of the very man Aunt Naomi fell for.

That's when Beth knew she must ask forgiveness for her attitude toward her dead aunt. How could she entertain judgmental thoughts against Aunt Naomi when she was almost as guilty? Even though Beth had not committed immorality as did her aunt, she still willfully went against a biblical principle and dated a non-Christian.

In His awesome grace, God forgave Aunt Naomi. Furthermore, Aunt Naomi forgave herself and didn't let her sin ruin her life. She had been a living example of

Christ's love to her family and clients. What an awesome God they served—One who could take even the worst sinner and, through Christ's death on the cross, make that person a living force for Him.

Lord, some days I wonder if I'm ever going to learn. I get over one hurdle and smack right into the next one. Forgive me for my judgmental thoughts toward Aunt Naomi. How could I have been so hypocritical? Help me to keep my eyes on You, not people, not Aunt Naomi or anybody else. We're all human. We've all failed You, including Aunt Naomi . . . and me. Thanks for Your continued patience and love and . . . and thanks for Your healing touch.

The bell over her bedroom door rang, signaling a customer's arrival at the front desk. Hiding her internal struggles with her most professional smile, Beth slipped on her casual navy flats, straightened her pantsuit, and descended the stairs.

"Welcome to McAllister's." She grinned at a graying, middle-aged couple and a pair of giggling teenage girls. Inside, though, Beth felt as if she were burying her dreams and resurrecting the rut that Aunt Naomi set before her. For Beth's smile, her greeting were those of her spinster aunt. Just like Aunt Naomi, Beth made an idiot of herself over an Alexander man, and just like Aunt Naomi, she would live alone. Every hour Scott didn't call drove that reality deeper into her heart like a cold stone snuffing out the flames of her desires.

"We're the Donners. We made reservations for tonight," the mother said.

"You mentioned you had two rooms available?" the father said, shifting his fond gaze toward his twin daughters. "Otherwise, we'd never get any sleep."

"That's exactly right. Two guests recently checked out." Beth's smile didn't match her thoughts. Michael Alexander had been one of those guests. Earlier today Beth purchased a piece of drywall to nail over the hole he created until she could have it fixed properly. The dresser covered her patching.

"Uh . . . I can't remember if I told you, our rates are eighty-five dollars a night for double occupancy. That includes a continental breakfast," she said, trying to keep her thoughts on the task at hand.

"Ask her, Mother," one of the blonde twins whispered, as her sister snickered.

Rolling her eyes, the mother complied. "Is your gardener married? My girls need to know."

"My gardener?" Beth asked, wondering if they were confused. "But I don't have a gardener."

"Well, there's a man planting a row of rose bushes in your front yard," the father supplied. "We assumed he was the gardener."

Beth walked to her front window to peer past the porch and into the front yard. Just as her customer said, a young man was pressing the dirt around a rose bush in a long line of rose bushes. A young man wearing a pair of baggy jogging shorts and a red T-shirt. A young man who made Beth's heart skip several beats.

"We'll be here a week," the father continued.

"Okay," Beth said absently, tearing herself away from the vision of her heart's longing. She automatically went through the routine of signing in the new guests and showing them their rooms. But her thoughts were with Scott, so handsome. Scott, so thoughtful. Scott, in her *front yard*. She had to get out there or she would simply explode.

As soon as the guests were settled, Beth rushed to the kitchen to prepare a glass of iced tea. How many times had she taken him tea when he was helping her with some odd task? Too many to count. Each time now seemed a moment to cherish.

As she opened the front door and paused to savor the view of him, a tiny breath of hope sprouted in her heart. Maybe his kiss was sincere. Maybe he did share her love.

Father, she breathed. *If this isn't Your will for me—us—I hope You'll let me know. Otherwise, I'm afraid I'm head over heels.* But Beth had an inner peace that witnessed to God's will.

"Hello," she called, her voice raspy even to her own ears, for her pulse had accelerated past the safety mark.

"Hi." Scott stood as she approached, his smile feeling stiff against his quivering lips. After several hours, he finally got the nerve to come over. He had never felt so vulnerable, had never been so afraid of rejection. But he had come too far to back up now. Seeing her welcoming smile made him wonder why he had been so fearful. After all, this was Beth, the same old Beth. *His* Beth.

"I, um, thought you might want some iced tea," she said, her smile showing no signs of her past desertion.

"I always want your tea, Bet." With a grin he took the tumbler to drain its sweet, cold contents.

"That's nice to hear."

With the smell of her rose perfume teasing his senses, Scott began the speech he all but memorized. "Before I say anything else, you need to know that I am not in love with Marilyn Douglas."

"You're not?" Her eyes widened.

"No. I'm not. I went out with her a few times. That's all it amounted to."

"Oh."

"Second, I meant that kiss this morning. And there's more where that came from if . . ." Scott paused.

"I was hoping you'd say that," she murmured, her eyes sparkling.

Scott reached for her hand to bring it to his lips. "And I kissed you, my dear Beth, because I'm in love with you and have been ever since I moved back from New York. That's the reason I went berserk when Michael arrived. And the reason I followed you to the Crescent Hotel. And the reason I came back even after you told me to get out of your life. It's also the reason I went out with Marilyn. I decided you could never love me and was trying to get you out of my blood." He grinned again. "But it was no use."

The joy welling in her eyes was like a shower of diamonds from heaven itself. "Oh Scott, I love you too. I'm so sorry I left after you kissed me this morning. I was just scared and confused and then there was Marilyn, and—"

"It's okay. It's okay," he crooned, pulling her into his arms, not caring that he was sweaty from his work or that the elderly Mr. Juarez might be watching from across the street. "You've had a stressful time. It's understandable."

"I'm glad you understand." She trembled against him. "Because I'm not sure I do."

"I don't think any of us ever fully understands each and everything we do. The thing that's important to me right now is that Michael Alexander is out of the picture. You don't know how scared I was that I was going to lose you to him. I was beside myself with jealousy."

"I thought you had lost your mind."

"I almost did."

"So did I. I can't believe I told you to get out of my life." She leaned her head against his shoulder. "You know I didn't mean it."

"I know."

"Now I understand why you got so mad when I suggested counseling over your father's death. I thought you were getting mad because I was right."

"Oh, I needed counseling all right, but it wasn't about my father." He chuckled. "It was about waiting on God to work in His own time."

"What do you mean?" she asked, wrinkling her brow.

"I mean that God and I had a little secret we were keeping from you."

"Oh?"

"Yes . . . um . . ." He paused, his stomach feeling as if the bottom had dropped out. The ring box in his pocket seemed to double in size and weight. "See, I've been praying for a godly wife for about a year. And, well, God seemed to point to you. Of course, it did help that I had fallen for you, but I still felt that God had promised you to me." Scott reached into his pocket to encircle the ring box with his fingers. "Well, when Michael came on the scene, I started doubting whether I could even interpret the will of God. Then, I hate to admit it, but I got mad at God for not fulfilling His promise. I'm really ashamed of it, and I think I've learned my lesson. First, to trust my ability to perceive God's will, and second, and most importantly, to trust God's promises." Rubbing his jaw, he said, "It's been a tough few weeks."

"Tell me about it." She looked up at him. "I don't ever plan to go against God's will and date a non-Christian again. I was miserable. All I could think was 'unequally yoked, unequally yoked.' It was like there was a broken record in me."

"If I have any say, you won't date anyone else again, *period.*"

"Oh?" she said with a teasing smile. "And what is that supposed to mean?"

"It's supposed to mean . . ." The ring box grew warm

against his clammy palm. ". . . that I want you to spend your time, all your time, with me. That I do believe you're the answer to my prayer for a godly wife, and that I want you to marry me. Will you?" He held his breath, waiting for her answer.

"Oh, Scott," she gasped, throwing herself into his arms. "You've talked so long about everything but the weather, I didn't think you would ever ask."

"I guess we can chalk it up to nerves." He pulled the box from his shorts pocket. "I know that your front yard in the middle of the afternoon isn't the most romantic setting for giving you this ring, but I can't wait another second."

He slipped the diamond solitaire from its cushioned home and slid it onto her finger.

"Well, what do you think?" he asked, not sure what her silent scrutiny of the diamond implied.

"It's beautiful," she breathed, staring up at him through tear-filled eyes.

"Hey, why the tears?" He brushed away the first drop staining her cheek.

"I just—I don't know—when I realized I was in love with you, I never dreamed you loved me too."

"What's not to love, Beth? You're a wonderful woman, a gift from God. And I want to kiss you so badly that I'm about to lose my mind."

"I bet Mr. Juarez is watching." She glanced toward the white frame house across the street. "I can see him at his living room window."

"Maybe Mr. Juarez needs a little spice in his life."

"Maybe you're right."

Not waiting for further invitation, Scott crushed her to him, reveling in the feel of her in his arms and the God-given passion that sprang between them like a rare violet awaiting the perfect moment to burst into bloom.

"We should go inside," she said after Scott purposefully cut the kiss short. "I wouldn't want to give poor old Mr. Juarez a heart attack." She tugged him toward the porch, then stopped. "I don't remember ordering roses," she said.

"You didn't. But I have a request from an ardent admirer to plant a dozen red rose bushes. He doesn't seem to think a dozen roses is enough. He wants to be able to look out the window every day and see a reminder of our love."

"Does that mean we'll live here?" she asked eagerly.

"Yes, if it's okay with you. I'd feel better about starting our marriage in a new environment, for me anyway. I've decided to sell my house. After a lot of prayer, I've realized that I can't completely heal while living there. It's like continually reliving the verbal abuse. I sense the Holy Spirit prompting me to close that part of my past, and I think selling the house will complete my healing."

"We could remodel the third floor," she said excitedly. "We could reduce the size of the library and increase the bathroom—maybe make two bathrooms, his and hers. And—and then we could turn the attic into a—a . . ." She hesitated, glancing up at him uncertainly. "I guess that's jumping too far ahead."

"What?" he asked, suspecting her thoughts.

She rushed up the mansion's steps and turned to face him. "Well, I was going to say we could turn the attic into a nursery, but—do you want children, Scott?" Her blue eyes begged him to affirm her desires.

"I want dozens of them, leagues of them." He picked her up to twirl her around the porch. "We could even start our own army!"

With the delighted laughter of a woman in love, Beth gripped his hand to pull him indoors. "Come on. We've got to call Mom and Dad and Lauren."

"Er . . . Don't be disappointed if they aren't surprised."

Her blank stare spanned only seconds. Then an understanding gleam ignited in her eyes. "That explains all the odd comments Lauren has been making. And when I told Dad how strange you'd been acting, all he could do was laugh. No wonder!" Beth giggled. "How long have they known?"

"Well, your dad figured me out the night I almost choked to death on your German chocolate cake. Remember, you said something about our getting married in our old age, and I swallowed a bit too fast after that one."

"Yeah, that was the night I unplugged the air conditioner in the pink room and called you over to fix . . ." She trailed off, her eyes rounding in mischief. "Oops."

"*You* unplugged that air conditioner?"

"Uh . . ."

"You knew it was unplugged?" Scott's heart soared.

"Well, it's just that I hadn't seen you in so long and I . . . I missed you." A helpless shrug. "That was the only way I knew to get you over here. Otherwise, I guess you would have stubbornly sat in your house the rest of the summer and never come back."

"That was a devious scheme." Scott grabbed her around the waist and pulled her close. "I feel used and manipulated," he growled.

"But I never lied." She held up her index finger for emphasis.

"Did my being here matter that much to you, Bet?" Scott's playful tone softened. "Even then?" Gently, he stroked her cheek. "Tell me you thought about me as much as I thought about you."

"More than you'll ever know."

Debra White Smith is a full-time writer who has published numerous novels, is working on several nonfiction books, and speaks at conferences and retreats. Debra's readers are comparing her Christian romatic suspense novels to Agatha Christie or Mary Higgins Clark. This best-selling author holds both a Bachelor and Master's degree in English. If you would like to write Debra or slate her for a speaking engagement, contact her at P.O. Box 1482, Jacksonville, TX 75766 or www.getset.com/debrawhitesmith.

Dear Reader:

We love to hear from our readers. Your response to the following questions will help us continue publishing the excellent Christian fiction that you enjoy.

1. What most influenced you to buy *Best Friends*?
   - ❏ Cover/title
   - ❏ Subject matter
   - ❏ Back cover copy
   - ❏ Author
   - ❏ Recommendation by friend
   - ❏ Recommendation by bookstore sales person

2. How would you rate this book?
   - ❏ Great
   - ❏ Good
   - ❏ Fair
   - ❏ Poor

Comments:

3. What did you like best about this book?
   - ❏ Characters
   - ❏ Plot
   - ❏ Setting
   - ❏ Inspirational theme
   - ❏ Other_____

4. Will you buy more novels in the **Promises** series?
   - ❏ Yes
   - ❏ No

Why?

5. Which do you prefer?
   - ❏ Historical romance
   - ❏ Contemporary romance
   - ❏ No preference

6. How many Christian novels do you buy per year?
   - ❏ Less than 3
   - ❏ 3-6
   - ❏ 7 or more

7. What is your age?
   - ❏ Under 18
   - ❏ 18-24
   - ❏ 25-34
   - ❏ 35-44
   - ❏ 45-54
   - ❏ Over 55

Please return to
Chariot Victor Publishing
Promises Editor
4050 Lee Vance View
Colorado Springs, CO 80918
Fax: (719) 536-3269

Airwaves
by Sherrie Lord
ISBN: 1-56476-706-X

So what if Colin Michaels is traffic-stopping gorgeous? So what if he represents every sin she knows to flee? Emily Erickson wants only the job Colin offers at *Diamond Country KDMD*. And so what if Emily goes out with Colin a few times? God isn't happy with her anyway. It won't matter that Colin's her boss. That he's definitely not a Christian. Or maybe a thief—*someone's* stealing from the station. So what if he's a man of his own invention, a man who can never tell what happened—*what he did*—in Oklahoma nine years before?

When will Emily learn that an unforgiven heart can't outrun God's love?

Freedom's Promise
by Suzanne D. Hellman
ISBN: 1-56476-718-3

Finding life in Victorian England stifling, Tabitha, a lonely young widow, sets out for America. The love she finds there for a handsome, widowed farmer and his young daughter is doomed—unless he can overcome his anger at God and put the tragic death of his wife behind him.

Suzanne D. Hellman lives in Arizona along with her family. She is an experienced novelist who researches her historical fiction thoroughly.

Only His Kiss
by Sherrie Lord
ISBN: 1-56476-707-8

Available
June
1999

"It's a girl, sir."

The wagon master's shoulders collapsed in exasperation. "I can see that," he said, eyes flashing ominously. "What I mean is, what's she doing here and where the...blazes did you find her? What's she doing all by herself, two weeks' ride from Independence?"

Sonja glanced from the train's commander to her captor then searched each bullwhacker's grimy face. Her heart fell. He wasn't here, the man with the brown eyes; no chance for another of his gallant rescues. *Please, Lord, make this the right train...*

If you liked this book,
check out these great titles from
Chariot Victor Publishing . . .

Promised Land
by John Culea
ISBN: 1-56476-722-1

Only Shelly Hinson knows that the "best small town" award is a lie—because she's the one who wrote the article. Braxton, CA is no better or worse than any other town in the state, or the country, for that matter. Little does she know the effect the hoax will have on people.

Caught in her lie, she watches with growing guilt the changes taking place. She is forced to come to grips with her life, including her spiritual condition, as she realizes how her article has changed the lives of so many people, including her own.

Days of Deception
by Lee Roddy
ISBN 1-56476-635-7

Being a spy for the famous Pinkerton Detectives suits Laurel
Bartlett's adventurous nature. During the Civil War, Laurel
had used her charm and cleverness to penetrate Confederate
lines and bring back military intelligence for the Union army
as a way to avenge her brother's death. But the war casts a
long shadow onto Laurel's future happiness.

On a train heading South through lawless lands, sparks fly
when she meets Ridge Granger, a handsome former rebel
cavalryman, and Laurel's secret past comes back to haunt her.
When Laurel stumbles upon a murder scene, both their lives
are threatened by an unknown killer.

Wings of Dawn
by Sigmund Brouwer
ISBN: 1-56476-756-6

In the year of our Lord 1312, in the remote North York Moors of England, Thomas pursues his destiny—the conquest of Magnus, an 800-year-old kingdom, an island castle that harbors secrets dating back to the days of King Arthur and Merlin.

Haunted by a beautiful woman he dare not trust, surrounded by enemies he cannot see, and with no army but a mysterious knight he has saved from the gallows, Thomas faces an insurmountable task. Yet armed with a powerful weapon he has concealed since his orphaned boyhood, there remains a glimmer of hope.